Stanzas

Theory and History of Literature
Edited by Wlad Godzich and Jochen Schulte-Sasse

For other books in the series, see p. 164.

Stanzas

Word and Phantasm

in Western Culture

Giorgio Agamben

Translated by Ronald L. Martinez

Theory and History of Literature, Volume 69

University of Minnesota Press, Minneapolis and London

Published by the University of Minnesota Press
2037 University Avenue Southeast, Minneapolis, MN 55414
Printed in the United States of America on acid-free paper

Library of Congress Cataloging-in-Publication Data

Agamben, Giorgio, 1942-
    [Stanze. English]
    Stanzas : word and phantasm in Western culture / Giorgio Agamben : translated by Ronald L. Martinez.
        p.   cm. — (Theory and history of literature ; v. 69)
    Includes bibliographical references and index.
    ISBN 0-8166-2037-7 (acid free). —
    ISBN 0-8166-2038-5 (pbk. : acid free)
    1. Civilization, Western.   2. Creation (Literary, artistic, etc.)
    3. Personality and culture.   I. Title.   II. Series.
    CB245.A3313   1993
    302.2—dc20   92-30970
                                                                       CIP

In memoriam Martin Heidegger

And here one must know that this term (stanza) *has been chosen for technical reasons exclusively, so that what contains the entire art of the canzone should be called* stanza, *that is, a capacious dwelling or receptacle for the entire craft. For just as the canzone is the container (literally lap or womb) of the entire thought, so the stanza enfolds its entire technique* . . .

Dante, *De vulgari eloquentia* II.9

Contents

IV. The Perverse Image: Semiology from the Point of View of the Sphinx

Illustrations

Notes and Acknowledgments

The essay "The Phantasms of Eros" appeared, in a shorter version, in *Paragone* (April 1974). The original nucleus of "In the World of Odradek" was published with the title "Il dandy e il feticcio" (The dandy and the fetish) in *Ulise* (February 1972).

The spellings "phantasm," "phantasy," and "phantastic" throughout the book indicate the technically precise use of these terms.

Translations that are not documented to a published English-language source may be assumed to be the translator's own.

The author wishes to thank Frances Yates of the Warburg Institute of London, whose courtesy made it possible for him to pursue research in the library of the Institute. He also thanks the conservators of the Bibliothèque Nationale in Paris and Professor Traini of the Caetani fund of the library of the Accademia Nazionale dei Lincei.

The University of Minnesota Press wishes to thank Michael Hardt for his invaluable assistance with the translation.

Introduction

It is possible, perhaps, to accept that a novel may never actually recount the story it has promised to tell. But it is common to expect results of a work of criticism, or at least arguable positions and, as they say, working hypotheses. Yet when the term "criticism" appears in the vocabulary of Western philosophy, it signifies rather inquiry at the limits of knowledge about precisely that which can be neither posed nor grasped. If criticism, insofar as it traces the limits of truth, offers a glance of "truth's homeland" like "an island nature has enclosed within immutable boundaries," it must also remain open to the fascination of the "wide and storm-tossed sea" that draws "the sailor incessantly toward adventures he knows not how to refuse yet may never bring to an end."

Thus for the Jena group, which attempted through the project of a "universal progressive poetry" to abolish the distinction between poetry and the critical-philological disciplines, a critical work worthy of the name was one that included its own negation; it was, therefore, one whose essential content consisted in precisely what it did not contain. The corpus of the European critical essay in the present century is poor in examples of such a genre. Leaving aside a work that by its very absence is "more than complete"—that of Félix Fénéon, *celui qui silence* (he who silences)—there is strictly speaking perhaps only a single book that deserves to be called critical: the *Ursprüng des deutschen Trauerspiel* (The origin of German tragic drama) of Walter Benjamin.

A certain sign of the extinction of such critical thinking is that among those who today draw their authority more or less from the same tradition there are many who proclaim the creative character of criticism—precisely when the arts have for some time renounced all pretense at creativity. If the formula of "both poet and critic" (*poietes hama kai kritikos*), applied for the first time in antiquity to the Alexandrian poet-philologist Philitas, may once again serve as an exemplary definition of the modern artist, and if criticism today truly identifies with the work of art, it is not because criticism itself is also "creative," but (if at all) insofar as criticism is also a form of negativity. Criticism is in fact nothing other than the process of its own ironic self-negation: precisely a "self-annihilating nothing," or a "god that self-destructs," according to Hegel's prophetic, if ill-willed, definition. Hegel's objection, that "Mister Friedrich von Schlegel," Solger, Novalis, and other theoreticians of irony remained stalled at "absolute infinite negativity" and would have ended by making of the least artistic "the true principle of art," marketing "the unexpressed as the best thing," misses the point: that the negativity of irony is not the provisional negative of dialectic, which the magic wand of sublation (*Aufhebung*) is always already in the act of transforming into a positive, but an absolute and irretrievable negativity that does not, for that, renounce knowledge. The claim that a posture genuinely both philosophical and scientific (which has provided an essential impetus to Indo-European linguistics, among other things) arose from Romantic irony, precisely with the Schlegels, remains to be questioned in terms of the prospects for giving a critical foundation to the human sciences. For if in the human sciences subject and object necessarily become identified, then the idea of a science without object is not a playful paradox, but perhaps the most serious task that remains entrusted to thought in our time. What is now more and more frequently concealed by the endless sharpening of knives on behalf of a methodology with nothing left to cut—namely, the realization that the object to have been grasped has finally evaded knowledge—is instead reasserted by criticism as its own specific character. Secular enlightenment, the most profound project of criticism, does not possess its object. Like all authentic quests, the quest of criticism consists not in discovering its object but in assuring the conditions of its inaccessibility.

European poets of the thirteenth century called the essential nucleus of their poetry the *stanza,* that is, a "capacious dwelling, receptacle," because it safeguarded, along with all the formal elements of the canzone, that *joi d'amor* that these poets entrusted to poetry as its unique object. But what is this object? To what enjoyment does poetry dispose its stanza as the receptive "womb" of its entire art? What does its *trobar* so tenaciously enclose?

   Access to what is problematic in these questions is barred by the forgetfulness of a scission that derives from the origin of our culture and that is usually accepted as the most natural thing—that goes, so to speak, without saying—when in fact it is the only thing truly worth interrogating. The scission in question is that between poetry and philosophy, between the poetic word and the word of thought. This split is so fundamental to our cultural tradition that Plato could already declare it "an ancient enmity." According to a conception that is only implicitly contained in the Platonic critique of poetry, but that has in modern times acquired a hegemonic character, the scission of the word is construed to mean that poetry possesses its object without knowing it while philosophy knows its object without possessing it. In the West, the word is thus divided between a word that is unaware, as if fallen from the sky, and enjoys the object of knowledge by representing it in beautiful form, and a word that has all seriousness and consciousness for itself but does not enjoy its object because it does not know how to represent it.

The split between poetry and philosophy testifies to the impossibility, for Western culture, of fully possessing the object of knowledge (for the problem of knowledge is a problem of possession, and every problem of possession is a problem of enjoyment, that is, of language). In our culture, knowledge (according to an antinomy that Aby Warburg diagnosed as the ''schizophrenia'' of Western culture) is divided between inspired-ecstatic and rational-conscious poles, neither ever succeeding in wholly reducing the other. Insofar as philosophy and poetry have passively accepted this division, philosophy has failed to elaborate a proper language, as if there could be a royal road to truth that would avoid the problem of its representation, and poetry has developed neither a method nor self-consciousness. What is thus overlooked is the fact that every authentic poetic project is directed toward knowledge, just as every authentic act of philosophy is always directed toward joy. The name of Hölderlin—of a poet, that is, for whom poetry was above all problematic and who often hoped that it would be raised to the level of the *mēchanē* (mechanical instrument) of the ancients so that its procedures could be calculated and taught—and the dialogue that with its utterance engages a thinker who no longer designates his own meditation with the name of ''philosophy'' are invoked here to witness the urgency, for our culture, of rediscovering the unity of our own fragmented word.

Criticism is born at the moment when the scission reaches its extreme point. It is situated where, in Western culture, the word comes unglued from itself; and it points, on the near or far side of that separation, toward a unitary status for the utterance. From the outside, this situation of criticism can be expressed in the formula according to which it neither represents nor knows, but knows the representation. To appropriation without consciousness and to consciousness without enjoyment criticism opposes the enjoyment of what cannot be possessed and the possession of what cannot be enjoyed. In this way, criticism interprets the precept of Gargantua: ''Science without consciousness is nothing but the ruin of the soul.'' What is secluded in the *stanza* of criticism is nothing, but this nothing safeguards unappropriability as its most precious possession.

In the following pages, we will pursue a model of knowledge in operations such as the desperation of the melancholic or the *Verleugnung* (disavowal) of the fetishist: operations in which desire simultaneously denies and affirms its object, and thus succeeds in entering into relation with something that otherwise it would

have been unable either to appropriate or enjoy. This is the model that has provided the frame both for an examination of human objects transfigured by the
commodity, and for the attempt to discover, through analysis of emblematic form
and the tale (*ainos*) of the Sphinx, a model of signifying that might escape the
primordial situation of signifier and signified that dominates Western reflection
on the sign. From this perspective, one can grasp the proper meaning of the central project of the present inquiry—the reconstruction of the theory of the phantasm that subtends the entire poetic project bequeathed by troubadour and Stilnovist lyric to European culture and in which, through the dense textual
entrebescamen (interlacing, interweaving) of phantasm, desire, and word, poetry
constructed its own authority by becoming, itself, the *stanza* offered to the endless joy (*gioi che mai non fina*) of erotic experience.

Each of the essays gathered here thus traces, within its hermeneutic circle, a
topology of joy (*gaudium*), of the *stanza* through which the human spirit responds to the impossible task of appropriating what must in every case remain
unappropriable. The path of the dance in the labyrinth, leading into the heart of
what it keeps at a distance, is the spatial model symbolic of human culture and its
royal road (*hodos basileie*) toward a goal for which only a detour is adequate.
From this point of view, a discourse that is aware that to hold "tenaciously what
is dead exacts the greatest effort" and that eschews "the magic power that transforms the negative into being" must necessarily guarantee the unappropriability
of its object. This discourse behaves with respect to its object neither as the master who simply negates it in the act of enjoyment nor like the slave who works
with it and transforms it in the deferral of desire: its operation is, rather, that of a
refined love, a *fin'amors* that at once enjoys and defers, negates and affirms,
accepts and repels; and whose only reality is the unreality of a word "qu'amas
l'aura / e chatz la lebre ab lo bou / e nadi contra suberna" [that heaps up the
breeze / and hunts the hare with the ox / and swims against the tide (Arnaut
Daniel, *canso* "En cest sonet coind' e leri," vv. 43-45)].

From this vantage one can speak of a topology of the unreal. Perhaps the *topos*,
for Aristotle "so difficult to grasp" but whose power is "marvelous and prior to
all others" and which Plato, in the *Sophist*, conceives as a "third genre" of being, is not necessarily something "real." In this sense we can take seriously the
question that Aristotle puts in the fourth book of the *Physics*: "Where is the ca-
pristag, where the sphinx?" (*pou gar esti tragelaphos he sphinx*). The answer, to
be sure, is "nowhere"; but perhaps only because the terms in question are themselves *topoi*. We must still accustom ourselves to think of the "place" not as
something spatial, but as something more original than space. Perhaps, following
Plato's suggestion, we should think of it as a pure difference, yet one given the
power to act such that "what is not, will in a certain sense be; and what is, will
in a certain sense not be." Only a philosophical topology, analogous to what in
mathematics is defined as an *analysis situs* (analysis of site) in opposition to

analysis magnitudinis (analysis of magnitude) would be adequate to the *topos outopos,* the placeless place whose Borromean knot we have tried to draw in these pages. Thus topological exploration is constantly oriented in the light of utopia. The claim that thematically sustains this inquiry into the void, to which it is constrained by its critical project, is precisely that only if one is capable of entering into relation with unreality and with the unappropriable as such is it possible to appropriate the real and the positive. Thus this volume is intended as a first, insufficient attempt to follow in the wake of the project that Robert Musil entrusted to his unfinished novel: a project that, a few years previously, the words of a poet had expressed in the formula "Whoever seizes the greatest unreality will shape the greatest reality."

Part I
The Phantasms of Eros

Now loss, cruel as it may be, cannot do anything against possession: it completes it, if you wish, it affirms it. It is not, at bottom, but a second acquisition—this time wholly internal— and equally intense.

Rilke

Many attempted in vain to say the most joyful things joyfully; here, finally, they are expressed in mourning.

Hölderlin

Chapter 1
The Noonday Demon

During the whole of the Middle Ages, a scourge worse than the plague that infested the castles, villas, and palaces of the cities of the world fell on the dwellings of spiritual life, penetrated the cells and cloisters of monasteries, the Thebaid of the hermits, the convents of recluses. *Acedia* (sloth), *tristitia* (sorrow), *taedium vitae* (weariness, loathing of life), and *desidia* (idleness) are the names the church fathers gave to the death this sin induced in the soul; and, although its desolate effigy occupies the fifth position in the lists of the *Summae virtutum et vitiorum* (Summa of virtues and vices), in the miniatures of manuscripts, and in the popular representations of the seven capital sins,[1] an ancient hermeneutic tradition considered it the most lethal of the vices, the only one for which no pardon was possible.

The fathers exercised themselves with particular fervor against the dangers of this "noonday demon"[2] that chose its victims among the *homines religiosi* (religious men), assailing them when the sun reached its highest point over the horizon. Perhaps for no other temptation of the soul do their writings show such a pitiless psychological penetration and such a punctilious and chilling phenomenology:

> The gaze of the slothful man rests obsessively on the window, and with his fantasy, he imagines the image of someone who comes to visit him. At the squeak of the door, he leaps to his feet. He hears a voice, runs to face the window and look out, and yet he does not descend to the street, but turns back to sit down where he was, torpid and as if dismayed. If he reads, he interrupts himself restlessly and, a minute later, slips into sleep. If he wipes his face with his hand, he extends the

3

fingers and, having removed his eyes from the book, fixes them on the wall. Again he gazes at the book, proceeds for a few lines, mumbling the end of each word he reads; and meanwhile he fills his head with idle calculations, he counts the number of the pages and the sheets of the bindings, and he begins to hate the letters and the beautiful miniatures he has before his eyes, until, at the last, he closes the book and uses it as a cushion for his head, falling into a brief and shallow sleep, from which a sense of privation and hunger that he must satisfy wakes him.[3]

As soon as this demon begins to obsess the mind of some unfortunate one, it insinuates into him a horror of the place he finds himself in, an impatience with his own cell, and a disdain for the brothers who live with him, who now seem to him careless and vulgar. It makes him inert before every activity that unfolds within the walls of his cell, it prevents him from staying there in peace and attending to his reading; and behold the wretched one begin to complain that he obtains no benefit from conventual life, and he sighs and moans that his spirit will produce no fruit so long as he remains where he is. Querulously he proclaims himself inept at facing any task of the spirit and afflicts himself with being always empty and immobile at the same point, he who might have been useful to others and guided them, and who has instead not concluded anything or benefited anyone. He plunges into exaggerated praise of distant and absent monasteries and evokes the places where he could be healthy and happy; he describes pleasant communities of brothers, burning with spiritual conversation; and on the other hand everything that he has within reach seems harsh and difficult, his brothers lack all good qualities, and even food seems difficult to obtain without effort. Finally he convinces himself that he will not be at ease until he abandons his cell and that if he were to remain there, he would perish. Then, toward the fifth or sixth hour, a languor seized his body, and a rabid hunger for food, as if he were exhausted from a long journey or a hard task, or as if he had fasted for two or three days. Then he begins to look about himself here and there, he enters and exits several times from the cell and fixes his eyes on the sun as if he could slow down the sunset; and finally, a senseless confusion comes over his mind, similar to the mist that envelops the earth, and leaves it inert and empty.[4]

In the evocation of the infernal train of the *filiae acediae* (daughters of sloth),[5] the allegorizing mentality of the church fathers magisterially fixed the hallucinated psychological constellations of *acedia*. In the first place there is *malitia* (malice, ill will), the ambiguous and unstoppable love-hate for good in itself, and *rancor* (resentment), the revolt of the bad conscience against those who exhort it to good; *pusillanimitas,* the "small soul" and the scruple that withdraws crestfallen before the difficulty and the effort of spiritual existence; *desperatio,* the dark and presumptuous certainty of being already condemned beforehand and the complacent sinking into one's own destruction, as if nothing, least of all divine grace, could provide salvation; *torpor,* the obtuse and somnolent stupor that paralyzes any gesture that might heal us; and finally, *evagatio mentis* (wandering of the mind), the flight of the will before itself and the restless hastening from fantasy to fantasy.[6] The latter manifests itself in *verbositas* (garrulity), the proliferation of vain and tedious speech; *curiositas,* the insatiable desire to see for seeing's sake that disperses in always new possibilities; *instabilitas loci vel propositi* (instability of place and purpose); and *importunitas mentis* (importunity of mind), the petulant incapability of fixing an order and a rhythm to one's own thought.

Modern psychology has to such a degree emptied the term *acedia* of its original meaning, making it a sin against the capitalist work ethic, that it is difficult to discern in the spectacular medieval personification of the noonday demon and its *filiae* the innocent mixture of laziness and unwillingness that we are accustomed to associate with the image of the slothful.[7] Nevertheless, as frequently happens, the misunderstanding and the minimization of a phenomenon, far from signifying that it is remote and extraneous, are rather symptoms of a proximity so intolerable as to require camouflage and repression. This is so true that very few will have recognized in the patristic evocation of the *filiae acediae* the same categories that served Heidegger in his celebrated analysis of daily banality and the collapse into the anonymous and inauthentic of the impersonal construction "one . . . " that has furnished the point of departure (not in fact always to the purpose) for innumerable sociological characterizations of our existence within so-called mass society—but in fact there is a concordance of terms. *Evagatio mentis* becomes the flight and diversion from the most authentic possibilities of Dasein; *verbositas* is the gossip that everywhere incessantly dissimulates that which it should disclose and that maintains Dasein within equivocation; *curiositas* is the curiosity that seeks what is new only to jump once again toward what is even newer, and that, incapable of taking care of what is truly offered to it, obtains, through this impossibility of sustaining attention (the *instabilitas* of the fathers), the constant availability of distraction.

The resurrection of the psychological wisdom that the Middle Ages crystallized in the typology of the slothful therefore risks being something more than an academic exercise: scrutinized close up, the repulsive mask of the noonday demon reveals features that are perhaps more familiar than we might have expected.

If we examine the interpretation the doctors of the church gave of sloth, we see that it was not placed under the rubric of laziness but under that of anguished sadness and desperation. According to Saint Thomas, who in the *Summa theologica* gathered the observations of the fathers in a rigorous and exhaustive synthesis, sloth was, in fact, a *species tristitiae* (kind of sorrow), and more exactly, sadness with regard to the essential spiritual good of man, that is, to the particular spiritual dignity that had been conferred on him by God. What afflicts the slothful is not, therefore, the awareness of an evil, but, on the contrary, the contemplation of the greatest of goods: *acedia* is precisely the vertiginous and frightened withdrawal (*recessus*) when faced with the task implied by the place of man before God.[8] Hence, that is, insofar as sloth is the horrified flight before that which cannot be evaded in any way, *acedia* is a mortal evil; it is, indeed, the mortal malady par excellence, whose distorted image Kierkegaard fixed in the description of the most fearful of its daughters: "the desperation that is aware of its being desperation, aware therefore of having an ego in which there is something eternal, and which now desperately wishes not to be itself, or desperately wishes to be itself."

The sense of this *recessus a bono divino* (withdrawal from divine good), of this flight before the richness of one's own spiritual possibilities, contains in itself a fundamental ambiguity, whose identification is among the most surprising results of medieval psychological science. That the slothful should withdraw from his or her divine destiny does not mean, in fact, that he or she manages to forget it or ceases, in reality, to desire it. If, in theological terms, what the slothful lacks is not salvation, but the *way* that leads to it, in psychological terms the *recessus* of the slothful does not betray an eclipse of desire but, rather, the becoming unobtainable of its object: *it is the perversion of a will that wants the object, but not the way that leads to it, and which simultaneously desires and bars the path to his or her own desire.*

Saint Thomas discerns perfectly the ambiguous relation of desperation to its own desire: "What we do not desire," he writes, "cannot be the object either of our hope or of our desperation." It is to his equivocal erotic constellation that we owe the fact that in the *Summa theologica* sloth is not opposed to *sollicitudo,* that is, to desire and attention, but to *gaudium,* to the satisfaction of the spirit in God.[9]

This persistence and exaltation of desire in the face of an object that the subject itself has rendered unobtainable is expressed in the ingenuous popular characterization of *acedia* by Jacopone da Benevento: "*Acedia* wants to have everything, but does not want to make an effort." Paschasius Radbertus includes it in one of those fantastic etymologies[10] to which medieval thinkers entrusted their most audacious speculative intuitions: "Desperatio dicta est, eo quod desit illi *pes* in via, quae Christus est, gradiendi" [Desperation is so named because it lacks the foot (*pes*) to walk in the way that is Christ]. Fixed in the scandalous contemplation of a goal that reveals itself in the act by which it is precluded and that is therefore so much the more obsessive to the degree that it becomes more unattainable, the *acidiosus* (slothful one) finds himself or herself in a paradoxical position in which, as in Kafka's aphorism, "There exists a point of arrival, but no path," and there is no escape because one cannot flee from what cannot even be reached.

This desperate sinking into the abyss that is opened between desire and its unattainable object was fixed by medieval iconography in the type of *acedia,* represented as a woman who desolately lets her gaze fall to earth and abandons her head to the support of her hand, or as a bourgeois or cleric who entrusts his discomfort to the cushion that the devil holds out for him.[11] What the mnemotechnical project of the Middle Ages offered here to the edification of the contemplator was not a naturalistic representation of the "guilty sleep" of the lazy person, but the exemplary gesture of allowing the head and glance to decline as an emblem of the desperate paralysis of the soul before its inescapable situation. Precisely because of this fundamental contradiction, however, *acedia* does not have only a negative value. With their intuition of the capacity for dialectical inversion proper to the categories of spiritual life, next to *tristitia mortifera* (deadly sorrow) [or *diabolica*, or *tristitia saecula* (weariness of the world)], the fathers placed a *tristitia salutifera* (saving sorrow) [or *utilis* (useful), or *secundum deum* (according to God)] that was the operator of salvation and the "golden goad of the soul," and, as such, "it should be counted not a vice but a virtue."[12] In the ecstatic ascension of the *Scala Paradisi* of John Climachus, the seventh step is thus occupied by the "grief that makes joy," defined as "a sadness of the soul and an affliction of the heart that seeks always that for which it is ardently thirsty; and, as long as it is deprived of it, anxiously follows it and goes after it with howls and laments."

The ambiguous negative value of *acedia* becomes in this manner the dialectical leavening capable of reversing privation as possession. Since its desire remains fixed in that which has rendered itself inaccessible, *acedia* is not only a flight from, but also a flight toward, which communicates with its object in the form of negation and lack. As in those illusory figures that can be interpreted now in one way, now in another, all of its features thus describe in its concavity the fullness of that from which it is turned away, and every gesture that it completes in its flight is a testimonial to the endurance of the link that binds it to its object.

Insofar as his or her tortuous intentions open a space for the epiphany of the unobtainable, the slothful testifies to the obscure wisdom according to which hope has been given only for the hopeless, goals only for those who will always be unable to reach them. The nature of the "noonday demon" is just that dialectical. As of a mortal illness containing in itself the possibility of its own cure, it can be said of *acedia* that "the greatest disgrace is never to have had it."

Notes

1. In the most ancient patristic tradition the capital sins are not seven, but eight. In the list of John Cassian, they are *gastrimargia* (gluttony), *fornicatio* (lust), *philargyria* (avarice), *ira* (wrath), *tristitia* (sorrow), *acedia* (sloth), *cenodoxia* (vainglory), and *superbia* (pride). In the Western tradition, beginning with Saint Gregory, *tristitia* is fused with *acedia*, and the seven sins take on the order that is found in popular illustrations and allegorical representations from the end of the Middle Ages, familiar to us through the frescoes of Giotto in Padua, the *tondo* of Bosch in the Prado, or the engravings

of Brueghel. When sloth is mentioned in the text, the reference is always to the complex resulting from this fusion, which should be rendered more precisely as *tristitia-acedia* (sadness-sloth).

2. "Maxime circa horam sextam monachum inquietans. . . . Denique nonnulli senum hunc esse pronuntiant meridianum daemonen, qui in psalmo nonagesimo nuncupatur" (The monk is made most restless at about the sixth hour. . . . Therefore not a few elders have judged this to be the noonday demon that is mentioned in the ninetieth psalm) (John Cassian, *De institutis coenobiorum*, book 10, chap. 1, in *Patrologia latina*, 49). Similarly, John Climachus (*Scala Paradisi*, gr. 13, in *Patrologia graeca*, 88): "Mane primum languentes medicus visitat, acedia vero monachos circa meridiem" (The doctor visits the sick in the early morning, and sloth visits the monks around noon). It is then no accident that in Brueghel's engraving representing sloth, an enormous clock face appears in the upper right of the painting, on which, in the place of the usual clock hands, the image of a hand indicates *circa meridiem* (near noon). On the noonday demon, consult Leopardi's, *Saggio sopra gli errori popolari degli antichi* (Essay on the popular errors of the ancients), chap. 7. The reference to the "ninetieth psalm" in Cassian is, to be precise, to the sixth verse, and the Hebrew word that corresponds is *Keteb*. According to Rohde, the noonday demon of Christian authors is a reincarnation of Empusa, one of the ogress figures in the spectral retinue of Hecate, which appears, in fact, at noon [See Erwin Rohde, *Psyche: The Cult of Souls and the Belief in Immortality among the Greeks* (New York: Harcourt, Brace, 1925)].

3. Sancti Nili, *De octo spiritibus malitiae*, chap. 14.

4. John Cassian, *De institutis coenobiorum*, book 10, chap. 2. Even at the distance of so many centuries, the patristic description of the slothful man has lost none of its exemplarity and contemporaneity and seems rather to have furnished the model for modern literature in the grips of its own *mal du siècle*. Thus the Chevalier d'Albert, the protagonist of that bible *avant la lettre* of decadentism that is *Mademoiselle de Maupin*, is presented by Gautier in terms that closely recall the medieval phenomenology of sloth. Even closer to the patristic model is the description of the states of feeling of Des Esseintes (who does not conceal his preference for the works of the church fathers) in Huysmans's *A rebours*. Similar traits, though garnered obviously at second hand, are to be found in Giorgio Aurispa's *Trionfo della morte*. In many respects, Baudelaire's annotations in *Mon coeur mis à nu* and in the *Fusées* reveal as well a singular proximity to the phenomenology of sloth. In any case, in the poem that opens *Les fleurs du mal*, Baudelaire places his poetic work under the sign of sloth (here appearing as *ennui*). Baudelaire's poetry in its totality may be understood, in this perspective, as a mortal struggle with sloth and, at the same time, as the attempt to transform it into something positive. The dandy, who represents, according to Baudelaire, the perfect type of the poet, may be considered, in a certain sense, as a reincarnation of the slothful. If it is true that the essence of dandyism consists in a religion of the trivial or in an art of carelessness (that is, in taking pains over carelessness itself), then it presents itself as a paradoxical reevaluation of sloth, whose etymological meaning is, in fact, lack of care (from *a-chedomai*).

5. According to Gregory, there are six daughters of sloth: *malitia, rancor, pusillanimitas, desperatio, torpor circa praecepta, evagatio mentis* (malice, rancor, pusillanimity, desperation, torpor with regard to rules and precepts, wandering of the mind). Isidore lists seven (*otiositas, somnolentia, importunitas mentis, inquietudo corporis, instabilitas, verbositas, curiositas;* idleness, somnolence, indecorousness of mind, bodily disquiet, instability, verbosity, curiosity), but, as Saint Thomas observes, these can be reduced to those enumerated by Gregory. In fact, "otiositas et somnolentia reducuntur ad torporem circa praecepta . . . omnia autem alia quinque, quae possint oriri ex acedia, pertinent ad evagationem mentis circa illicita" (*idleness* and *somnolence* reduce to *torpor regarding precepts* . . . all the other five that can originate from sloth, pertaining to the *wandering of the mind toward unlawful things*) (see *Summa theologica*, IIa IIae 35, 4th article). In *Aurora*, the first novel of one of the most acute and "slothful" of living French writers, Michel Leiris, it is possible to find a distinctly abundant list of *filiae acediae* (sixty-eight), but it is easy to establish that they can almost be subsumed under the patristic categories.

6. The inability to control the incessant discourse (the *co-agitatio*) of the interior phantasms is among the essential traits in the patristic characterization of sloth. All the *Vitae patrum* (Lives of the fathers) (*Patrologia latina,* 73) echo to the cry of the monks and anchorites whom solitude confronts with the monstrous proliferation of the fantasy: "Domine, salvari desidero, sed cogitationes variae non permittunt" (Lord, I wish to be saved, but the fluctuating thoughts do not permit it); "Quid faciam, pater, quoniam nulla opera facio monachi, sed in negligentia constitutus comedo et bibo et dormio, et de hora in horam transgredior de cogitatione in cogitationem" (What shall I do, father, since I perform no works fitting for a monk; rather, established in my negligence I eat and drink and sleep, and hour by hour I flit from one thought to another). *Cogitatio,* in medieval terminology, refers always to the phantasy and to its phantasmatic discourse; only with the disappearance of the Greek and medieval notion of the separate intellect does *cogitatio* begin to describe intellectual activity.

We will see later that this hypertrophy of the imagination is one of the traits that links the sloth of the fathers to the melancholic syndrome and to the love-disease of humoral medicine; like these, sloth could be defined as *vitium corruptae imaginationis* (a fault of corrupted imagination). Whoever, under the effect of this melancholic depression, induced by a disease or a drug, has experienced this disorder of the phantasy, knows that the uncontrollable flux of interior images is, for the consciousness, one of the most arduous and dangerous trials. Flaubert, who suffered through his adolescence with an atrocious imaginative disorder, represented in his most ambitious work (*La tentation de Saint Antoine*) the condition of a soul at grips with the "temptations" of the phantasy. The discovery, familiar to the mystic tradition of every country, of a possible positive value implicit in the abundance of phantasms was, as we shall see, a significant event in the history of Western culture.

One of the few modern attempts to construct something that corresponds to medieval phantasmology is owed to that unique mixture of genius and idiocy that characterized Léon Daudet (an author dear to Walter Benjamin), whose analysis of interior phantasms (defined as *personimages*) gives rise to an authentic biological theory of the human spirit as a "system of congenital images and figures" that deserves to be developed further. From this point of view, a reading of his now unobtainable *Le monde des images* (1919) and *Le rêve eveillé* (1926) is of considerable interest.

7. For an interpretation of sloth that restores its original meaning, see Josef Pieper, *Hope and History,* trans. Richard and Clara Winston (London: Burns and Oates/Herder and Herder, 1969).

It is surely not a coincidence if, parallel to the bourgeois travesty of sloth as laziness, laziness (along with sterility, which is crystallized in the ideal of the lesbian) comes to be the emblem that artists oppose to the capitalist ethic of productivity and usefulness. The poetry of Baudelaire is dominated throughout by the idea of *paresse* (laziness, idleness) as a cipher of beauty. One of the fundamental effects that Moreau attempted to realize in his painting was *la belle inertie* (beautiful inertia). The obsessive return, in his work, of an emblematic female figure (as fixed, in particular, in the hieratic gesture of his Salome) cannot be understood if one ignores his conception of femininity as the cryptography of idleness and unproductive tedium: "Cette femme ennuyée, fantasque," he writes, "à nature animale, se donnant le plaisir, très peu vif pour elle, de voir son ennemi à terre, tant elle est degoutée de toute satisfaction de ses désirs. Cette femme se promenant nonchalamment d'une façon végetale . . . " (This bored, capricious woman, of animal nature, giving herself the pleasure, scarcely vivid enough for her, of seeing her enemy prostrated, so much is she disgusted by every satisfaction of her desires. This woman strolling nonchalantly in a vegetal manner . . .). In the great unfinished canvas of *Les chimères* (Chimaeras), where Moreau wished to represent all the sins and temptations of mankind, a figure can be detected that strikingly corresponds to the traditional representation of sloth-melancholy.

8. "Acedia non est recessus mentalis a quocumque spirituali bono, sed a bono divino, cui oportet mentem inhaerere ex necessitate" (Sloth is not a mental withdrawal from any spiritual good, but from the divine good, to which it behooves the mind to cleave out of necessity) (*Summa theologica* 2, 2.35). The account of Guillaume d'Auvergne said that the slothful man is sickened by God himself: "Deum igitur ipsum fontem omnium suavitatem in primis fastidit accidiosus" (God, therefore, the fount of all sweetness, first of all sickens the slothful man) (Guiliemi Parisiensis, *Opera omnia,* Ve-

netiis, 1591, p. 168). The image of the *recessus,* of drawing back, constant in the patristic descriptions of sloth, also appeared, as we will see, in the medical accounts of melancholy, from humoral medicine through Freud.

9. "Ergo acedia nihil aliud est quam pigritia, quod videtur esse falsum; nam pigritia sollicitudini opponitur, acediae autem gaudium" (Therefore sloth is nothing but laziness, which is false; for laziness is opposed to zeal, sloth, rather, to joy) (*Summa theologica* 2, 2.35). Alcuin, too, insists on the aggravation of desire as an essential characteristic of sloth: the slothful man "is stupefied in carnal desires and takes no joy in spiritual works, nor is gladdened in the desire of his soul, nor rejoices in the assistance of fraternal labor; but yet he craves and desires, and his idle mind flits over every thing." The link between sloth and desire, and therefore between sloth and love, is among the most inspired intuitions of medieval psychology and is essential to understanding the nature of this sin. This explains why Dante, in *Purgatorio* XVII, understood sloth as a form of love, to be precise, as that love "that runs to the good in a disordered manner" (v. 126).

10. The unsurpassed model of this fantastic science of etyma is in Plato's *Cratylus,* whose richness of material on the science of language is far from completely explored. Among the many playful etymologies (which are not, however, to be taken only as jokes) that Plato proposes, deserving of being remembered here are at least those of *onoma* (name) from *on ou masma estin* ("the being that is avidly sought"); *istoria* (history), *hoti histesi ton hroun* ("because it stops the flow of time"); and *alētheia* (truth) from *theia alē* ("divine race").

11. Panofsky and Saxl, in their study on the genealogy of Dürer's *Melencolia* (see figure 1) [*Dürer's "Melencolia I". Eine quellen- und typengeschichtliche Untersuchung* (Leipzig-Berlin, 1923)], misunderstood the medieval concept of sloth, which they interpreted simply as the guilty sleep of the lazy. *Somnolentia* (as an aspect of *torpor circa praecepta*) is only one of the consequences of sloth and in no way characterizes its essence. The easy refuge of sleep is but the "pillow" that the devil holds out to the slothful man to deprive him of all resistance to sin. The gesture of allowing the head to recline on one hand signifies not sleep, but desperation. And it is precisely to this emblematic gesture that the old German equivalent of the term *acedia* alludes: *truricheit,* from *trûren = den Blick, das Haupt gesenkt halten* (allow the gaze and head to fall toward the earth). Only later does the essence of sloth become blurred and confused with laziness. It is possible that the pathway of this conversion was the assimilation of the noonday demon of sloth to the *somnus meridianus,* which the Salernitan *Regimen sanitatis* (Rule of health) recommended be avoided as the cause of many evils: "Let your noonday sleep be none, or brief. / Sloth, headaches, catarrhs, and fever / all these come to the noonday sleeper."

12. Already in a work attributed to Saint Augustine (*Liber de conflictu vitiorum et virtutum,* in *Patrologia latina,* 40), *tristitia* is defined as *gemina* (twin): "I discovered sadness to be double, indeed I knew two kinds of sorrow: one that works salvation, the other, evil; one that draws to penitence, the other that leads to desperation." So also Alcuin: "There are two kinds of sadness: one that brings salvation, one that brings plagues" (*Liber de virtutis,* chap. 33); and Jonas d'Orléans: "Sadness occurs in two ways, that is, sometimes healthful, sometimes lethal; when it is healthful, it should be counted not a vice but a virtue." In the alchemical terminology sloth also appears with a double polarity: in the *Clavis totius philosophiae* at Dorn (in *Theatrum chemicum,* Argentorari 1622, vol. 1), the alchemical oven is called *acedia* because of its slowness, which, however, appears as a necessary quality ("Now we have the oven filled up [or fully prepared], which we sometimes call sloth, because it is slow in operation, on account of the slow fire").

Chapter 2
Melencolia I

The list of the four humors of the human body was condensed by the *Regimen sanitatis* of Salerno into an aphorism of three verses:

Quatuor humores in humano corpore constant:
Sanguis cum cholera, phlegma, melancholia.
Terra melancholia, aqua phlegma, aer sanguis, cholera ignis.

[Four humors coexist in the human body:
Blood, with choler, phlegm, and melancholy.
Earth melancholy, water phlegm, air blood, choler fire.]

Melancholy[1] or black bile (*melaina chole*) is the humor whose disorders are liable to produce the most destructive consequences. In medieval humoral cosmology, melancholy is traditionally associated with the earth, autumn (or winter), the dry element, cold, the north wind, the color black, old age (or maturity); its planet is Saturn, among whose children the melancholic finds himself with the hanged man, the cripple, the peasant, the gambler, the monk, and the swineherd. The physiological syndrome of *abundantia melancholiae* (abundance of melancholy humor) includes darkening of the skin, blood, and urine, hardening of the pulse, burning in the gut, flatulence, acid burping, whistling in the left ear,[2] constipation or excess of feces, and gloomy dreams; among the diseases it can induce are hysteria, dementia, epilepsy, leprosy, hemorrhoids, scabies, and suicidal mania. Consequently the temperament that derives from its predominance in the human body is presented in a sinister light: the melancholic is *pexime com-*

plexionatus (worst complected), sad, envious, malevolent, avid, fraudulent, cowardly, and earthly.

Nevertheless, an ancient tradition associated the exercise of poetry, philosophy, and the arts with this most wretched of all humors. "Why is it," asks one of the most extravagant of the Aristotelian *problemata*, "that all men who are outstanding in philosophy, poetry, or the arts are melancholic, and some to such an extent that they are infected by the disease arising from black bile?" The answer Aristotle gave to his own question marks the point of departure of a dialectical process in the course of which the doctrine of genius came to be joined indissolubly to that of the melancholic humor under the spell of a symbolic complex whose emblem ambiguously established itself in the winged angel of Dürer's *Melencolia* (see figure 1):

> Those for instance in whom the bile is considerable and cold become sluggish and stupid, while those with whom it is excessive and hot become mad, good-natured or amorous, and easily moved to passion and desire. . . . But many, because this heat is near to the seat of the mind, are affected by the diseases of madness or frenzy, which accounts for the Sibyls, Bacis, and all inspired persons, when their condition is due not to a disease but to a natural mixture. Maracus, the Syracusan, was an even better poet when he was mad. But those with whom the excessive heat has sunk to a moderate amount are melancholic, though more intelligent and less strange, but they differ from the rest of the world in many ways, some in education, some in the arts, and others again in statesmanship.[3]

This double polarity of black bile and its link to the "divine mania" of Plato were gathered and developed with particular fervor in that curious miscellany of mystic sects and avant-garde cabals that gathered, in the Florence of Lorenzo the Magnificent, around Marsilio Ficino. In the thought of Ficino, who recognized himself as a melancholic and whose horoscope showed "Saturnum in Aquario ascendentem" (Saturn ascendant in Aquarius), the rehabilitation of melancholy went hand in hand with an ennobling of the influence of Saturn,[4] which the astrological tradition associated with the melancholic temperament as the most malignant of planets, in the intuition of polarized extremes where the ruinous experience of opacity and the ecstatic ascent to divine contemplation coexisted alongside each other. In this context, the elemental influence of the earth and the astral influence of Saturn were united to confer on the melancholic a natural propensity to interior withdrawal and contemplative knowledge:

> The nature of the melancholic humor follows the quality of earth, which never dispersed like the other elements, but concentrated more strictly in itself . . . such is also the nature of Mercury and Saturn, in virtue of which the spirits, gathering themselves at the center, bring back the

apex of the soul from what is foreign to it to what is proper to it, fix it in contemplation, and allow it to penetrate to the center of things.[5]

Thus the cannibal and castrated god, represented in medieval imagery as lame and brandishing the harvesting scythe of death, became the sign under whose equivocal domination the noblest species of man, the "religious contemplative" destined to the investigation of the supreme mysteries, found its place next to the "rude and material" herd of the wretched children of Saturn.

It is not easy to discern the precise moment when the moral doctrine of the noon-day demon emerged from the cloister to join ranks with the ancient medical syndrome of the black-biled temperament. When the iconographic types of the slothful and the melancholic appeared fused in calendar illustrations and popular almanacs at the end of the Middle Ages, the process must have already been un-der way for some time; only a poor understanding of sloth, one that identifies it with its late travesty as the "guilty sleep" of the lazy person, can explain why Panofsky and Saxl, in their attempt to reconstruct the genealogy of Dürer's *Melencolia,* reserved such scant space for the patristic literature on the "noonday demon." To this poor understanding we also owe the erroneous opinion (repeated by all who have traditionally preoccupied themselves with this problem)[6] that *acedia* had a purely negative valuation in the Middle Ages. It may be supposed, on the contrary, that the patristic discovery of the double polarity of *tristitia-acedia* prepared the ground for the Renaissance reevaluation of the atrabilious temperament within the context of a vision in which the noonday demon, as the temptation of the religious, and black humor, as the specific malady of the con-templative, should appear assimilable, and in which melancholy, having under-gone a gradual process of moralization, presented itself as, so to speak, the lay heir of cloistral sorrow and gloom.[7]

In the *Medicine of the Soul* of Hugh of St. Victor, the process of allegorical transfiguration of humoral theory appeared close to completion. If in Hildegard von Bingen the negative polarity of melancholy was still interpreted as the sign of original sin, in Hugh the black bile was now identified rather with the *tristitia utilis* (useful sorrow) in a perspective where the humoral pathology became the corporeal vehicle of a mechanism of redemption:

> The human soul uses four humors: sweetness like blood, bitterness like red bile, sadness like black bile. . . . Black bile is cold and dry, but ice and dryness can be interpreted now in a good, now in an evil sense.
> . . . It renders men now somnolent, now vigilant, that is, now grave with anguish, now vigilant and intent on celestial desires. . . . You obtained, through blood, the sweetness of charity; have now, through black bile, O melancholy, sorrow for your sins![8]

This reciprocal penetration of sloth and melancholy maintained intact their double polarity in the idea of a mortal risk latent in the noblest of human intentions, or the possibility of salvation hidden in the greatest danger. With this in mind we can understand why the "greedy desire to see the supreme good" should be found in the writings of Constantine the African, the master of the medical school of Salerno, as one of the causes of melancholy of the religious, and why, on the other hand, the theologian Guillaume d'Auvergne could affirm that in his day "many pious and religious men ardently desired the melancholy disease."[9] In the stubborn contemplative vocation of the saturnine temperament reappears the perverse Eros of the slothful, who keeps his or her own desire fixed on the inaccessible.

Notes

1. The most complete study on melancholy remains that of Klibansky, Panofsky, and Saxl, *Saturn and Melancholy* (London, 1964), whose omissions and doubtful points will be noted in the course of this chapter.

2. This symptom (and not, as Panofsky seems to hold, slothful somnolence, especially given that the authoritative Aristotle—*De somno et vigilia,* 457a—affirmed that melancholics were not lovers of sleep) perhaps best explains the gesture of holding up the head with the left hand, so characteristic of the depictions of the melancholic temperament (in the oldest representations, the melancholic often appeared standing, in the act of squeezing his left ear with his hand). This attitude probably came to be misunderstood as an indication of sleepiness and assimilated to depictions of sloth; the path of this convergence may be sought in the medical theory of the harmful effects of the *somnus meridianus* (midday sleep) placed in relation with the noonday demon of sloth.

3. These two quotations from Problem 30 of Aristotle's *Problems* are from the translation by W. S. Hett (Cambridge: Harvard University Press, 1937), 953a and 954a-b.

Bringing up to date the list of melancholics listed by Aristotle in his Problem 30 [Hercules, Bellerophon, Heraclitus (see figure 3), Democritus, Maracus] would risk excessive length. After its first reappearance among the love poets of the duecento, the great return of melancholy began with humanism. Among artists, the cases of Michelangelo, Dürer, and Pontormo are exemplary. A second epidemic struck in Elizabethan England (see L. Babb, *The Elizabethan Malady,* Lansing, 1951); the case of John Donne is a good example. The third epoch of melancholy was the nineteenth century: among the victims were Baudelaire, Nerval, De Quincey, Coleridge, Strindberg, and Huysmans. During all three periods, melancholy was interpreted with daring polarization as something at once positive and negative.

4. The rediscovery of the importance of the astrological theory of influences of Saturn for the interpretation of Dürer's *Melencolia* was the work of K. Giehlow (*Dürers Stich 'Melencholia I' und der maximilianische Humanistenkreis,* Vienna, 1903) and A. Warburg ("Heidnisch-antike Weissagung in Wort und Bild zu Luthers Zeiten" in *Sitzungsberichte der Heidelberg Akademie der Wissenschaften,* vol. 26, Heidelberg, 1920). Warburg's interpretation of Dürer's image as a "pamphlet of humanistic comfort against the fear of Saturn," which transforms the effigy of the planetary demon into the plastic incarnation of the contemplative man, strongly influenced the conclusions of the aforementioned study by Panofsky and Saxl.

5. Marsilio Ficino, *Theologia platonica de animarum immortalitate,* critical edition by R. Marcel, Paris, 1964, book 13, chap. 2.

6. The error is thus repeated even by careful students such as Edgar Wind (*Pagan Mysteries in the Renaissance,* Harmondsworth, 1967) and Rudolf Wittkower.

7. Proof of the early convergence of melancholy and *tristitia-acedia,* which appeared rather as two aspects of the same reality, is found in a letter of Saint Jerome: "Sunt qui humore cellarum,

immoderatisque jeiunis, taedio solitudinis ac nimia lectione, dum diebus ac noctibus auribus suis per-sonant, vertuntur in melancholiam et Hippocratis magis fomentis quam nostris monitis indigent'' (There are those who, because of the dampness of the cells, immoderate fasts, the boredom of soli-tude, and the excessive reading sounding in their ears day and night, are given to melancholy, and need the poultice of Hippocrates more than our admonitions) (Epistle 4).

8. The author is actually Hugo de Folieto (*Patrologia latina,* 176, 1183ff.).

9. Guilielmi Parisiensis, *De universo,* 1, 3.7 (in *Opera omnia*).

Chapter 3
Melancholic Eros

The same tradition that associated the melancholic temperament with poetry, philosophy, and art attributed to it an exasperated inclination to Eros. Aristotle, after having affirmed the genial vocation of melancholics, placed lustfulness among their essential characteristics:

> Now the liquid and the mixing of the black bile is due to breath . . .
> and the melancholic are usually lustful. For sexual excitement is due to
> breath. The penis proves this as it quickly increases from small to large
> because of the breath in it. (*Problems,* trans. W. S. Hett, 953b)

From this moment on, erotic disorder figures among the traditional attributes of black bile.[1] If, analogously, the slothful man was also represented in medieval treatises on the vices as *philedonos* (pleasure-loving), and Alcuin could say that "he becomes sluggish in carnal vices," in the strongly moralizing interpretation of humoral theory by Hildegard von Bingen the abnormal Eros of the melancholic assumed no less than the aspect of a feral and sadistic disturbance:

> Melancholics have great bones that contain little marrow, which
> nevertheless burns so strongly that they are incontinent with women like
> vipers . . . they are excessive in lust and without restraint with women,
> like asses, so much so that if they ceased from the depravation they
> would readily become mad . . . their embrace is hateful, twisted, and
> mortal like that of predatory wolves . . . they have commerce with
> women, but nevertheless they despise them.[2]

But the nexus between love and melancholy had long since found its theoretical foundation in a medical tradition that constantly considered love and melancholy as related, if not identical, maladies. In this tradition, fully articulated in the *Viaticum* of the Arab physician Haly Abbas (who, through the tradition of Constantine the African, profoundly influenced medieval European medicine), love, which appeared with the name *amor hereos* or *amor heroycus,* and melancholy were catalogued in contiguous rubrics among the mental diseases.[3] On occasion, as in the *Speculum doctrinale* of Vincent de Beauvais, they appeared in fact under the same rubric: "de melancolia nigra et canina et de amore qui ereos dicitur" (of black and canine melancholy and of love that is called *ereos*). The substantial proximity of erotic and melancholic pathology found its expression in the *De amore* of Ficino. The very process of falling in love here became the mechanism that unhinges and subverts the moral equilibrium, while, conversely, the determined contemplative inclination of the melancholic pushes him or her fatally toward amorous passion. The willful figural synthesis that emerged from this mechanism and that pushed Eros to assume the obscure saturnine traits of the most sinister of the temperaments must have remained operative for centuries in the popular conception of the amorous melancholic, whose emaciated and ambiguous caricature made its timely appearance among the emblems of black humor on the frontispiece of sixteenth-century treatises on melancholy:

> Wherever the assiduous intentions of the soul bear themselves, there also the spirits direct themselves, which are the vehicles or the instruments of the soul. The spirits are produced in the heart with the most subtle part of the blood. The soul of the lover is pulled toward the image of the beloved written in the imagination and toward the beloved itself. Thither are attracted also the spirits, and, in their obsessive flight, they are exhausted. Because of this a constant refurbishing of pure blood is necessary to replace the consumed spirits, there where the most delicate and transparent particles of blood are exhaled each day in order to regenerate the spirits. Because of this, pure and bright blood is dissolved, and nothing remains but impure, thick, arid, and black blood. Then the body dries out and dwindles, and the lovers become melancholic. It is in fact the dry, thick, and black blood that produces melancholic or black bile, which fills the head with its vapors, dries out the brain, and ceaselessly oppresses, day and night, the soul with dark and frightening visions. . . . It is because of having observed this condition that the doctors of antiquity have affirmed that love is a passion that resembles the melancholy disease. The physician Rasis prescribes therefore, in order to recover, coitus, fasting, drunkenness, walking.[4]

In the same passage, the specific character of melancholic Eros was identified by Ficino as disjunction and excess. "This tends to occur," he wrote, "to those who, misusing love, transform what rightly belongs to contemplation into the desire of the embrace." The erotic intention that unleashes the melancholic disorder presents itself as that which would possess and touch what ought merely to be the object of contemplation, and the tragic insanity of the saturnine temperament thus finds its root in the intimate contradiction of a gesture that would embrace the unobtainable. It is from this perspective that we should interpret the passage from Henry of Ghent that Panofsky placed in relation to Dürer's image and according to which melancholics "cannot conceive the incorporeal" as such, because they do not know "how to extend their intelligence beyond space and size." This is not, as some have claimed, merely a matter of a static limit in the mental structure of melancholics that excludes them from the metaphysical sphere, but rather of a dialectical limit tied to the erotic impulse to transgress, which transforms the contemplative intention into the "concupiscence of the embrace." That is, the incapacity of conceiving the incorporeal and the desire to make of it the object of an embrace are two faces of the same coin, of the process in whose course the traditional contemplative vocation of the melancholic reveals itself vulnerable to a violent disturbance of desire menacing it from within.[5]

It is curious that this erotic constellation of melancholy should have so persistently escaped scholars who have attempted to trace the genealogy and meaning of Dürer's *Melencolia*. Any interpretation—whatever its ability to decipher one by one the figures inscribed in its field of vision—that fails to consider the fundamental relevance of black bile to the sphere of erotic desire is bound to be excluded from the mystery so emblematically fixed in Dürer's image. Only when it is understood that the image is placed under the sign of Eros is it possible simultaneously to keep and reveal the secret of the emblem, whose allegorical intention is entirely subtended in the space between Eros and its phantasms.

Notes

1. The association between melancholy, sexual perversion, and nervous excitability (erethism) is still found among the symptoms of melancholy in modern psychiatric texts, testifying to the curious immutability over time of the atrabilious syndrome.

2. *Causae et curae,* ed. Kaiser, Leipzig, 1903, p. 73; see also 20ff.

3. Thus Arnaldo of Villanova (*Liber de parte operativa,* in *Opera,* Lugduni, 1532, fol. 123-50) distinguished five types of *alienatio*: the third is melancholy, the fourth is "alienatio quam concomitatur immensa concupiscentia et irrationalis: et graece dicitur heroys . . . et vulgariter amor, et a medicis amor heroycus" (alienation that is accompanied by enormous and irrational concupiscence: and in Greek it is called *heroys* . . . and more commonly love, and by the doctors heroical love).

4. Marsilio Ficino, *De amore,* critical edition by R. Marcel, Paris, 1956, oration 6, chap. 9.

5. From this point of view, the "melancolia illa heroica" (that heroic melancholy) that Melanchthon (in a passage of the *De anima* that did not escape Warburg) attributed to Dürer plausibly contains a reference to the *amor heroycus* that was, according to the medical tradition passed on by Ficino, a kind of melancholy. This proximity of love and melancholy, according to medieval medicine, also explained the appearance of *Dame Melencolie* (Lady Melancholy) in the love poetry of the thirteenth and fourteenth centuries.

Chapter 4
The Lost Object

In 1917, in the *Internationale Zeitschrift für Psychoanalyse* (vol. 4), the essay "Mourning and Melancholia" was published, one of the rare texts in which Freud affronted thematically the psychoanalytic interpretation of the ancient saturnine humor. The distance that separates psychoanalysis from the last sixteenth-century offshoots of humoral medicine coincides with the birth and the development of modern psychiatric science, which classifies melancholia among the grave forms of mental disease. Therefore it is not without some surprise that we rediscover in the Freudian analysis of the mechanism of melancholia—translated naturally into the language of libido—two elements that appeared traditionally in the patristic descriptions of *acedia* and in the phenomenology of the black-biled temperament, and whose persistence in the Freudian text testifies to the extraordinary stability over time of the melancholy constellation: the withdrawal from the object and the withdrawal into itself of the contemplative tendency.

According to Freud, the dynamic mechanism of melancholy borrows its essential characteristics in part from mourning and in part from narcissistic regression. As when, in mourning, the libido reacts to proof of the fact that the loved one has ceased to exist, fixating itself on every memory and object formerly linked to the loved object, so melancholy is also a reaction to the loss of a loved object; however, contrary to what might be expected, such loss is not followed by a transfer of libido to another object, but rather by its withdrawal into the ego, narcissistically identified with the lost object. According to the succinct formula of Abraham, whose conclusions on melancholia, published five years earlier, constituted the basis of Freud's study, "after being withdrawn from the object, the libidinal investment returns to the ego and the object is simultaneously incorporated in the ego.''[1]

Nevertheless, with respect to the genetic process of mourning, melancholia presents a relationship to its origin that is especially difficult to explain. Freud does not conceal his embarrassment before the undeniable proof that, although mourning follows a loss that has really occurred, in melancholia not only is it unclear what object has been lost, it is uncertain that one can speak of a loss at all. "It must be admitted," Freud writes, with a certain discomfort, "that a loss has indeed occurred, without it being known what has been lost." Shortly thereafter, in the attempt to gloss over the contradiction posed by a loss without a lost object, Freud speaks of an "unknown loss" or of an "object-loss that escapes consciousness." In fact, the examination of the mechanism of melancholia, as described by Freud and Abraham, shows that the withdrawal of libido is the original datum, beyond which investigation can go no further; if we wish to maintain the analogy with mourning, we ought to say that melancholia offers the paradox of an intention to mourn that precedes and anticipates the loss of the object. Here psychoanalysis appears to have reached conclusions very similar to those intuited by the church fathers, who conceived of sloth as the withdrawal from a good that had not yet been lost and who interpreted the most terrible of its daughters, despair, as an anticipation of unfulfillment and damnation. As, in the case of *acedia,* the withdrawal not from a defect, but from a frantic exacerbation of desire that renders its object inaccessible to itself in the desperate attempt to protect itself from the loss of that object and to adhere to it at least in its absence, so it might be said that the withdrawal of melancholic libido has no other purpose than to make viable an appropriation in a situation in which none is really possible. From this point of view, melancholy would be not so much the regressive reaction to the loss of the love object as the imaginative capacity to make an unobtainable object appear as if lost. If the libido behaves *as if* a loss had occurred although *nothing* has in fact been lost, this is because the libido stages a simulation where what cannot be lost because it has never been possessed appears as lost, and what could never be possessed because it had never perhaps existed may be appropriated insofar as it is lost. At this point the specific ambition of the ambiguous melancholy project, which the analogy with the exemplary mechanism of mourning had in part disfigured and rendered unrecognizable, becomes understandable: it is what the ancient humoral theory rightly identified in the will to transform into an object of amorous embrace what should have remained only an object of contemplation. Covering its object with the funereal trappings of mourning, melancholy confers upon it the phantasmagorical reality of what is lost; but insofar as such mourning is for an unobtainable object, the strategy of melancholy opens a space for the existence of the unreal and marks out a scene in which the ego may enter into relation with it and attempt an appropriation such as no other possession could rival and no loss possibly threaten.

If this is true, if melancholy succeeds in appropriating its own object only to the extent that it affirms its loss, it is understandable why Freud remained so struck by the ambivalence of the melancholic tendency, so much so as to make it one of the essential characteristics of the malady. In melancholia, love and hate— engaged in pitched battle around the object, "one to separate the libido from it, the other to defend from attack this position of the libido"—coexist and reconcile in one of those compromises possible only under the laws of the unconscious, a compromise whose identification remains among the most fecund acquisitions psychoanalysis has bequeathed to the sciences of the spirit.

In the case of the fetishist *Verleugnung* (disavowal), in the conflict between the perception of reality (which forces the child to renounce his phantasy) and his desire (which drives him to deny its perception), the child does neither one thing nor the other (or, rather, does both things simultaneously, repudiating, on the one hand, the evidence of his perceptions, and recognizing reality, on the other hand, through the assumption of a perverse symptom). Similarly, in melancholia the object is neither appropriated nor lost, but both possessed and lost at the same time.[2] And as the fetish is at once the sign of something and its absence, and owes to this contradiction its own phantomatic status, so the object of the melancholic project is at once real and unreal, incorporated and lost, affirmed and denied. It does not surprise us then that Freud was able to speak, in regard to melancholia, of a "triumph of the object over the ego," clarifying that "the object has been, yes, suppressed, but it has shown itself stronger than the ego." This is a curious triumph, which consists in conquering through autosuppression; however, it is precisely in the gesture that abolishes the object that the melancholic demonstrates his or her extreme fidelity to it.

From this perspective we can also understand in what sense ought to be taken both Freud's correlation (made in Abraham's footsteps) between melancholy and "the oral or cannibal phase in the evolution of the libido," where the ego aspires to incorporate its object by devouring it, and the singular obstinacy with which eighteenth-century legal psychiatry classified as forms of melancholia the cases of cannibalism that fill with horrors the criminal chronicles of the period. The ambiguity of the melancholic relationship to the object was thus assimilated to the cannibalizing that destroys and also incorporates the object of libido. Behind the "melancholic ogres" of the legal archives of the nineteenth century, the sinister shadow of the god who devours his children rises again, that Chronos-Saturn whose traditional associations with melancholy find here an additional basis in the identification of that phantasmatic incorporation of the melancholic libido with the homophagic meal made of that deposed monarch of the Golden Age.[3]

Notes

1. K. Abraham, "Notes on the Psycho-Analytical Investigations and Treatment of Manic-Depressive Insanity and Allied Conditions," *Selected Papers on Psycho-Analysis* (London, 1927).

2. On this characteristic of the fetish according to Freud, see chapter 6 of this volume.

3. On the links between cannibalism and melancholia, see the *Nouvelle Revue de Psychanalyse* 6 (1972), on the topic "Destins du cannibalisme."

Chapter 5
The Phantasms of Eros

In his essay "Mourning and Melancholia" Freud barely hints at the eventual phantasmatic character of the melancholic process, observing that the revolt against the loss of the loved object can be so intense that a turning away from reality takes place, a clinging to the object through the medium of a hallucinatory wishful psychosis."[1] It is necessary therefore to refer to his "A Metapsychological Supplement to the Theory of Dreams" (which, with the essay on melancholia published with it, was to have formed part of the projected volume of *Preparations for a Metapsychology*) to find sketched, next to an analysis of the mechanism of the dream, an investigation into the process through which the phanthoms of desire manage to elude that fundamental institution of the ego, the reality test, and penetrate into consciousness. According to Freud, in the development of psychic life, the ego passes through an initial stage in which it does not yet dispose of a faculty that will permit it to differentiate real from imaginary perceptions:

> At the beginning of our mental life we did in fact hallucinate the satisfying object when we felt the need for it. But in such a situation, satisfaction did not occur, and this failure must very soon have moved us to create some contrivance with the help of which it was possible to distinguish such wishful perceptions from a real fulfillment and to avoid them for the future. In other words, we gave up hallucinatory satisfaction of our wishes at a very early period and set up a kind of "reality-testing." ("Metapsychological Supplement" 231)

In certain cases, however, the reality test can be evaded or temporarily set aside. This is what occurs during the hallucinatory psychoses of desire, which present themselves as a reaction to a loss, affirmed by reality, but which the ego must deny because it finds the loss unbearable:

> The ego then breaks its link to reality and withdraws its own investment to the conscious system of perceptions. It is through this distortion of the real that the reality test is avoided and the phantasms of desire, not removed, but perfectly conscious, can penetrate into the consciousness and come to be accepted as a superior reality.

Freud, who in none of his writings elaborates a proper organic theory of the phantasm, does not specify what part the phantasm plays in the dynamic of melancholic introjection. Nevertheless, an ancient and tenacious tradition considered the syndrome of black bile to be so closely tied to a morbid hypertrophy of the imaginative (or phantasmatic, phantastic) faculty that only if situated within the fundamental complex of the medieval theory of the phantasm could all of its aspects be understood. It is probable that contemporary psychoanalysis, which has reevaluated the role of the phantasm in the psychic processes and which seems intent on considering itself, always more explicitly, as a general theory of the phantasm, would find a useful point of reference in a doctrine that, many centuries previously, had conceived of Eros as an essentially phantasmatic process and had prepared a large place in the life of the spirit for the phantasm. Medieval phantasmology was born from a convergence between the Aristotelian theory of the imagination and the Neoplatonic doctrine of the pneuma as a vehicle of the soul, between the magical theory of fascination and the medical theory of the influences between spirit and body. According to this multiform doctrinal complex, which is found already variously enunciated in the pseudo-Aristotelian *Theologia,* in the *Liber de spiritu et anima* of Alcher, and in the *De insomniis* of Synesius, the phantasy (*phantasikon pneuma, spiritus phantasticus*) is conceived as a kind of subtle body of the soul that, situated at the extreme point of the sensitive soul, receives the images of objects, forms the phantasms of dreams, and, in determinate circumstances, can separate itself from the body and establish supernatural contacts and visions. In addition the phantasy is the seat of astral influences, the vehicle of magical influences, and, as *quid medium* between corporeal and incorporeal, makes it possible to account for a whole series of phenomena otherwise inexplicable, such as the action of maternal desire on the "soft matter" of the fetus, the apparition of demons, and the effect of sexual fantasies on the genital member. The same theory also permitted an explanation of the genesis of love; it is not possible, in particular, to understand the amorous ceremonial that the troubadour lyric and the poets of the "dolce stil novo" (sweet new style) left as a legacy to modern Western poetry unless notice is taken that since its origins this ceremonial presented itself as a phantasmatic process. Not an external body, but an internal image, that is, the phantasm impressed on the phantastic spirits by the gaze, is the origin and the object of falling in love; only the attentive elaboration and immoderate contemplation of this phantasmatic mental simulacrum were held capable of generating an authentic amorous passion. Andreas Cappellanus, whose *De amore* is considered the exemplary theorization of courtly love, thus defines love as the "immoderata cogitatio" (immoderate contemplation) of the interior phantasm, and adds that "ex sola cogitatione . . . passio illa procedit" ("passion derives . . . from contemplation alone").

It should be no surprise then, given the fundamental pertinence of the black bile in the erotic process, that the melancholic syndrome should have been since its origin traditionally joined to phantasmatic practice. The "imaginationes malae" (wicked phantasies) have long appeared in the medical literature among the "signa melancoliae" (signs of melancholy) in such an eminent position that it can be said that the atrabilious disease configures itself essentially, according to the expression of the Paduan doctor Girolamo Mercuriale, as a "vitium corruptae imaginationis" (fault of corrupt imagination).[2] Already Ramon Llull mentioned the affinity between melancholy and the imaginative faculty, specifying that the saturnine "a longo accipiunt per ymaginacionem, quae cum melancolia maiorem habet concordiam quam cum alia compleccione" (perceive from afar through the imagination, which has greater agreement with melancholy than with other complexions). In Albertus Magnus we find that melancholics "multa phantasmata inveniunt" (make up many phantasms) because dry vapor holds images more firmly. But once again, however, it is in Ficino and in Florentine Neoplatonism that the capacity of black bile to hold and fix the phantasms was asserted from the perspective of a medical-magical-philosophical theory that explicitly identifies the amorous contemplation of the phantasm with melancholy, whose pertinence to the erotic process here finds its reasons for being precisely in an exceptional phantasmatic disposition. If one thus reads in the *Theologia platonica* that melancholics "because of the earthy humor fix the phantasy more stably and more efficaciously with their desires," in the passage quoted in chapter 3 from Ficino's *De amore* it is the obsessive and exhausting hastening of the vital spirits around the phantasm impressed in the fantastic spirits that characterizes, at once, the erotic process and the unleashing of the atrabilious syndrome. In this context, melancholy appears essentially as an erotic process engaged in an ambiguous commerce with phantasms; and the double polarity, demonic-magic and angelic-contemplative, of the nature of the phantasm is responsible not only for the melancholics' morbid propensity for necromantic fascination but also for their aptitude for ecstatic illumination.

The influence of this conception, which indissolubly bound the saturnine temperament to commerce with the phantasm, quickly extended itself beyond its original range. It is still evident, for example, in a passage of the *Trattato della nobiltà della pittura* of Romano Alberti, frequently cited in regard to the history of the concept of melancholy. More than four centuries before psychoanalysis, this passage laid the foundations for a theory of art understood as a phantasmatic operation:

Painters become melancholics because, wishing to imitate, they must retain the phantasms fixed in the intellect, so that afterward they can express them in the way they first saw them when present; and, being their work, this occurs not only once, but continually. They keep their minds so much abstracted and separated from nature that consequently melancholy derives from it. Aristotle says, however, that this signifies genius and prudence, because almost all the ingenious and prudent have been melancholics.[3]

The traditional association of melancholy with artistic activity finds its justification precisely in the exacerbated phantasmatic practice that constitutes their common trait. Both place themselves under the sign of the *spiritus phantasticus,* the subtle body that not only furnishes the vehicle of dreams, of love, and of magical influence, but which also appears closely and enigmatically joined to the noblest creations of human culture. If this is true, then it is also significant that one of the texts in which Freud lingers longest in his analysis of the "wishful phantasies" should be the essay "Creative Writers and Day-Dreaming," in which he attempts to delineate a psychoanalytic theory of artistic creation and formulates a hypothesis according to which the work of art would be, in some manner, a continuation of infantile play and of the unconfessed but never abandoned phantasmatic practice of the adult.

At this point, we can begin to see the region whose spiritual configuration was the object of an itinerary that, having begun on the traces of the noonday demon and its infernal retinue, has led us to the winged genius of Dürer's melancholy and in whose domain the ancient tradition crystallized in this emblem can perhaps find a new foundation. The imaginary loss that so obsessively occupies the melancholic tendency has no real object, because its funereal strategy is directed to the impossible capture of the phantasm. The lost object is but the appearance that desire creates for its own courting of the phantasm, and the introjection of the libido is only one of the facets of a process in which what is real loses its reality so that what is unreal may become real. If the external world is in fact narcissistically denied to the melancholic as an object of love, the phantasm yet receives from this negation a reality principle and emerges from the mute interior crypt in order to enter into a new and fundamental dimension. No longer a phantasm and not yet a sign, the unreal object of melancholy introjection opens a space that is neither the hallucinated oneiric scene of the phantasms nor the indifferent world of natural objects. In this intermediate epiphanic place, located in the no-man's-land between narcissistic self-love and external object-choice, the creations of human culture will be situated one day, the interweaving (*entrebescar*) of symbolic forms and textual practices through which man enters in contact with a world that is nearer to him than any other and from which depend, more directly than from physical nature, his happiness and his misfortune. The *locus severus* (austere place) of melancholy, which according to Aristotle signifies genius and prudence, is also the *lusus severus* (serious play) of the word and of the symbolic forms through which, according to Freud, man succeeds in "enjoying [his] own day-dreams without self-reproach or shame" ("Creative Writers" 153). The topology of the unreal that melancholy designs in its immobile dialectic is, at the same time, a topology of culture.[4]

It is not surprising, in this perspective, that melancholy should have been identified by the alchemists with *Nigredo* (blackness), the first stage of the Great Work, which consisted, according to the ancient spagyritic maxim, in giving a body to the incorporeal and rendering the corporeal incorporeal.[5] In the space opened by its obstinate phantasmagoric tendency originates the unceasing alchemical effort of human culture to appropriate to itself death and the negative and to shape the maximum reality seizing on the maximum unreality.

If we turn now to the engraving of Dürer (see figure 1), it is entirely fitting to the immobile winged figure intent on its own phantasms, and at whose side sits the *spiritus phantasticus*[6] represented in the form of a cherub, that the instruments of the active life should lie abandoned on the ground, having become the cipher of an enigmatic wisdom. The troubling alienation of the most familiar objects is the price paid by the melancholic to the powers that are custodians of the inaccessible. The meditating angel is not, according to an interpretation by now traditional, the symbol of the impossibility for geometry (or for the arts based on it) to reach the incorporeal metaphysical world but, on the contrary, the emblem of man's attempt, at the limit of an essential psychic risk, to give body to his own phantasies and to master in an artistic practice what would otherwise be impossible to be seized or known. The compass, the sphere, the millstone, the hammer, the scales, and the straightedge, which the melancholic project has emptied of their habitual meaning and transformed into images of its own mourning, have no other significance than the space that they weave during the epiphany of the unattainable. Since the lesson of melancholy is that only what is ungraspable can truly be grasped, the melancholic alone is at his leisure among these ambiguous emblematic spoils. As the relics of a past on which is written the Edenic cipher of infancy, these objects have captured forever a gleam of that which can be possessed only with the provision that it be lost forever.

Notes

1. From "Mourning and Melancholia," *The Standard Edition of the Complete Psychological Works of Sigmund Freud,* vol. 14 (London: Hogarth Press, 1957), 244. Subsequent translations of passages from Freud's essays that appear with page references are also from this source; undocumented translations are the translator's own.

2. See G. Tanfani, "Il concetto di melancolia nel '500," *Revista di storia delle scienze mediche e naturali,* Florence (July-December 1948).

3. The mannerist theory of the "inner design" must be placed against the background of this psychological doctrine in order to be fully intelligible.

4. The topological operation of melancholy can be represented in the following schema:

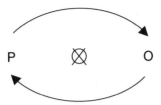

where P = phantasm, O = external object, and ⊗ = unreal object. The space they demarcate is the symbolic *topos* of melancholy.

5. An illustration in the first Ripley Scrowle, painted at Lübeck in 1588 (Ms. Add. Sloane 5025, British Museum), shows the alchemist as a melancholic by way of representing the first phase of the alchemical work.

6. A systematic revision of the iconographic interpretation of Panofsky and Saxl was not among the thematic objects of this essay; nevertheless it is impossible not to bring into relief here the aspects of that interpretation that have been gradually brought into question in the course of this study, which has derived its domain and its measure precisely from an incessant confrontation with Dürer's emblem. The greatest innovation of this present study is to have resituated the melancholic syndrome against the background of the medieval and Renaissance theory of the *spiritus phantasticus* (melancholy, in the strict sense, was but a disorder of the phantasmatic activity, a "vitium corruptae imaginationis") and to have consequently returned it to the context of the theory of love [as the phantasm was, at once, the object and vehicle of the act of falling in love, and love itself a form of *solicitudo melancholica* (melancholy diligence)]. The affinity between imagination and melancholy temperament is recognized by Panofsky and Saxl, insofar as it is explicitly affirmed in the text of Agrippa on which their interpretation is based, but it is in no way pursued.

The first consequence that, on the iconographical plane, derives from the link between the image produced by Dürer and the theory of the phantasm, is that the winged cherub (*putto*) cannot be identified any longer with *Brauch,* "Practice." Klein, who saw in the drawing cherub a personification of drawing/design ["Saturne: croyances et symboles," in *Mercure de France* (1964): 588-94; reprinted in *La forme et l'intelligible* (Paris, 1970), 224-30], had already noticed the lack of congruence between the small winged figure and Practice, which should have been logically represented blind and without wings. The cherub may be suitably identified with the *spiritus phantasticus* depicted in the act of imprinting the phantasm in the phantasy. This explains why Dürer's cherub undoubtedly belongs to the iconographic type of the *erotes: spiritus phantasticus* is, as we have seen, the magic vehicle of love and belongs to the same family as the "spiritelli d'amore" (little love-spirits) of Stilnovist lyric.

The semantic rotation that the phantasmological perspective effects on Dürer's image, from a static limit (the inability of geometry to reach metaphysics) to a dialectical one (the attempt of the phantasy to possess the unattainable), also permits us to understand correctly the meaning of the bat holding the scroll with the inscription "Melencolia I." This can be considered an authentic minor emblem that holds the key to the larger emblem that contains it. In the *Hieroglyphica* of Horapollo (see figure 2), the bat in flight is interpreted as representing man's attempt to boldly transcend the misery of his condition by daring the impossible: "Imbecillum hominem lascivientem, tamen et audacius aliquid molientem, cum monstrare voluerint, verpertilionem pingunt. Haec enim etsi alas non habeat volare tamen conatur" (When they wished to show weak and wanton man, but more daring and attempting something, they paint the bat. For this creature, although lacking wings, attempts to fly).

Another important innovation that has emerged in the course of this study is the reevaluation of the role of the patristic theorization of *tristitia-acedia* (which Panofsky interprets simply as "the guilty sleep of the lazy'') in the genesis of the Renaissance doctrine of melancholy. As we have seen, not only is *tristitia-acedia* not identified with laziness in patristic thought, but it has the same ambiguous polarity (*tristitia salutifera-tristitia mortifera*) that characterizes the Renaissance concept of melancholy.

Part II
*In the World of Odradek:
The Work of Art Confronted
with the Commodity*

Chapter 6
Freud; or, The Absent Object

In 1927 a brief article appeared in the *Internationale Zeitschrift für Psychoanalyse* (vol. 13) with the title "Fetischismus." It is one of the rare texts in which Freud posed thematically the problem of those individuals "whose object-choice was dominated by a fetish."[1] The results furnished by the analyses in the cases he observed seemed so concordant and unequivocal that they persuaded him to conclude that all cases of fetishism could be reduced to a single explanation. According to Freud, the fetishistic fixation arises from the refusal of the male child to acknowledge the absence of the penis of the female (of the mother). Confronted with the perception of this absence, the child refuses [Freud used the term *Verleugnung* (disavowal)] to admit its reality, because to do so would permit a threat of castration against his own penis. The fetish is therefore the "substitute for the woman's (the mother's) penis that the little boy once believed in and—for reasons familiar to us—does not want to give up" (152-53).

Nevertheless, according to Freud, the sense of this *Verleugnung* is not as simple as it might seem and in fact implies an essential ambiguity. In the conflict between the perception of reality, which urges him to renounce his phantasm, and the counterdesire, which urges him to deny his perception, the child does neither one nor the other; or, rather, he does both simultaneously, reaching one of those compromises that are possible only under the rule of the laws of the unconscious. On the one hand, with the help of a particular mechanism, he disavows the evidence of his perception; on the other, he recognizes its reality, and, through a perverse symptom, he assumes the anguish he feels before it. The fetish, whether a part of the body or an inorganic object, is, therefore, at one and the same time, the presence of that nothingness that is the maternal penis and the sign of its absence. Both symbol of something and its negation, the fetish can maintain itself only thanks to an essential laceration in which two contrary reactions constitute the nucleus of an authentic fracture of the ego (*Ichspaltung*).

It is interesting to observe how a mental process of fetishistic type is implicit in one of the most common tropes of poetic language: synecdoche (and in its close relative, metonymy). The substitution, in synecdoche, of part for whole (or of a contiguous object for another) corresponds, in fetishism, to the substitution of one part of the body (or of an object annexed to it) for the whole sexual partner. That we are not dealing with a superficial analogy is proved by the fact that the metonymic substitution is not exhausted in the pure and simple substitution of one term for another: the substituted term is, rather, at once negated and evoked by the substitution through a process whose ambiguity closely recalls the Freudian *Verleugnung*, and it is precisely from this kind of "negative reference" that the peculiar poetic character that invests the word arises. The fetishistic character of the phenomenon becomes evident in that particular kind of metonymic operation that, since Vasari and Condivi first gave it critical recognition with respect to the "unfinished" sculptures of Michelangelo, has become one of the essential stylistic instruments of modern art: the nonfinished.[2] Gilpin, who pushed the pre-Romantic taste for the nonfinished to the point of proposing the partial destruction of Palladian villas so as to transform them into artificial ruins, had become aware that what he called the "laconism of genius" consisted precisely in "giving a part for the whole." Schlegel, to whom we owe the prophetic affirmation that "many works of the ancients have become fragments, and many works of the moderns are fragments at their birth," thought, as did Novalis, that every finite work was necessarily subject to a limit that only the fragment could transcend. It is superfluous to recall that, in this sense, almost all modern poems after Mallarmé are fragments, in that they allude to something (the absolute poem) that can never be evoked in its integrity, but only rendered present through its negation.[3] The difference with respect to normal linguistic metonymy is that the substituted object (the "whole" to which the fragment alludes) is, like the maternal penis, nonexistent or no longer existent, and the nonfinished therefore reveals itself as a perfect and punctual pendant of the fetishist denial.

Analogous remarks can be formulated for metaphor, which Ortega y Gasset, in a book often cited but rarely read, considered "the most radical instrument of dehumanization" of modern art. As Ortega noted, metaphor substitutes one thing for another, not so much in order to reach the second, as to escape from the first. If it is true, as it has been argued, that the metaphoric substitute is originally a nominal replacement for an object that should not be named, then the analogy with fetishism is even stronger than in the case of metonymy.[4] Given that Freud was simply attempting to trace the phenomenon of fetishism to the unconscious processes that constituted its origin, we cannot be surprised that he did not unduly preoccupy himself with the consequences that the ambiguity of the infantile *Verleugnung* might have on the status of the fetish object, or that he neglected to put this object in relation to the other objects that make up the world of human culture insofar as it is an activity that creates objects.[5]

Considered from this point of view, the fetish confronts us with the paradox of an unattainable object that satisfies a human need precisely through its being unattainable. Insofar as it is a presence, the fetish object is in fact something concrete and tangible; but insofar as it is the presence of an absence, it is, at the same time, immaterial and intangible, because it alludes continuously beyond itself to something that can never really be possessed.

This essential ambiguity in the status of the fetish perfectly explains a fact that observation had already revealed some time ago, that is, that the fetishist unfailingly tends to collect and multiply fetishes.[6] Whether the object of perversion be an article of lingerie of a certain kind or a small leather boot or a woman's head of hair, the perverse subject will be equally satisfied (or, if you wish, equally unsatisfied) by all the objects that present the same characteristics. Precisely because the fetish is a negation and the sign of an absence, it is not an unrepeatable unique object; on the contrary, it is something infinitely capable of substitution, without any of its successive incarnations ever succeeding in exhausting the nullity of which it is the symbol. However much the fetishist multiplies proofs of its presence and accumulates harems of objects, the fetish will inevitably remain elusive and celebrate, in each of its apparitions, always and only its own mystical phantasmagoria.

The fetish reveals a new and disturbing mode of being of objects, of the *facticia* manufactured by human efforts.[7] However brief our consideration of the phenomenon, we realize that it is more familiar than we first imagined.

Scholia

The birth of fetishism

1. From "Fetishism," *The Standard Edition of the Complete Psychological Works of Sigmund Freud,* vol. 21, trans. and ed. James Strachey (London: Hogarth Press, 1961), 152.

The first to use the term fetishism to designate a sexual perversion was Alfred Binet, whose study *Le fétichisme dans l'amour* (Paris, 1888) was attentively read by Freud during the period of his composition of *Three Essays on the Theory of Sexuality* (1905). "Such substitutes," Freud writes with Binet's words in mind, "are with some justice likened to the fetishes in which savages believe that their gods are embodied" (*Standard Edition,* vol. 7, 153). The psychological connotations of the term are more familiar to us today than the original religious meaning, which appeared for the first time in the work of Charles de Brosses, *Du culte des dieux fétiches, ou parallèle de l'ancienne religion de l'Egypte avec la religion actuelle de Nigritie* (Paris, 1760). Neither Restif de la Bretonne [whose *Pied de Fanchette ou le soulier couleur de rose* (Fanchette's foot, or the pink slipper), centering on shoe fetishism, appeared only nine years after de Brosses's study] nor the Marquis de Sade, although they both mentioned numerous cases of sexual "fetishism" in their works, used this term. Even Charles Fourier, who, in the chapter on erotic manias in his *Le nouveau monde amoureux,* several times mentioned the case of a heel fetishist (a "mania" worthy, according to the author, of the "Golden Age") did not use the word fetish. It should be noted that along with the diffusion of the psychoanalytic use of the term, anthropologists, who had accepted the term proposed by de Brosses, gradually abandoned it in response to the strict disapproval of Mauss (according to whom "the notion of fetish ought to disappear completely from science").

The nonfinished

2. Giorgio Vasari, speaking of the Virgin in the Medici Chapel, writes that "although its parts are not finished, one recognizes . . . in the imperfection of the sketch the perfection of the work"; and Condivi, in regard to the sculptures of the New Sacristy, states, "nor does the rough sketch stand in the way of the perfection and beauty of the work" [see Renato Bonelli, "Il non-finito di Michelangiolo" and Piero Sanpaolesi, "Michelangelo e il non-finito" in *Atti del Convegno di studi michelangioleschi* (Rome: Editore dell' Ateneo, 1966)]. On the nonfinished in art and literature see also the volume of essays *Das Unvollendete als kunstlerische Form* (The unfinished as artistic form), edited by J. Adolf Eisenwerth (Bern: Francke, 1959), and the acute observations of Edgar Wind in *Art and Anarchy* (London: Faber and Faber, 1963).

Absolute poetry

3. "But of what do I properly speak, when from *this* direction, in *this* direction, with these words, I speak of a poetry—no, *of* poetry? I speak, yes, of the poetry that does not exist!

"Absolute poetry—no, certainly it does not exist, it cannot exist!

"But it does exist, yes, in every existing poem, it exists in every poem without pretense, this question that cannot be evaded, this unheard-of pretense" [Paul Celan, *Der meridian,* in *Ausgewählte Gedichte* (Frankfurt am Main, 1970)].

Metaphor and perversion

4. Ortega's definition of metaphor might well refer to the fetishist *Verleugnung*: "A strange thing, indeed, this human mental activity of replacing one thing for another—not so much out of haste to reach the latter as out of determination to escape the former." The theory of metaphor as a "substitutive name" for a taboo is found in Heinz Werner, *Die Ursprüng der Metapher* (The origin of metaphor) (1919). The analogy of sexual perversions and metaphor was noted, with his usual acumen, by Kraus: "There are metaphors in the erotic language as well. The illiterate call them perversions."

Objects of fetishism

5. Even recently, in the issue of the *Nouvelle Revue de Psychanalyse* entitled *Objets du fétichisme* (vol. 2, 1970), only two of the psychoanalysts contributing

to the volume appeared to realize, though but fleetingly, the possible implications of the phantomatic status of the fetish object, suggestively characterized as *objet de perspective* (perspective object) or *objet de manque* (object of lack), or to perceive the closeness of the fetish object to the domain of cultural creation. See Guy Rosolato, "Le fétichisme dont se dérobe l'objet" (The fetishism whose object disappears), and V. N. Smirnoff, "La transaction fétichique" (The fetishist transaction).

The collector

6. As Krafft-Ebing records, actual warehouses of braids and shoes were found in the dwellings of the "braid-cutters" or of the shoe fetishists. In this sense, the fetishist displays many resemblances with a figure not usually listed among perverts: the collector. What the collector seeks in the object is something absolutely impalpable to the noncollector, who only uses or possesses the object, just as the fetish does not coincide in any way with the object in its material aspect.

Etymology

7. The Portuguese word *feitiçio* (from which the word fetish is coined) does not derive, as de Brosses thought, from the Latin root of *fatum, fari, fanum* (with the meaning, therefore, of "enchanted thing") but from the Latin *facticius* ("artificial"), from the same root as *facere*. Saint Augustine even referred to a *genus facticiorum deorum* with regard to the pagan idols, where the term *facticius* surely anticipates the modern meaning. The Indo-European root **dhē-* of *facere* is linked with that of *fas, fanum, feria* and has an originally religious value, which can still be perceived in the archaic sense of *facere* ("make a sacrifice"). See Alfred Ernout and Alphonse Meillet, *Dictionnaire étymologique de la langue latine*, s.v. "facio" and "feriae." In this sense, everything that is *factitious* belongs by rights to the religious sphere, and the astonishment of de Brosses before the fetish not only has no reason to exist, it betrays a forgetfulness of the original status of objects.

Chapter 7
Marx; or, The Universal Exposition

In 1925, two years before the publication of Freud's article on fetishism, Rainer Maria Rilke, in a letter to Witold von Hulewicz (particularly important for Rilke's attempt to explain what he had expressed poetically in the *Duino Elegies*), revealed his apprehension before what was according to him a change in the status of objects:

> Even for our grandparents a "house," a "well," a familiar tower, their very clothes, their coat: were infinitely more, infinitely more intimate; almost everything a vessel in which they found the human and added to the store of the human. Now, from America, empty indifferent things are pouring across, sham things, *dummy life* . . . A house, in the American sense, an American apple or a grapevine over there, has *nothing* in common with the house, the fruit, the grape into which went the hopes and reflections of our forefathers . . . Live things, things lived and conscient of us, are running out and can no longer be replaced. *We are perhaps the last still to have known such things.*
> [*Letters of Rainer Maria Rilke*, vol. 2 (New York: W. W. Norton, 1947), 374-75; emphasis in the original][1]

In the fourth part of the first chapter of *Capital*, which has the title "The Fetishism of the Commodity and Its Secret," Marx is explicitly concerned with this transformation of the products of human labor into "appearances of things," in a "phantasmagoria . . . that is subject, and also not subject, to the senses":

> A commodity appears at first sight an extremely obvious, trivial thing.
> . . . So far as it is a use-value, there is nothing mysterious about it,

whether we consider it from the point of view that by its properties it satisfies human needs, or that it first takes on these properties as the product of human labour. It is absolutely clear that, by his activity, man changes the forms of the materials of nature in such a way as to make them useful to him. The form of wood, for instance, is altered if a table is made out of it. Nevertheless the table continues to be wood, an ordinary, sensuous thing. But as soon as it emerges as a commodity, it changes into a thing which transcends sensuousness. It not only stands with its feet on the ground, but, in relation to all other commodities, it stands on its head, and evolves out of its wooden brain grotesque ideas, far more wonderful than if it were to begin dancing of its own free will. [*Capital,* vol. 1, trans. Ben Fowkes (New York: Vintage Books, 1977), 163-64]

This "mystical character" that the product of labor acquires as soon as it takes on the form of the commodity depends, according to Marx, on an essential doubling of the relation to the object, for which the product does not now represent only a use-value (its suitability to satisfy a determinate human need), but this use-value is, at the same time, the material substrate of something else: the exchange value. Since the commodity presents itself under this double form of useful object and bearer of value, it is an essentially immaterial and abstract piece of goods, whose concrete enjoyment is impossible except through accumulation and exchange:

In obvious contrast with the materiality of the body of the commodity, not a single atom of matter penetrates to its value . . . Metamorphosed into identical sublimates, samples of the same undifferentiated labor, all objects manifest but one thing, which is that a certain force of labor has been expended in producing them. Insofar as they are crystals of this common social substance, they are reputed to be value.

This doubling of the product of work, which presents us now with one face now with another, without making both visible in the same instant, constitutes what Marx calls the "fetishistic character" of the commodity. The commodity thus presents more than a simply terminological analogy with the fetishes that are objects of perversion. The superimposition of the use-value corresponds, in fetishism, to the superimposition of a particular symbolic value on the normal use of the object. Just as the fetishist never succeeds in possessing the fetish wholly, because it is the sign of two contradictory realities, so the owner of a commodity will never be able to enjoy it simultaneously as both useful object and as value: the material body in which the commodity is manifest may be manipulated in all manner of ways, and it may be materially altered so far as to destroy it, but in this disappearance the commodity will once again reaffirm its unattainability.

The fetishization of the object effected by the commodity becomes evident in the Universal Expositions, which Walter Benjamin defined as "pilgrimage-sites of the commodity-fetish.'' Marx was in London in 1851 when the first Universal Exposition, in Hyde Park, was inaugurated with great fanfare, and it is probable that his memory of that occasion contributed to his reflections on the character of the commodity-fetish. The "phantasmagoria" of which he speaks in relation to the commodity can be discovered in the intentions of the organizers, who chose, from among the various possibilities presented, Paxton's project for an enormous palace constructed entirely out of glass. The *Guide* to the Paris Exposition of 1867 reiterated the supremacy of this phantasmagorical character: "The public needs a grandiose concept that will strike its imagination; its spirit must halt, astonished, before the marvels of industry. It wishes to contemplate *an enchanted scene (un coup d'oeil féerique)* and not similar products, uniformly grouped." The postcards of the period increased the effect even more, swathing the buildings of the Exposition in a luminous halo.

The transfiguration of the commodity into *enchanted object* is the sign that the exchange value is already beginning to eclipse the use-value of the commodity. In the galleries and the pavilions of its mystical Crystal Palace, in which from the outset a place was also reserved for works of art, the commodity is displayed to be enjoyed only through the glance at the *enchanted scene*.

Thus at the Universal Exposition was celebrated, for the first time, the mystery that has now become familiar to anyone who has entered a supermarket or been exposed to the manipulation of an advertisement: the epiphany of the unattainable.[2]

Scholia

Rilke and things

1. In a letter of 1912, Rilke wrote of the change that had come over things in terms that closely recall Marx's analysis of the fetishistic character of the commodity. "The world contracts," Rilke writes, "because even things, for their part, do the same, in that they continuously displace their existence into the vibration of money, developing a kind of spirituality that from this moment on outstrips their tangible reality. In the period that I am treating (the fourteenth century), money was still gold, metal, something beautiful, the most easily handled, the most intelligible of all things." In Rilke, a poet that certainly does not have the reputation of a revolutionary, we discover again the same nostalgia for use-value that characterizes Marx's critique of the commodity. Nevertheless, faced with the impossibility of a return to the past, this nostalgia in Rilke translates into the program for a transformation of the world of visible things into the invisible. "The earth," continues the previously cited letter to Hulewicz, "has no way out other than to become invisible: *in* us who with a part of our natures partake of the invisible, have (at least) stock in it, and can increase our holdings in the invisible during our sojourn here—*in* us alone can be consummated this intimate and lasting conversion of the visible into an invisible. . . . The angel of the *Elegies* is

that creature in whom the transformation of the visible into the invisible, which we are accomplishing, appears already consummated" (*Letters of Rainer Maria Rilke* 2:375). From this point of view, the Rilkean angel is the symbol of the transcendence in the invisible of the commodified object, that is, the cipher of a relation to things that goes beyond both the use-value and the exchange value. As such, it is the metaphysical figure that succeeds the merchant, as Rilke put it in one of the late poems: "When from the hand of the merchant / the scales pass / to the Angel in heaven / they are appeased and balanced with space . . . "

The Universal Exposition

2. The organizers of the 1851 London Exposition were perfectly conscious of the phantasmagorical character of Paxton's palace. In the essay "The Armony [*sic*] of Colours as Exemplified in the Exhibition," which accompanied the Exposition catalogue, Merrifield writes that the Crystal Palace "is perhaps the only building in the world in which the *atmosphere* is perceptible; and the very appropriate style of decoration chosen by Mr. Owen Jones greatly adds to the general effect of the edifice. To a spectator situated in the gallery at the eastern or western end, who looks directly before himself, the most distant parts of the building appear enveloped in a bluish halo . . . "

Even a passing glance at the illustrations of the catalogue produces an indefinite sense of discomfort that, little by little, is shown to be caused by the monstrous hypertrophy of ornament that transforms the simplest objects into nightmarish creatures (see figures 4 and 5). Many of the objects displayed are devoured by ornament to such an extent that Warnum (whose essay "The Exhibition as a Lesson in Taste," a peroration on the necessity of ornament, concludes the catalogue) took it as his duty to place the public on its guard against the arbitrary substitution of the object by ornament. In an incredible eclecticism, all the styles and all the periods are invited to feast, in the extratemporal temple of the commodity, on the spoils of the object. As the "bluish halo" that envelops the Crystal Palace is but a visualization of the aura that bathes the commodity-fetish, so the elephantiasis of ornament betrays the new character of the commodified objects. If seen in relation to the spectacle of the Exposition, the Marxian theory of the fetishistic character of the commodity—which has appeared to at least one incautious modern reader as "a flagrant and extremely harmful Hegelian influence" (the infelicitous remark is Althusser's)—requires neither explication nor philosophical references.

It is interesting to note that the first reactions of the intellectuals and artists to the Universal Exposition were generally of concealed distaste and aversion. Ruskin's decidedly unfavorable opinions of the Exposition of 1851 are in this sense symptomatic. A certain intention to compete with the Exposition can be discerned in Courbet's decision, in 1855, to display his works in a pavilion within sight of the Exposition grounds. The example was later followed by Manet and in 1889 by Gauguin, who organized a show of his own works in a café not far from the Exposition site. For their part, the organizers of the Exposition did not tire of entreating artists not to disdain "le voisinage des produits industriels qu'ils ont si souvent enrichis et où ils peuvent puiser encore nouveaux élements d'inspiration et de travail" (the proximity of industrial products that they had so often enriched and from which they might still draw new elements of inspiration and labor).

The construction in 1889, on the occasion of the fifth Universal Exposition, of the Eiffel Tower, whose elegant shape today seems inseparable from Paris, excited protest from a substantial group of artists, among whom were personalities as diverse as Zola, Meissonier, Maupassant, and Bonnat. They had probably realized what the fait accompli prevents us from perceiving today: that the tower (in addition to giving the coup de grace to the labyrinthine character of old Paris by offering a reference point visible everywhere) transformed the whole city into a commodity that could be consumed at a single glance. In the Exposition of 1889, the most precious commodity was the city itself.

Chapter 8
Baudelaire; or, The Absolute Commodity

We have an exceptional witness to the Paris Universal Exposition of 1855. Charles Baudelaire left his impressions in a series of three articles that appeared at brief intervals in two Paris dailies. Though Baudelaire restricted his comments to the fine arts, and although his articles do not apparently differ much from the reports he had written for the Salons of 1845 and 1846, we see on closer inspection that the novelties and the importance of the challenge offered to the work of art by the commodity did not escape his prodigious sensitivity.

In the first article of the series [which carries the significant title "De l'idée moderne du progrès appliquée aux beaux arts" (On the modern idea of progress applied to the fine arts)] he describes the sensation created in an intelligent visitor by the spectacle of an exotic commodity and shows his awareness of the new kind of attention the commodity requires of the viewer. "What would a modern Winckelmann say," he asks himself, "before a Chinese product, a strange and bizarre product, shapely in its form, intense in color, and sometimes delicate to the point of evanescence?" "Nonetheless," he answers, "it is a sample of universal beauty; but for it to be understood it is necessary for the spectator to work in himself a transformation that is somewhat mysterious . . ." It is no accident that the idea on which the sonnet "Correspondances" is based (a poem that is usually interpreted as the quintessence of Baudelairean esotericism) should be articulated at the beginning of the article on the 1855 Exposition. Like Bosch, who at the dawn of capitalism had drawn from the spectacle of the first great international fairs in Flanders the symbols to illustrate his mystical Adamic conception of the millenarian kingdom, Baudelaire, at the beginning of the second industrial revolution, drew from the transfiguration of the commodity during the Universal

Exposition the emotional atmosphere and the symbolic elements of his poetics.[1] The great novelty that the Exposition had made obvious to Baudelaire's perceptive eye was that the commodity had ceased to be an innocent object, whose enjoyment and perception were exhausted in the practical use of it, and had charged itself with that disturbing ambiguity to which Marx would allude twelve years later when speaking of the "fetishistic character," the "metaphysical subtleties," and "theological witticisms" of the commodity. Once the commodity had freed objects of use from the slavery of being useful, the borderline that separated them from works of art—the borderline that artists from the Renaissance forward had indefatigably worked to establish, by basing the supremacy of artistic creation on the "making" of the artisan and the laborer—became extremely tenuous.

Before the enchantment (*féerie*) of the Universal Exposition, which began to draw toward the commodity the kind of interest traditionally reserved for the work of art, Baudelaire took up the challenge and carried the battle to the ground of the commodity itself. As he had implicitly admitted when speaking of the exotic product as a "sample of universal beauty," he approved of the new features that commodification impresses on the object and he was conscious of the power of attraction that they would inevitably have on the work of art. At the same time, however, he wanted to withdraw them from the tyranny of the economic and from the ideology of progress. The greatness of Baudelaire with respect to the invasion of the commodity was that he responded to this invasion by transforming the work of art into a commodity and a fetish. That is, he divided, within the work of art itself, use-value from exchange value, the work's traditional authority from its authenticity. Hence his implacable polemic against every utilitarian interpretation of the artwork and the ferocious zeal with which he proclaimed that poetry has no end except itself. Hence, too, his insistence on the intangible character of the aesthetic experience and his theorization of the beautiful as an instantaneous and impenetrable epiphany. The aura of frozen intangibility that from this moment began to surround the work of art is the equivalent of the fetishistic character that the exchange value impresses on the commodity.[2]

But what gives his discovery a genuinely revolutionary character is that Baudelaire did not limit himself to reproducing within the artwork the scission between use-value and exchange value, but also proposed to create a commodity in which the form of value would be totally identified with the use-value: an *absolute* commodity, so to speak, in which the process of fetishization would be pushed to the point of annihilating the reality of the commodity itself as such. A commodity in which use-value and exchange value reciprocally cancel out each other, whose value therefore consists in its uselessness and whose use in its intangibility, is no longer a commodity: the absolute commodification of the work of art is also the most radical abolition of the commodity. Baudelaire understood that if art wished to survive industrial civilization, the artist had to attempt to reproduce that destruction of use-value and traditional intelligibility that was at the origin of the experience of shock. In this way the artist would succeed in making the work the vehicle of the unattainable and would restore in unattainability itself a new value and a new authority. This meant, however, that art had to begin to give up the guarantees that derived from its insertion in a tradition, for whose sake artists constructed the places and the objects in which the incessant welding of past and present, old and new, was accomplished, in order to make of its own self-negation its sole possibility of survival. As Hegel had already understood by defining the most advanced experiences of the Romantic poets as "self-annihilating nothingness," self-dissolution was the price that the work of art must pay to modernity. For this reason Baudelaire seems to assign to the poet a paradoxical task: "he who cannot grasp the intangible," he writes in the essay on Poe, "is not a poet," and he defines the experience of creation as a duel to the death, "where the artist cries out in terror before being overcome."

It is a stroke of luck that the founder of modern poetry should have been a fetishist.[3] Without his passion for feminine clothing and hair, for jewels and cosmetics (which he expresses without hesitation in the essay "Le peintre de la vie moderne" and to which he intended to devote a detailed catalogue, never completed, of human dress), Baudelaire could scarcely have emerged victorious from his encounter with the commodity. Without the personal experience of the miraculous ability of the fetish object to make the absence present through its own negation, he would perhaps not have dared to assign to art the most ambitious task that any human being has ever entrusted to one of his or her creations: the appropriation of unreality.

Scholia

Correspondences and the commodity

1. The entire sonnet "Correspondances" can be read as a transcription of the estrangement produced by impressions of the Universal Exposition. In the cited article, Baudelaire evokes, with regard to the impressions of the visitor before the exotic commodity, "ces odeurs qui ne sont plus celles du boudoir, ces fleurs mystérieuses dont la couleur profonde entre dans l'oeil despotiquement, pendant qui leur forme taquine le régard, ces fruits dont le goût trompe et déplace les sens, et revèle au palais des idées qui apartiennent à l'odorat, tout ce monde d'harmonies nouvelles entrera lentement en lui, le pénétrera patiemment . . . toute cette vitalité inconnue sera ajoutée à sa vitalité propre; quelques milliers d'idées et de sensations enrichiront son dictionnaire de mortel" (those smells that are no longer those of the bedroom, those mysterious flowers whose deep color imperiously enters the eye while its form teases the glance, those fruits whose taste fools and displaces the sense, that whole world of new harmonies will slowly enter him, will patiently penetrate him . . . all that unknown vitality will be added to his own vitality; some thousands of ideas and sensations will enrich the dictionary of his mortal existence). He speaks with disdain of the pedant that,

faced with such a spectacle, is unable to "courir avec agilité sur l'immense clavier des *correspondances*" (run with agility over the immense keyboard of *correspondences*).

In a certain sense, even the *Garden of Delights* of Hieronymus Bosch can be seen as an image of the universe transfigured by the commodity. Like Grandville four centuries later [and as, contemporary with Bosch, the authors of the innumerable books of emblems and of *blasons domestiques* (domestic escutcheons, coats of arms) who, confronted with the first massive appearances of the commodity, represented objects by alienating them from their contexts], Bosch transformed nature into "speciality," and the mixture of organic and inorganic of his creatures and fantastic architecture seems to anticipate the *féerie* of the commodity in the Universal Exposition. From this point of view, the mystical Adamic theories that according to the interpretation of W. Fraenger [*Hieronymus Bosch: Das tausendjährige Reich* (Winkler-Verlag, 1947); trans. *The Millennium of Hieronymus Bosch: Outlines of a New Interpretation* (London: Faber and Faber, 1952)] Bosch intended to express symbolically in his paintings, manifest, like a mystical Land of Cockaygne, certain analogies with the erotico-industrial utopias of Fourier. In *Un autre monde* (Another world) Grandville left us some of the most extraordinary ironic transcriptions (which is not to say that an ironic intention was foreign to Bosch where Adamic doctrines were concerned) of the prophecies of Fourier—for example, the northern lights and seven artificial moons as children flying around in the sky, nature transformed into the land of Cockaygne, and winged human beings who adhere to the "butterflying" passion (see figures 6, 7, and 8).

Benjamin and the aura

2. Walter Benjamin, though he had perceived the phenomenon through which the traditional value and authority of the work of art began to vacillate, did not realize that the "decay of the aura"—the phrase with which he synthesized this process—in no way implied as a result "the liberation of the object from its cultural scabbard" or its grounding, from that moment on, in political praxis, but rather the reconstitution of a new "aura" through which the object, re-creating and exalting to the maximum its authenticity on another plane, became charged with a new value, perfectly analogous to the exchange value, whose object is doubled by the commodity.

For once, Benjamin had not obtained the concept of "aura"—one of his most typical concepts—from mystical-esoteric texts alone, but also from a French writer, Léon Daudet, unjustly forgotten today, whose unusual intelligence Benjamin appreciated while of course distrusting his cloddish political ideas. Daudet's book *La melancholia* [*sic*] (1928) contains a meditation on the aura (which also appears with the name *ambiance*) that deserves more than a casual reappraisal. Specifically, Daudet's definition of Baudelaire as a "poet of the aura" is almost certainly the source of one of the central motifs of Benjamin's great study on Baudelaire. Benjamin's considerations on odors are anticipated by Daudet's intuition that "the olfactory is of our senses the closest to the aura and the best suited to give us an idea or a representation. Olfactory hallucinations are the rarest and most profound of all." Moreover, the passage in the essay "The Work of Art in the Age of Mechanical Reproduction" [see Benjamin, *Illuminations,* trans. Harry Zohn (New York: Schocken Books, 1968), 217-51] where Benjamin writes of old photographs as means to capture the aura, has a precedent in Daudet's reflections on photography and the cinema as "transmitters of aura." It should be recalled that the ideas on the aura of the author-physician Léon Daudet have been noted with interest by the psychiatrist E. Minkowski, who cites them liberally in the chapter on the sense of smell in his *Vers une cosmologie* (Toward a cosmology) (1936).

Baudelaire the fetishist

3. A catalogue enumeration of the fetishist motifs in Baudelaire should include, in addition to his celebrated poem "Les bijoux" (Jewelry)—"La très-chère était nue, et, connaissant mon coeur / elle n'avait gardé que ses bijoux sonores" (The dearest one was naked, and aware of my desire she had kept only her sonorous jewels)—at least the prose poem "Un hémisphère dans une chevelure," whose concluding phrase contains more information on fetishism than an entire psychological treatise: "Quand je mordille tes cheveux lastiques et rebelles, il me semble que je mange des souvenirs" (When I graze on your flexible, rebellious hair, it seems I am feeding on memories). In the essay on Constantin Guys, which is the summa of Baudelaire's poetics, the poet speaks of *maquillage* (makeup) in these terms: "La femme est bien dans son droit, et même elle accomplit une espèce de devoir en s'appliquant à paraître magique et surnaturelle; il faut qu'elle étonne, qu'elle charme; idole, elle doit se dorer pour être adorée. Elle doit donc emprunter à tous les arts les moyens de s'élever au-dessus de la nature. . . . L'enumeration en serait innombrable; mais, pour nous restreindre à ce que notre temps appelle vulgairement *maquillage,* qui ne voit que l'usasge de la poudre de riz, si niaisement anathématisé par les philosophes candides, a pour but et pour résultat de faire disparaître du teint toutes les taches que la nature y a outrageusement semées, et de créer une unité abstraite dans le grain et la couleur de la peau, laquelle unité, comme celle produite par le maillot, rapproche immédiatement l'être humain de la statue, c'est dire d'un être devin et supérieur" (The women is well within her rights, and indeed she fulfills a kind of duty, in her attempt to appear magical and supernatural; she must astonish, she must charm. An idol, she must adorn herself [literally, "gild"] so that she will be adored. She must then borrow from all the arts the means of raising herself above nature. . . . An enumeration of the means would be innumerable; but, to restrict ourselves to what our period commonly refers to as makeup, who cannot see that the use of rice powder, so foolishly excoriated by candid philosophers, has as its goal and result the disappearance from the hue of all the spots that nature has

outrageously sown there, and the creation of an abstract unity in the texture and color of the skin, which unity, like that produced by hosiery [more specifically: the leotard, the dancer's body stocking], immediately assimilates the human being to the statue, that is to say, to a divine and superior being).

Chapter 9
Beau Brummell; or, The Appropriation of Unreality

In 1843 Grandville published *Petites misères de la vie humaine,* based on a text by his friend Forgues. In a series of genially perverse illustrations, Grandville gave us one of the first representations of a phenomenon that would become increasingly familiar to the modern age: a bad conscience with respect to objects. In a leaky faucet that cannot be turned off, in an umbrella that reverses itself, in a boot that can be neither completely put on nor taken off and remains tenaciously stuck on the foot, in the sheets of paper scattered by a breath of wind, in a coverlet that does not cover, in a pair of pants that tears, the prophetic glance of Grandville discovers, beyond the simple fortuitous incident, the cipher of a new relation between humans and things. No one has shown better than he the human discomfort before the disturbing metamorphoses of the most familiar objects (see figure 9). Under his pen, objects lose their innocence and rebel with a kind of deliberate perfidy. They attempt to evade their uses, they become animated with human feelings and intentions, they become discontented and lazy. The eye is not surprised to discover them in lecherous attitudes.

Rilke, who had described the same phenomenon in the episode of the coverlet from *Notebooks of Malte Laurids Brigge,* observed, with a revealing expression, that the "relations of men and things have created confusion in the latter." The bad human conscience with respect to commodified objects is expressed in the mise-en-scène of this phantasmagorical conspiracy. The degeneration implicit in the transformation of the artisanal object into the mass-produced article is constantly manifest to modern man in the loss of his own self-possession with respect to things. The degradation of objects is matched by human clumsiness, that is, the fear of their possible revenge, to which end Grandville lends his pen.[1]

It is perfectly understandable that the dandy, the man who is never ill at ease, would be the ideal of a society that had begun to experience a bad conscience with respect to objects. What compelled the noblest names of England, and the regent himself, to hang on every word that fell from Beau Brummell's lips was the fact that he presented himself as the master of science that they could not do without. To men who had lost their self-possession, the dandy, who makes of elegance and the superfluous his raison d'être, teaches the possibility of a new relation to things, which goes beyond both the enjoyment of their use-value and the accumulation of their exchange value. He is the redeemer of things, the one who wipes out, with his elegance, their original sin: the commodity.[2]

Baudelaire, who was actually frightened by the animated objects of Grandville and who thought of dandyism as a kind of religion, understood that in this respect the poet (he who, according to Baudelaire's own words, should know how to "manage the intangible") might have something to learn from the dandy.

The Marxist analysis of the fetishistic character of the commodity is founded on the idea that "no object can be invested with value if it is not something useful. If it is useless, the labor that it contains has been uselessly spent and therefore creates no value." According to Marx, "production itself is directed in all its development toward use-value, not toward exchange value, and it is therefore only through the exceeding of the measure in which use-values are required for consumption that they cease to be use-values and become means of exchange, commodities." Coherently with these premises, the enjoyment of use-value is opposed by Marx to the accumulation of the exchange value as something natural to something aberrant, and it can be said that his whole critique of capitalism is conducted on behalf of the concreteness of the object of use against the abstraction of the exchange value.[3] Marx evokes with a certain nostalgia the case of Robinson Crusoe and of the autarkic communities for whom exchange value is unknown and in which the relations between producers and things are therefore simple and transparent. He thus writes in *Capital* that "capitalism is suppressed from the outset if it is postulated that the enjoyment, and not the accumulation, of goods is its motive force." Marx's critique is limited in that he does not know to separate himself from the utilitarian ideology, which decrees that the enjoyment of use-value is the original and natural relation of man to objects; consequently the possibility of a relation to things that goes beyond both the enjoyment of use-value and the accumulation of exchange value escapes him.[4]

Modern ethnography has discredited the Marxian prejudice that "no object can be invested with value if it is not something useful" and the idea serving as its basis, according to which the utilitarian principle is the psychological motive of economic life. The study of archaic economies has demonstrated that human activity is not reducible to production, conservation, and consumption, and that archaic man seems in fact to have been dominated in all activity by what has been defined, perhaps with some exaggeration, as a principle of unproductive loss and expenditure.[5]

Mauss's studies on the potlatch and on ritual prodigality do not merely reveal what Marx did not know—that the gift, and not exchange, is the original form of exchange—but also reveal a whole series of behaviors (which range from the ritual gift to the destruction of the most precious goods). From the point of view of economic utilitarianism, these behaviors appear inexplicable, and on the basis of them one might say that primitive man could attain the rank to which he aspired only through the destruction or negation of wealth. Archaic man gave gifts because he wished to lose, and his relation to objects was not governed by the principle of usefulness, but by that of sacrifice. On the other hand, Mauss's research shows that, in primitive societies, the thing was never simply an object of use, but was endowed with a power, a *mana*, equivalent to that of living beings, and was profoundly implicated in the religious sphere. Where the object had been withdrawn from its original sacred order, sacrifice and the gift always intervened to restore it to that order. This requirement was so universally dominant that an ethnographer has been able to affirm that, in primitive cultures, the gods existed only to give structure to the human need for sacrifice and self-expropriation.

Baudelaire was perhaps alluding to behavior of this kind when he spoke of "a kind of dandy encountered by the travelers in the forests of North America." What is certain is that he hated "repugnant usefulness" too much to think that the world of the commodity could be abolished by means of a simple return to use-value. For Baudelaire, as for the dandy, the enjoyment of use is already an alienated relation to the object, scarcely different from commodification. The lesson that Baudelaire bequeathed to modern poetry is that the only way to go beyond the commodity was to press its contradictions to the limit, to the point at which the commodity as such would be abolished and the object would be restored to its own truth. As sacrifice restores to the sacred sphere what servile use has degraded and profaned, so, through poetic transfiguration, the object is pulled away both from the enjoyment of its use and from its value as accumulation, and is restored to its original status. For this reason Baudelaire saw a great analogy between poetic activity and sacrifice, between "the man that sings" and "the man that sacrifices," and he planned the composition of a "theory of sacrifice" of which the notes in *Fusées* are but fragments. As it is only through destruction that sacrifice consecrates, so it is only through the estrangement that makes it unattainable, and through the dissolution of traditional intelligibility and authority, that the falsehood of the commodity is changed into truth. This is the sense of "art for art's sake," which means not the *enjoyment* of art for its own sake, but the *destruction* of art worked by art.

The redemption that the dandy and the poet bring to things is their evocation of the imponderable act in which the aesthetic epiphany is realized. The reproduction of the dissolution of the transmissibility of culture in the experience of the shock thus becomes the last possible source of meaning and value for things themselves. To the capitalist accumulation of exchange value and to the enjoyment of the use-value of Marxism and the theorists of liberation, the dandy and modern poetry oppose the possibility of a new relation to things: the appropriation of unreality.

The condition of success of this sacrificial task is that the artist should take to its extreme consequences the principle of loss and self-dispossession. Rimbaud's programmatic exclamation "I is an other" (je est un autre) must be taken literally: the redemption of objects is impossible except by virtue of becoming an object. As the work of art must destroy and alienate itself to become an absolute commodity, so the dandy-artist must become a living corpse, constantly tending toward an *other,* a creature essentially nonhuman and antihuman.[6]

Balzac, in his *Traité de la vie élégante* (Treatise of the elegant life), writes that "making himself a dandy, man becomes a piece of boudoir furniture, an extremely ingenuous mannequin." Barbey d'Aurevilly made the same remark about George Brummell: "He elevated himself to the rank of object." And Baudelaire compared dandyism (which for him was of a piece with the exercise of writing poetry) to the "most severe monastic rule, the irresistible order of the Old Man of the Mountain, who commanded his adepts to commit suicide."

The creative activity and the creator cannot be spared the process of alienation. In modern poetry, the emergence into the foreground of the creative process, and its establishment as an autonomous value independent of the work produced (Valéry: "Why not conceive of the production of a work of art as a work of art in itself?") is above all an attempt to reify the nonreifiable.[7] After having transformed the work into a commodity, the artist now puts on the inhuman mask of the commodity and abandons the traditional image of the human. What reactionary critics of modern art forget when they reproach it with dehumanization is that during the great periods of art, the artistic center of gravity has never been in the human sphere.[8] What is new about modern poetry is that, confronted with a world that glorifies man so much the more it reduces him to an object, modern poetry unmasks the humanitarian ideology by making rigorously its own the *boutade* that Balzac puts in George Brummell's mouth: "Nothing less resembles man than man." Apollinaire perfectly formulated this proposition in *Les peintres cubistes,* where he writes that "above all, artists are men who wish to become inhuman." Baudelaire's antihumanism, Rimbaud's call "to make one's soul monstrous," the marionette of Kleist, Lautréamont's "it is a man or a stone or a tree," Mallarmé's "I am truly decomposed," the arabesque of Matisse that confuses human figures and tapestries, "my ardor is rather of the order of the dead and the unborn" from Klee, "the human doesn't come into it" of Gottfried Benn, to the "nacreous snail's trace" of Eugenio Montale and "the head of medusa and the Robot" of Paul Celan, all express the same need: there are still figures beyond the human!

Whatever the name given to the object of its search, the quest of modern poetry points in the direction of that disturbing region where there are no longer either men or gods, where there is but a presence, rising incomprehensibly over itself like a primitive idol, at once sacred and miserable, enchanting and terrifying, a presence that possesses at once the fixed materiality of a dead body and the phantomatic elusiveness of a living one. Fetish or grail, site of an epiphany or a disappearance, it reveals and once again dissolves itself in its own simulacrum of words until the program of alienation and knowledge, of redemption and dispossession, entrusted to poetry over a century ago by its first lucid devotees, will be accomplished.

Scholia

Grandvilliana; or, The world of Odradek

1. As usual, Poe was among the first to register this new relation between man and objects. In a tale, translated by Baudelaire, entitled "L'ange du bizarre" (The angel of the bizarre) he makes an improbable creature of nightmare appear, the ancestor of the Odradek bobbin of Kafka, whose body is constituted by utensils joined together in a vaguely anthropomorphic manner (a small flask of wine, two bottles, a funnel, a kind of tobacco case, two barrels) and which presents itself as "the genius that presides over the annoyances and bizarre incidents of humanity." Because of having refused to believe in the existence of the creature, the protagonist of the tale is led on by a series of insignificant incidents until he nearly has one foot in the grave.

The discomfort of man with respect to the objects that he himself has reduced to "appearances of things" is translated, as it was already in the time of Bosch, into the suspicion of a possible "animation of the inorganic" and into the placing in doubt of the bond that unites each thing to its own form, each creature to its familiar environment. In these two stylistic procedures the prophetic excellence of Grandville excels: they are confused and add up to a single disquieting effect in the "animated flowers," in the military decorations transformed into marine plants, in the personified musical instruments, in the "heraldic animals," in the eyes removed from their sockets, and in the anguished chain reaction of metamorphoses that populate his "otherworld."

Baudelaire, who was fascinated and frightened by the "illegitimate crossings" of Grandville and who saw in his designs "nature transformed into apocalypse," spoke of him with a kind of reverent fear. "There are superficial persons," he writes in *Quelques caricaturistes français* (Some French caricaturists), "whom Grandville amuses. As for myself, he terrifies me."

At this moment was born, as a mass-consumption commodity, the genre of "disturbing" literature, which relies on the discomfort and unconfessed fears of the reader. The theme of the portrait that comes to life, which Grandville had anticipated in the *Louvre des marionettes* (The puppet museum), is developed by Gautier in a story that was to be imitated in innumerable variations. It is therefore not surprising that Offenbach should have chosen as the libretto of one of his most fortunate operettas *The Tales of Hoffmann*, in which Olympia, the chilly animated puppet of Hoffmann's *Sandmann*, appears. Thus, in the "ironic utopia of a permanent domination of capital'' (which is Benjamin's characterization of the operetta), is manifest the menacing presence of the animated object, destined to have a second existence in the age of advanced mechanical development.

Freud dedicated an ample study, which appeared in the fifth volume of *Imago* and whose conclusions are highly significant, precisely to the uncanny (*Das Unheimliche,* of which he finds notable examples in two topics dear to Grandville: the eye out of its socket and the animated puppet, discovered in the novels of Hoffmann). Freud saw in the uncanny (*Unheimliche*) the distanced familiar (*heimliche*): "This uncanny is not in reality anything new or strange, but rather something that has always been familiar to the psyche and that only the process of distancing has rendered other." The refusal to acknowledge the degradation of commodified artifacts (*facticia*) is expressed cryptographically in the menacing aura that surrounds the most familiar things, with which it is not possible to feel safe.

The liberty style, which transforms dead matter into an organic creature, lifts this discomfort into a stylistic principle ("a washbasin of Pankok," a benevolent critic of that new style wrote in 1905, "with its cartilaginous and swollen members, appears to us a living organism. When Hermann Obrist designs an easy chair, the arms seem to be muscular limbs that seize and immobilize"). A few decades later, surrealism would make estrangement the fundamental character of the work of art. Grandville was claimed by the surrealists as their precursor; a lithography of Max Ernst reads: "Un nouveau monde est né, que Grandville soit loué (A new world is made, may Grandville be praised).

Brummelliana

2. One of the most celebrated remarks of Beau Brummell ("Do you call this thing a coat?", also related in the variant "What are these things on your feet?") is based on the assumption of a radical difference between an item of clothing and a "thing," thanks to which a useful item like a coat, apparently so ordinary, is raised to an indescribable essence.

Contemporaries could not be aware that the ultimate foundation on which the Brummell phenomenon rested was the commodification of the real. This is true of even the most acute contemporaries, like Hazlitt, who was among the first to examine the mechanism of Beau Brummell's wit, which that critic defined as "minimalism": "He has arrived at the *minimum* of wit, managing to take it, with felicity or pain, to an almost invisible point. All of his bons mots are founded on a single circumstance, the exaggeration of the purest trifles into something important . . . their significance is so attenuated that 'nothing lives' between them and nonsense: they are suspended on the edge of the void and in their shadowy composition they are very close to nothingness . . . His is truly the art of extracting something from nothing." Brummell's jacket is opposed to the "thing" as the commodity is to the useful object. What is more, suppressing any ambiguous survival of use-value, the jacket overtakes the commodity itself and renders transparent, so to speak, its fetishistic character, abolishing it in a kind of dialectical *Aufhebung* (sublation). At the same time, with his exaggeration of the irrelevant, the dandy reinvents a particular kind of use-value, which cannot be grasped or defined in utilitarian terms.

In a period that submitted hypocritically to the elephantiasis of ornament, the absence of every kind of bad conscience with respect to objects explains the almost ascetical sobriety of Beau's wardrobe and his foundation of the criterion of elegance on elusive nuances, like the accidental folds of a cravat. The technique of tying a cravat—worthy of a Zen master—invented by Beau Brummell was rigorous in the elimination of any intentionality: it is related that his valet Robinson could be seen every evening emerging from the dressing room, his arms laden with barely wrinkled neckwear. "They are our failures," he would explain. Beau himself, whom some of the greatest poets of modernity have not disdained to consider their teacher, can, from this point of view, claim as his own discovery the introduction of chance into the artwork so widely practiced in contemporary art (see figure 10).

In the abolition of any trace of subjectivity from his own person, no one has ever reached the radicalism of Beau Brummell. With an asceticism that equals the most mortifying mystical techniques, he constantly cancels from himself any trace of personality. This is the extremely serious sense of a number of his witticisms, such as "Robinson, which of the lakes do I prefer?"

That something very significant for the spirit of the age was revealed in Beau Brummell did not escape his more intelligent contemporaries. Byron once said that he would have preferred to be Brummell than Napoleon (the spirit of the world in the boudoir set against the spirit of the world on horseback: it is no small compliment). Bulwer-Lytton, in his novel *Peelham; or, The Adventures of a Gentleman* (whose protagonist is a reincarnation of Beau) wrote about the "trifles" of the dandy: "Flowers may be woven not only in an idle garland, but, as in the thyrsus of antiquity, also on a sacred instrument," and "in the folds of a collar there can be more pathos than fools imagine."

Marx and use-value

3. The position of Marx on this point is not clear and was modified over time. In the *Manuscripts* of 1844, he still seemed to consider use-value as something unnatural on a par with exchange value. "Private property," he writes, "has made us so stupid and one-sided that an object is only *ours* when we have it— when it exists for us as capital, or when it is directly possessed, eaten, drunk, worn, inhabited, etc.—in short, when it is *used* by us" [*The Economic and Philosophic Manuscripts of 1844* (New York: International Publishers, 1964), 139].

Natural and unnatural needs

4. It is curious that N. O. Brown and the other theorists of "liberation," although recognizing that Marx neither explained what was meant by "excess of

use-value'' nor understood the sacred origin of money, should nevertheless appeal to common sense in affirming the necessity of distinguishing between natural and unnatural needs, between the necessary and the superfluous. These theorists thus substitute for the bourgeois repression of the ''natural'' a moralistic repression of the superfluous. What is most revolutionary in modern art with regard to the theorists of liberation is the understanding, from the outset, that only by pushing to the extreme limits both ''unnatural need'' and ''perversion'' could one rediscover oneself and overcome repression.

Bataille and unproductive expenditure

5. The most rigorous attempt to define this principle and found upon it a science of economy is found in Bataille's essay ''La notion de dépense'' (The notion of expenditure) (*La critique sociale,* n. 7, January 1933), taken up and developed later in *La part maudite* (1949) [*The Accursed Share,* trans. Robert Hurley (New York: Zone Press, 1988)]. Mauss, whose magisterial ''Essai sur le don'' (Essay on the gift) (*L'année sociologique,* 1923-24) was behind the idea of Bataille, did not simply oppose ritual prodigality and the potlatch to the utilitarian principle, but, more wisely, demonstrated the inadequacy of this opposition in accounting for social behavior.

Genealogy of the antihero

6. Antihumanist traits are evident in an imaginary genealogical tree of the characters (or, rather, the anticharacters) in which modern artists have represented themselves: Igitur—Doctor Faustroll—Monsieur Croche—Stephen Dedalus—Monsieur the Vivisectionist—Plume—Loplop, chief of birds—Werfüronne—Adrian Leverkuhn.

Eclipse of the work

7. Gottfried Benn rightly observes, in his essay on the ''Problem of Lyricism'' (1951), that all modern poets, from Poe to Mallarmé to Valéry and Pound, appear to bring to the process of creation the same interest they bring to the work itself. An analogous preoccupation can be noted in one of the masters of the new American poetry, William Carlos Williams. His *Paterson* is, perhaps, with *The Age of Anxiety* of Auden, the most successful attempt at the long poem in contemporary poetry: ''The writing is nothing, the being / in a position to write . . . is nine tenths / of the difficulty.'' It is interesting to observe that the reification of the creative process is born precisely from the refusal of reification implicit in every work of art. Thus Dada, which seeks constantly to deny the artistic object and to abolish the very idea of the ''work,'' finishes by paradoxically commodifying spiritual activity itself [see Tristan Tzara, ''Essai sur la situation de poésie'' (Essay on the situation of poetry), 1931]. The same can be said of the situationists who, in the attempt to abolish art by realizing it, finish rather by extending it to all human existence. The origin of this phenomenon is probably to be found in the theories of Schlegel and Solger on so-called Romantic irony, which was founded precisely on the assumption of the superiority of the artist (that is, on the

creative process) with respect to the work and which led to a kind of constant negative reference between expression and the unexpressed, comparable to a mental reserve.

Antihumanistic, not antihuman

8. Ortega y Gasset, writing in *La deshumanización del arte,* was perfectly conscious of this fact and it is curious that his authority should have been invoked to criticize the antihumanism of modern art. The polemic of modern art is not directed against man, but against his ideological counterfeiting; it is not antihuman, but antihumanistic. Besides, as Edgar Wind acutely observed, art historians are scarcely immune from the process of dehumanization. The elaboration of the formal method in the second half of the past century (which can be summarized in Wölfflin's famous remark that the essence of the Gothic style is as evident in a pointed shoe as in a cathedral) is obvious proof.

Chapter 10
Mme Panckoucke; or, The Toy Fairy

The history of the semantic migration of the term "fetish" conceals some instructive insights. What is initially confined to the otherness of a "savage" culture as "something so absurd that it offers hardly any purchase to the discourse that would combat it" returns first, in the economic sphere, as an article of mass consumption and subsequently as the choice of perverse desire in the intimacy of sexual life. The proliferation of cases of fetishism at the end of the nineteenth century and the beginning of the twentieth (cutters of braids, coprophiliacs, sniffers of clothing, and fetishists of footwear, nightcaps, mourning crepe, lingerie, spots on lingerie, furs, wigs, leather objects, rings, and finally words and symbols) goes hand in hand with the complete commodification of objects and, after the transformation of things endowed with religious power into useful objects and of useful objects into commodities, announces a new transformation of the *facticia* produced by human labor.

The entrance of an object into the sphere of the fetish is always the sign of a transgression of the rule that assigns an appropriate use to each thing. It is easy to identify this transgression: for de Brosses, it concerned the transfer of a material object into the impalpable sphere of the divine; for Marx, the violation of the use-value; for Binet and Freud, the deviation of desire from its proper object. The map of the migration of the concept of fetishism traces thus, in filigree, the system of the rules that codify a type of repression that the theorists of liberation have not yet considered: that which exercises itself on objects and fixes the norms of their use. In our culture, even if not apparently sanctioned, this system of rules is so rigid that, as ready-made products demonstrate, the simple transfer of one object to the sphere of another is sufficient to render it unrecognizable and disquieting. But objects exist that have always been destined to such a particular function that they can be said to be withdrawn from all rules of use. I am speaking of toys. Once again, it was Baudelaire who noticed that an intelligent artist might find in toys material for reflection. In "The Moral of the Toy," published in the *Monde littéraire* of 17 April 1853, he recounts his visit, as a child, to the house of a certain Mme Panckoucke:

> She took me by the hand and, together, we traversed several rooms. Then she opened the door of a room that offered me an extraordinary spectacle, worthy of a fairy tale. The walls were no longer visible, so covered they were with toys. The ceiling disappeared under an efflorescence of toys that hung down like marvelous stalactites. The floor scarcely yielded a small path on which to walk . . . It is because of this adventure that I cannot pause before a toy shop and scan the inextricable medley of the bizarre forms and disparate colors without thinking of the woman, dressed in velvet and fur, who appeared to me as the Toy Fairy.

The evocation of this infantile recollection offered Baudelaire the pretext for a classification of the possible uses and abuses of toys. In children who transform a chair into a stagecoach, in those who meticulously order their toys, as in a museum, without touching them, but above all in those who, following "a first metaphysical tendency," wish rather "to see the soul" and, to this end, turn the toys in their hands, shake them, strike them against the wall, and finally eviscerate them and tear them to pieces ("but *where is the soul?*"—and this is where torpor and sadness set in), he saw the emblem of the relationship—of impenetrable joy mixed with stupefied frustration—that is the basis of artistic creation as of every relation between human and objects.

A text like Rilke's on dolls eloquently proves that children maintain a fetishistic relation to their toys. Developing Baudelaire's observations on toys, Rilke juxtaposed dolls—"soulless supports" and "empty sacks"—to handy and grateful objects. Dolls

> fed on fictitious food, like *ka*; befouling themselves, like spoiled children, with reality, every time that one attempted to make them ingest it; impenetrable and, at the extreme stage of a precocious plumpness, incapable of absorbing at any point even a single drop of water . . . It [the doll] makes us almost indignant at its tremendous and crass forgetfulness; that hatred that, unconscious, has always constituted a part of our relation to it, breaks forth, the doll lies before us unmasked like the horrible strange body on which we have dissipated our purest warmth; like the drowned corpse painted on the surface that allowed itself to be lifted up and borne along by the floods of our tenderness, until we would dry up again, abandoning it in some hedge . . . Are we not singular creatures, we who have allowed ourselves to

be guided to place our first inclination where it remains deprived of hope?

With respect to things, the doll is, on the one hand, infinitely lesser, because it is distant and beyond our grasp ("of you only, soul of the doll, it could never be said where you really were"), but, perhaps precisely because of this, it is on the other hand infinitely more, because it is the inexhaustible object of our desire and our fantasies ("in it [the doll] we would mix, as in a test tube, whatever unknowable things happened to us, which we would see boil up and turn colors there"). If one keeps in mind how much Rilke had written on the eclipse of authentic "things" and on the task falling to the poet to transfigure them into the invisible, the doll, at once absent and present, appears then as the emblem—suspended between this world and the other—of the object that has lost its weight "in the hands of the merchant" and has not yet transformed itself in the hands of the angel. From this derives its disturbing character, on which Rilke projects the implacable memory of a terrible infantile frustration. But from this also derives the doll's aptitude for providing us with information on the essence of the thing that has become an object of desire, which Rilke, with his morbid sensitivity to relationships with things, registered almost unawares.

If toys are not, as is apparent, simple and reassuring, then their situation in the world of objects is also not as definite as it seems. Ariès, in a chapter of his book *L'enfant et la vie familiale sous l'Ancien Régime* (Family life and the child under the ancien régime) informs us that the border between toys and objects for adults has not always been as rigid as might be imagined. Until the eighteenth century, adult Europe avidly sought out miniature objects: dollhouses, the *jouets d'Allemagne* (German playthings), and the *petites besognes d'Italie* (little Italian necessities). As the name shows (*bimbelot;* from *bimbe,* baby), the *bibelots* that burdened eighteenth-century interiors and that today populate petit-bourgeois decors are but a residue of these toys for adults. If we attempt to find out their origin, toys send us still further back in time, to a moment when they cannot be distinguished from other things. As Ariès writes:

> The historians of toys, the collectors of dolls and miniature objects, always encounter great difficulties in distinguishing the doll-toys from all the other images and statuettes that excavations restore in almost industrial quantities. In the greater number of cases these had a religious significance: domestic ritual, funerary ritual, ex voto, and so on.

Things that to us appear as toys were originally objects of such seriousness that they were placed in the tomb to accompany the deceased during the otherworldly sojourn. The greater antiquity of tombs that contain miniature objects with respect to those that contain real objects shows that the presence of the former is by no means a consequence of substitution based on "economic" motives (see figures 11 and 12).

If the foregoing is true, then the treasure guarded in Mme Panckoucke's room points to a more originary status of the thing, about which the dead, children, and other fetishists can give us precious information. Winnicott's research on the first relations between the child and the external world have led to the identification of a kind of object, by him defined as "transitional," that comprises the first things (pieces of bed linen, of cloth, or the like) that the child separates from external reality and appropriates, and whose place is "in the zone of experience which is between the thumb and the teddy-bear, between oral eroticism and the real object-relation." These objects, however, apparently properly belong neither to the internal and subjective nor to the external and objective spheres, but to something that Winnicott defined as "the area of illusion," in whose "potential space" they will subsequently be able to situate themselves both in play and in cultural experience. The localization of culture and play is therefore neither within nor outside of the individual, but in a "third area," distinct both "from interior psychic reality and from the effective world in which the individual lives."

The topology that is here expressed tentatively in the language of psychology has always been known to children, fetishists, "savages," and poets. It is in this "third area" that a science of man truly freed of every eighteenth-century prejudice should focus its study.[1] Things are not outside of us, in measurable external space, like neutral objects (*ob-jecta*) of use and exchange; rather, they open to us the original place solely from which the experience of measurable external space becomes possible. They are therefore held and comprehended from the outset in the *topos outopos* (placeless place, no-place place) in which our experience of being-in-the-world is situated. The question "where is the thing?" is inseparable from the question "where is the human?" Like the fetish, like the toy, things are not properly anywhere, because their place is found on this side of objects and beyond the human in a zone that is no longer objective or subjective, neither personal nor impersonal, neither material nor immaterial, but where we find ourselves suddenly facing these apparently so simple unknowns: the human, the thing.

Scholia

Where is the thing?

1. The Greek word *'agalma*, which designated statues, expresses well this original status of human *facticia* (products, man-made objects). As Kerényi writes (*Agalma, eikon, eidolon* in *Archivio di filosofia*, 1962), "this term does not indicate, for the Greeks, something solid and determinate, but . . . the perpetual source of an event, in which the divinity takes part no less than man." The etymological meaning of *'agalma* (from *'agllomai*) is "joy, exultation." Willamowitz tells of archaic statues that bear the inscription *Chares, 'eim, 'agalma toû Apollonos*, which must be translated "I am Chares, statue and joy of Apollo."

The genitive is here subjective and objective in exactly the same degree. In the presence of these statutes it is wholly impossible to decide if we find ourselves before "objects" or "subjects," because they gaze at us from a place that precedes and transcends our distinction subject/object. This is the more true if we take, rather than a Greek statue, any object whatsoever from a primitive culture: such an object stands on this side not only of our distinction between subjective and objective, but also of that between human and nonhuman. At the limit, however, the same is true of every human creation, be it statue or poem. Only in this perspective will future anthropology be able to arrive at a definition of the status of the cultural object and to localize in its *topos* precisely the products of human "making."

1. Dürer, *Melencolia I.*

2. *Vespertilio* (bat), in Ori Apollinis Niliaci,
De sacris Aegyptorium notis, 1574.
3. Rubens, *Heraclitus as a Melancholic.*
Madrid, Prado.

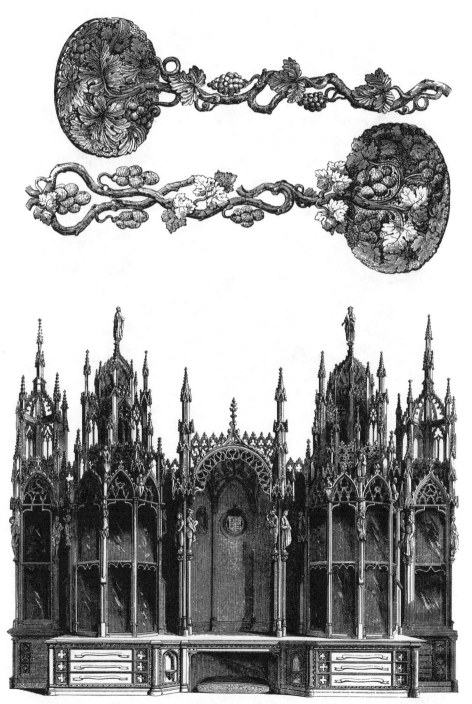

4-5. *Place settings* and *bookstore,* from the *Illustrated Catalogue* of the Universal Exposition of London, 1851.

6-7. Grandville, illustrations from
*Un autre mond*e (Another world).

8. Grandville, *Système de Fourier* (The system of Fourier), illustration from *Un autre monde*.

9. Grandville, illustrations from *Petites misères de la vie humaine*
(The small miseries of human life).

10. *Beau Brummell.*

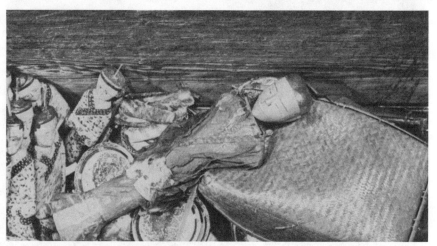

11-12. Figure in miniature of an archaic Chinese tomb.

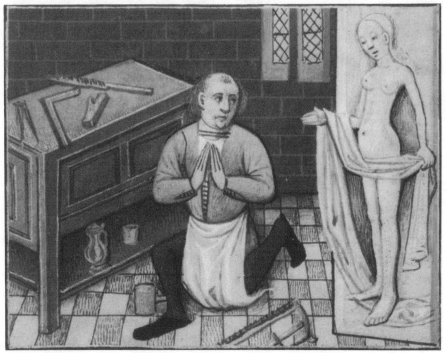

13. *The Lover at the Fountain of Narcissus* (Ms. fr. 12595, fol. 12v). Paris, Bibliothèque Nationale.
14. *Narcissus* (Ms. fr. 12595, fol. 12v). Paris, Bibliothèque Nationale.
15. *Pygmalion as Idolater* (Ms. Douce 195, fol. 149v). Oxford, Bodleian Library.

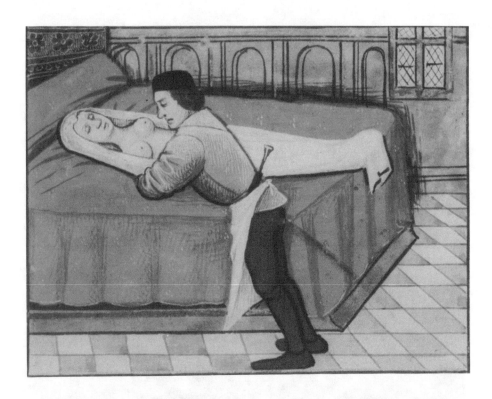

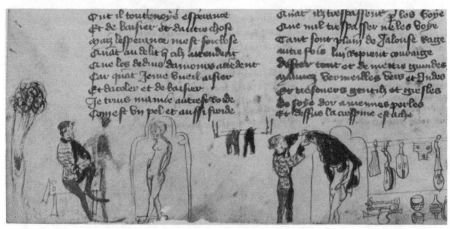

16. *Pygmalion and the Image* (Ms. Douce 195, fol. 150r). Oxford, Bodleian Library.
17. *Stories of Pygmalion* (Ms. fr. 12592, fol. 62v). Paris, Bibliothèque Nationale.

18. *The Lover and the Image* (Ms. 387, fol. 146v). Valencia.

19. *Venus and the Image* (Ms. 387, fol. 144r). Valencia.
20. *Venus and the Image* (Ms. fr. 380, fol. 135v). Paris, Biliothèque Nationale.

21. *The Lover, the Image, and the Rose* (Ms. 387, fol. 146v). Valencia.
22. *"Fol amour* as Idolatry," detail from the left side of the central portal of the Cathedral of Notre-Dame, Paris.

23. *Lovers as Idolaters,* birth salver attributed to the Master of Saint Martin. Paris, Louvre.

24-25. *Industrious Man* and *The Future Work*, from Ori Apollinis Niliaci,
De sacris Aegyptorum notis, 1574.

26. *What is Grave, Delights,* from J. Catz, *Proteus* (Rotterdam 1627).

27. *Love Is the Father of Elegance,* from J. Catz, *Proteus.*

Part III
The Word and the Phantasm:
The Theory of the Phantasm
in the Love Poetry of the Duecento

Manibus Aby Warburg et Robert Klein
"Der gute Gott steckt im Detail"
geniisque Henry Corbin et Jacques Lacan
"C'est li miroërs perilleus"

formando di disio nova persona
Guido Cavalcanti

If the spirit does not become an image, it will be annihilated along with the world.
Simon Magus

Les polissons sont amoureux, les poètes sont idolâtres.
Baudelaire

Chapter 11
Narcissus and Pygmalion

Toward the end of the *Roman de la Rose,* Love's army, in which the poem's protagonist is enlisted, after fruitlessly attempting to reduce the castle in which the flower is guarded, calls the goddess Venus to its aid. The hastily expedited messengers reach her on Mount Cithaeron as she lounges in the company of Adonis. On her golden coach, drawn by doves and embellished with pearls, the goddess swiftly reaches the battlefield and menacingly orders Shame and Fear, the defenders of the keep, to surrender. At their refusal, Venus, whom the poet represents with charming realism as an angry woman who, in her fury, has drawn up her dress above her ankles ["'la sua roba ha soccorciata,'" says the author of the Italian imitation of the *Roman* known as the *Fiore,* rendering almost literally Jean's "lors s'est Venus haut secourciee" (then Venus girded herself up high)], takes up her bow and prepares to shoot her incendiary shaft at the castle. At this decisive point in his narrative, Jean de Meung begins a digression of more than five hundred verses; the edition of the *Roman* attributed to Clément Marot introduces this passage with the concise but eloquent rubric: "Ci commence la fiction / de l'ymage Pigmalion" (Here begins the tale / of the statue of Pygmalion). The story of the sculptor in love with his statue derives, in its general outlines, from Ovid's *Metamorphoses;* but Jean gives it such a rich and peculiar treatment that it is permissible to suppose that the digression is more than a rhetorical expedient to increase, through delay, the tension in the reader before the happy conclusion of the poem.

Above all Pygmalion's falling in love is described so as to recall at every step of the way the *fol amour* (mad love) of the courtly love poets, which Jean even recalls literally, as when the unhappy sculptor bewails his love for "une ymage sourde et mue / qui ne se crole ne se mue" (a deaf and dumb statue, / that neither changes nor moves) and adds that she "ne ja de moi merci n'avra" (will never have mercy [concede her favors] on me).[1] This is almost a stereotypical formula of troubadour lyric; we need only think of "Ja n'aura un jor / merci de moi" (She will never one day have mercy on me) of Gaucelm Faidit or "celeis don ja pro non aurai" (she from whom I will never gain advantage) of Bernart de Ventadorn.[2] In the delicate verse of Ovid there is no trace of sadness, but the passion of Pygmalion is already here unmistakably that ambiguous mixture of not disinterested hope and grim desperation that the Stilnovists would call *dottanza* (anxious doubt):

> Ainsinc Pygmalion estrive
> n'an son estrif n'a pes ne trive
> En un estat point ne demeure:
> or aime, or het, or rit, or pleure
> or est liez, or est a mesese,
> or se tourmente, or se rapese. (vv. 20901-20906)

> [Thus Pygmalion struggles
> and his strife has no peace or truce
> He does not rest in one state:
> now he loves, now hates, now laughs, now weeps,
> now he is happy, now disturbed;
> now he torments himself, now calms himself.]

In general the entire scene seems to place the emphasis on the morbid and perverse character of the love for the *ymage* (image or statue), which at one and the same time resembles the sin of lust and a kind of religious cult. In his monologue, Pygmalion compares himself to Narcissus in love with his own form (see figures 13 and 14), which was certainly even more foolish (see vv. 20843-20855), and he describes crudely the attempts and frustrations of a passion that is *trop horrible:*

> car quant je me veull aesier
> et d'acoler et de besier,
> je truis m'amie autresine roide
> comme est uns pex, et si tres froide
> que, quant por lui besier i touche
> toute me refredist la bouche. (vv. 20871-20876)

> [because when I want to please myself
> and embrace and kiss her,
> I find my friend stiff like
> a stick, and so cold
> that when I touch to kiss her
> I wholly freeze my mouth.]

The description of putting clothing on the naked statue is dispatched in three verses by Ovid, but Jean lingers over this passage for more than seventy, thus punctiliously elaborating a scene in which the lover tries different garments and items of footwear on his *pucelle* (girl, virgin). If we did not know that (at least in the case of the footwear) a reference to troubadour lyric is at stake,[3] we would be surprised to find here such episodes of fetishism as would be characteristic of a novel of Restif:

> Autre foiz li reprent corage
> d'oster tout et de metre guindes
> jaunes, vermeilles, verz et indes,
> et treçoers gentez et grelles
> de saie et d'or, a menuz pelles;
> et desus la crespine estache,
> une mout precieuse estache,
> et par desus la crespinete
> une courone d'or grellete
> ou mout ot precieuses pierres . . .
> Et par grant antante li chauce
> en chascun pié soler et chauce,
> antailliez jolivetement,
> a deus doie du pavemant;
> n'est pas de houseaus estrenee
> car el n'iert pas de Paris nee;
> trop par fust rude chaucemante
> a pucele de tel jouvante. (vv. 20932-20968)

[Another time he desires
to take all off her and fits her with bows
yellow, red, green, and purple
and thin beautiful fillets
of silk and gold, with little pearls;
and under the crest he attaches
a very precious ribbon,
and above the crest
a crown of beaten gold
with many precious stones . . .
And with great care he fits her
on both feet with hose and shoes
beautifully chased
two fingerbreadths from the floor;
he does not give her boots
because she isn't Paris-born;

such would be footwear too coarse
for a girl of such grace.]

A grotesque religious pathos charges the scene in which Pygmalion offers to his image a gold ring and celebrates with her a wedding that is a parody of the Christian sacrament, with "love songs in place of the Mass" and with the accompaniment of all the instruments of profane medieval music. Afterward, as appropriate for a husband on his wedding night, he lays himself in bed with the new bride:

> Puis la rambrace, si la couche
> antre ses braz dedanz sa couche,
> et la rebese et la racole,
> mes ce n'est pas de bone escole
> quant II persones s'antrebesent
> et li besier aus II ne plesent. (vv. 21029-21032)

> [Then he embraces her again, and takes
> her between his arms and beds her,
> and he kisses her again and hugs her;
> but it's not good form
> when two people kiss each other
> and the kisses don't please both equally.]

We can confirm that this perverse and, at the same time, almost ceremonial character of Pygmalion's love as described by Jean is not just an impression of the modern reader by referring to the illustrations of the ancient manuscripts of the poem. In, for example, Oxford, Ms. Douce 195, fol. 150r (see figure 16), or Valencia, Ms. 387, fol. 146r, Pygmalion is represented both as the foolish lover who caresses his naked statue lasciviously and lies down next to her, and as a faithful devotee kneeling in ecstatic adoration before the *ymage* (in Douce 195, fol. 149v; see figure 15), at times (as in Douce 364, fol. 153v) in an interior that strongly resembles a church.[4]

If it is evident from what we have said thus far that the story of Pygmalion had a special importance for Jean de Meung, this also results, were further proof needed, from the fact that the story actually is not a digression, but serves to introduce and make more accessible the conclusive episode of the poem that immediately follows it. We had left Venus as she prepared to fire her arrow. The target at which the goddess aims is a kind of arrowslit (*une archiere; una balestriera* in the already-cited Italian version of the *Roman*) located between two pilasters that hold up

> une ymage en leu de chaase,
> qui n'iert trop haute ne trop basse,
> trop grosse ou trop grelle, non pas,
> mes toute tailliee a conpas

de braz, d'espaules et de mains,
qu'il n'i failloit ne plus ne mains. (vv. 20769-20774)

[a statue, in lieu of prey,
neither too high nor too low,
neither too fat nor too thin,
but sculpted all with such proportion
of arms, shoulders, and hands
that there was no need of more or less.]

When the incendiary shaft penetrates the arrowslit and sets fire to the castle, it is precisely this statue that unexpectedly reveals itself to be the object of the amorous quest of the protagonist, who, while the defenders flee on all sides, directs himself toward it in the guise of a pilgrim, with scrip and staff. The narrative that follows leaves little doubt about what is happening, however repugnant it seems to us: the lover, after kneeling down, simulates a coupling with the statue, using his staff in place of his virile member.

Once again the ancient illustrators of the *Roman* represented the scene without false modesty. The *ymage* (Valencia, Ms. 387, fols. 144r, 146v; see figures 17, 18 and 19) is the bust of a naked woman, the columns serving for legs, and the *archiere* is placed exactly where the female sex ought to be; the lover, semi-reclining between the ruins of the castle of Love next to the overthrown idol, pushes his staff into the arrowslit (see also figures 20 and 21).

If we keep in mind that the poem begins at the fountain of Narcissus and that the protagonist falls in love with an image reflected in this *miroërs perilleus* (dangerous mirror; see vv. 1569-1595), then love for the *ymage* will appear as the proper ruling motif of the *Roman*. With a symmetry that for numerous reasons appears calculated,[5] the story of Pygmalion and his statue is paralleled by the episode of the *demoisiaus* (pubescent male) in love with his image reflected in a mirror. Inaugurating a tradition that typically defines the medieval conception of love,[6] the mirror is identified with the fountain of Love, such that the whole poem appears from this viewpoint as an erotic itinerary that goes from the mirror of Narcissus to the workshop of Pygmalion, from a reflected image to an artistically constructed one, both objects of the same mad passion. But what meaning can we give to a love of this kind, and what does the *ymage* represent? And why, in this poem where according to the principles of allegory everything is animated and personified, is the object of love represented by an inert image and not by a flesh-and-blood woman?

The topic of love for an image is not infrequent in medieval Romance literature. Remaining within the limits of Old French literature, we find it in one of the most delicate works of thirteenth-century love poetry, the little poem that bears the title "Lai de l'ombre" (Lay of the reflection). The poet, Jean Renart, introduces us to a knight—a model of courtesy and prowess—whom Love has pierced with its arrow and rendered more besotted than Tristan was for Iseult. After several episodes, the knight, who has been received in the castle where his lady is, declares his love to her and is rebuffed. During a long colloquy, which is a proper amorous debate (*contrasto*), the knight, taking advantage of a momentary distraction on the lady's part, succeeds in placing a ring on her finger. When, later, she becomes aware of the ruse, she angrily sends for the knight and demands that he take back the ring. At this point the lover, as he takes back the ring, performs an act of such extraordinary courtesy that the lady is persuaded to change her mind and concede what she had so long refused. It is best to relate the scene in the words of Jean Renart himself, for it is without a doubt one of the most successful poetic passages in the poem and perhaps in all Old French literature:

> Au reprendre dist: «Granz merciz!
> Por ce n'est pas li ors noirciz—
> fet il—s'il vient de cel biau doit».
> Cele s'en sozrist, qui couidoit
> qu'il le deüst remetre el suen;
> mes il fist ainz un mout grant sen,
> qu'a grant joie li torna puis.
> Il s'est acoutez sor le puis,
> qui n'estoit que toise et demie
> parfonz, si meschoisi mie
> en l'aigue, qui ert bele et clere,
> l'ombre de la dame qui ere
> la riens el mont que miex amot.
> «Sachiez—fet il—tout a un mot,
> que je n'en reporterai mie,
> ainz l'avera ma douce amie,
> la riens que j'aim plus après vous.»
> «Diex!—fet ele—ci n'a que nous:
> ou l'avrez vous si tost trovee?»
> «Par mon chief, tost vous ert moustree
> la preus, la gentiz qui l'avra.»
> «Ou est?» «En non Dieu, vez le la,
> vostre bel ombre qui l'atent.»
> L'anelet prent et vers li tent.
> «Tenez—fet il—ma douce amie;
> puis que ma dame n'en veut mie,
> vous le prendrez bien sans meslee.»
> L'aigue s'est un petit troublee
> au cheoir que li aniaus fist,
> et, quant li ombres se desfit:
> «Veez—fet il—dame, or l'a pris.» (vv. 871-901)

[Taking it back, he said: "Many thanks;
Surely the gold has not tarnished,
if it returns from that lovely hand."
She smiled, for she thought that
he would replace the ring on his;
but instead he did a shrewd thing
that later brought him great joy.
He leaned over the pool,
which was but a span and a half
in depth, so he did not fail
to see in the clear water
the reflection of that lady
whom he loved more than anything
in the world. "Know then," he said,
"in a word, I will not take it back,
but my sweet friend will have it, whom
I love best after yourself."
"God!" she answered, "we are alone here,
where will you find her so quickly?"
"I swear it, soon you will be shown
the valorous and noble one who will have it."
"Where is she?" "By God, see her there, look
at your beautiful reflection that awaits.
For you," he said, "my sweet friend!
As my lady does not wish it,
You will take it—do not refuse."
The water was a bit troubled,
as the ring fell into it;
and, when the reflection was dissolved:
"Behold," he said, "lady, now she has it."]

It is not clear to us why this gesture of the knight should be an act of prowess and courtesy so full of meaning ("un mout grant sen") that it succeeds where other persuasion had failed. Nevertheless, we must assume that this was perfectly intelligible to Jean Renart's reading public and that the courtship of a "reflection" (how can we not think here of Pygmalion, who offers a ring to his statue?) had a significance that in part escapes us.

If we leave Provençal poetry to one side, where this topic appears most frequently, often in extravagant guises (as in the legend of the *domna soisebunda,* the imaginary lady, assembled from parts of other women, that Bertran de Born composed for himself when rebuffed by one of his ladies), we again come up against the theme of the image in a canzone of Giacomo de Lentini, the leader of that Sicilian school that is at the origin of Italian vernacular poetry. Here it is not a question of a statue or of an image reflected in the water, but of a figure painted in the lover's own heart. This motif must have had sufficient importance for the "Notaro" (Notary), as Dante would call him antonomastically in a famous passage of the *Purgatorio,* because the "image in the heart" became a commonplace among the Sicilian versifiers and was bequeathed by them to the Italian courtly poets who succeeded. Let us listen to Giacomo:

> Com'om che pone mente
> in altro exemplo pinge
> la simile pintura,
>   cosí, bella, facc'eo,
> che 'nfra lo core meo
> porto la tua figura.
>
>   In cor par ch'eo vi porti
> pinta como in parete,
> e non pare di fore . . .
>
>   Avendo gran disio
> dipinsi una pintura,
> bella, voi simigliante,
>   e quando voi non vio,
> guardo 'n quella figura,
> e par ch'eo v'aggia avante . . .

> [As a man who attends
> to an exemplar paints
> a similar picture,
> so, beauty, do I,
> for within my heart
> I bear your figure.

> In my heart it seems I bear you
> painted as if on a wall,
> and such painting does not appear outside . . .

> Having great desire
> I painted a picture,
> beauty, similar to you,
> And when I do not see you,
> I gaze on that figure,
> and I seem to have you before me . . .][7]

In this example too, as in the two preceding, the topic of love appears strictly and enigmatically linked to that of the image. But Giacomo furnishes us with clues that permit us to guess in which direction we are to seek for the meaning of this link. In a sonnet that begins "Or come pote sí gran donna entrare" (Now how can such a great lady enter) Giacomo asks himself rather seriously how it can be possible that his lady, who is so large, has entered him through his eyes, "che si piccioli sono" (which are so small), and answers saying that as light passes through glass, so "no la persona, ma la sua figura" (not her person, but her figure) penetrates his heart through his eyes. In another celebrated sonnet written for a poetic dispute (*tenzone*) with Jacopo Mostacci and Pier della Vigna, the Notary, after having reiterated, according to the erotic physics current in his day, that "the eyes first generate love," adds that the eyes represent what they see to the heart,

> e lo cor, che di zo è concepitore,
> imagina, e li piace quel desio.
>
> [and the heart, which of this conceives,
> imagines, and that desire pleases it.]

These affirmations send us back to a theory of sensation that is well known to medieval psychology and physiology, and which is, among other things, incidentally expounded by Dante in the *Convivio* (III.9) in not dissimilar terms when he says that "queste cose visibili, sí le proprie come le comuni in quanto sono visibili, vengono dentro a l'occhio—non dico le cose, ma le forme loro—per lo mezzo diafano, non realmente ma intenzionalmente, sí quasi come in vetro trasparente" (these visible things, both proper and common alike insofar as they are visible, come inside the eye—I do not say the things themselves, but their forms—through the diaphanous medium, not in reality but intentionally, almost as if through transparent glass).

According to this theory, and we restrict ourselves here to its most general outlines, sensible objects impress their forms on the senses, and this sensible impression, or image, or phantasm (as the medieval philosophers prefer, in the wake of Aristotle) is then received by the phantasy, or imaginative virtue, which conserves it even in the absence of the object that has produced it. The image "painted as if on a wall" in the heart, of which Giacomo speaks, is perhaps precisely this "phantasm," which, as we will see, accomplishes a very important function in medieval psychology. From Giacomo we learn (if we did not know it from other sources) that the phantasm, for reasons that thus far escape us, also has a conspicuous role in the process of falling in love ("and the heart, which of this conceives, / imagines, and that desire pleases it"). If this is true, perhaps we now begin to grasp in some way why the homage to the image of the beloved in the poem of Renart was not only not such an extravagant gesture, but on the contrary a very concrete proof of love. From this viewpoint, it will perhaps become more comprehensible why in the *Roman de la Rose* the protagonist falls in love when looking at a reflected image in the fountain of Narcissus and why, at the end of his long erotic meanderings, he finds himself once again, like Pygmalion, in front of an *ymage*. But before hazarding hypotheses that might appear fanciful, it is necessary to reconstruct medieval phantasmology in all of its complexity and to seek, insofar as it is possible, to trace its genealogy and follow its developments. This is what we shall attempt to do in the following chapters.

Notes

1. Guillaume de Lorris and Jean de Meung, *Le Roman de la Rose,* edited by F. Lecoy (Paris, 1970-73), vv. 20821-20822. Subsequent quotations of this work are from this edition.

2. Bernart de Ventadorn, *Seine Lieder,* edited by Carl Appel (Halle, 1915), 43, v. 12. This stereotype is found again among the Stilnovists [see G. Cavalcanti: "che neente / par che pietate di te voglia udire" (who seems not at all willing / to hear of pity toward you), in *Rimatori del dolce stil novo* (Poets of the sweet new style), edited by L. Di Benedetto (Bari, 1939), 6].

3. "qu'eu sia per sa comanda / pres de leih, josta l'esponda, / e. lh traya. ls sotlars be chaussans, / a genolhs et umilians, / si. lh platz que sos pes me tenda" (that I might be at her behest / near to her, next to the bed, / and might remove her well-fitting slippers / while humbly kneeling, / if it should please her to extend her foot to me) (Bernart de Ventadorn, *Seine Lieder,* 26, vv. 31-35).

4. For a good while now the iconological science born thanks to the efforts of Aby Warburg has used literary texts for the interpretation of images. It is to be hoped that, in the context of a global history of culture similar to what Warburg had in mind, the philological sciences too will begin to use images (in particular, illustrations) as an auxiliary instrument for the interpretation of literary texts. On the importance of the illustrations for the reading of the *Roman de la Rose,* see J. Fleming, *The "Roman de la Rose": A Study in Allegory and Iconography* (Princeton: Princeton University Press, 1969).

5. That Jean de Meung conceived the episode of Pygmalion as a *pendant* to that of Narcissus is proved not only by the fact that the two episodes share an analogous situation within the *Roman* (the first occurs immediately after the protagonist falls in love, the second immediately before he is united with his Rose) and are introduced in an identical way ["Narcissus fu uns demoisiaus" (Narcissus was a youth), "Pigmalion, ens antailleires" (Pygmalion, a sculptor)], but also because the episode of Pygmalion, like that of Narcissus, follows the description of a fountain that "makes the dead revive," which is explicitly contrasted to that of Narcissus, "that intoxicates the living with death." Thus the two episodes, at the beginning and end of the *Roman,* stand as two emblems, similar and opposed, of *fol amour* for an image (see figure 22).

6. The identification of the "dangerous mirror" of Narcissus with the fountain of Love appears to be an invention of Guillaume de Lorris. It is clear, however, that it reflects a concept widely disseminated in the poetry of the twelfth and thirteenth centuries, which saw in Narcissus the emblematic figure of love (keeping in mind that—as we will see shortly—the Middle Ages saw in Narcissus not simply love in itself, but above all love for an image).

7. *Poeti del duecento,* vol. 1, edited by G. Contini (Milano-Napoli, 1960), 55-56.

Chapter 12
Eros at the Mirror

SOCRATES: Memory unites with the senses, and the passions (*pathēmata*) connected with these write words in our souls, so to speak. When this passion writes truly, then true opinions and discourse are produced in us; but when the scribe within us writes what is false, the result is contrary to the truth.

PROTARCHUS: It seems the same way to me, and I accept what you have said.

SOCRATES: Accept then also the presence within our souls of another artist at the same time.

PROTARCHUS: Who?

SOCRATES: A painter who, after the scribe, draws in the mind the images of things said.

PROTARCHUS: But when and how?

SOCRATES: When a man, after having received from the sight or from some other sense the objects of opinion and discourse, sees within himself in some way the images of these objects. Is it not this way that it occurs?

That our quest for the phantasm should begin with this passage in Plato's *Philebus* (39a) will not appear too surprising to those who have a certain familiarity with medieval culture and its disguises. Epochs gifted with strong imagination frequently need to conceal their most original impulses and creative obsessions behind forms and figures borrowed from other eras, and ages that lack imagination are generally also those less disposed to compromise the affirmation

73

of their own originality. Through a phenomenon that has been improperly but suggestively defined as "pseudomorphosis,"[1] medieval Arabic civilization conceived of itself as a kind of gloss or appendix to classical texts. From this point of view, Aristotle is doubtless the most important of the medieval philosophers. At first glance, Plato does not appear to hold an equally important place in medieval thought, but the frequent assertion that the Middle Ages had but scant and in any case secondhand knowledge of his works is certainly exaggerated. In the first place, in the case of medieval culture it is meaningless to distinguish between first- and secondhand knowledge, given that it is a culture of "pseudomorphosis" and commentary. Second, although the publication of the *Plato latinus* undertaken by Klibansky for the Warburg Institute shows that the *Parmenides,* the *Meno,* the *Phaedo,* and the *Timaeus* were surely available in Latin translation, it would be impossible to furnish a complete list of works of writers in Latin — Eastern Fathers and above all Arabic and Neoplatonic philosophers — who transmitted directly or indirectly the thought of Plato.[2] For the Middle Ages, the works of an author do not occupy a well-defined place in time; rather, like Proust's characters in the *Recherche,* described as disproportionately prolonged in their duration "in that they simultaneously touch, like giants wallowing in the years, epochs so distant," they coincide with their own tradition. Despite the offense to our philological sensibilities, the consistency of these works cannot be verified once and for all: as Proust says of human bodies, they are literally made up of time. Thus, if it is true that the Middle Ages was dominated by a principle of authority, this authority must be understood in a very special way, which has nothing to do with the vicious circle of authority and citation (the authority is the source of the citation but the citation is the source of authority), which renders impossible the birth of real authority in the modern world (or, more exactly, only renders possible its "authoritarian" counterfeit): for the Middle Ages there is not, in fact, any possibility of citing a text in the modern sense of the word, because the work of the *auctor* also comprehends its own citation, such that it is possible to say, despite the apparent paradox, that the medieval texts are contained as citations within the *antiqui auctores* (ancient authors), which explains, among other things, the medieval predilection for the gloss as a literary form.

The artist who, in Plato's text, draws the images (*eikonas*) of things in the soul is the phantasy; these pictures are in fact shortly thereafter defined as "phantasms" (*phantasmata*) (40a). The central theme of the *Philebus* is not, however, knowledge, but pleasure, and, if Plato here evokes the problem of memory and the phantasy, it is because he was anxious to show that desire and pleasure are impossible without this "painting in the soul" and that a purely corporeal pleasure does not exist. Thus, from the beginning of our study, thanks to an intuition that strikingly anticipates the Lacanian thesis according to which "le phantasme fait le plaisir propre au désir" (the phantasm makes the pleasure suited to the desire),[3] the phantasm places itself under the banner of desire — a detail we would do well not to forget.

In another dialogue (*Theaetetus* 191d-e), Plato explained the metaphor of the "interior painting" with another metaphor, whose legacy was to be so rich that we can still discern its echo in the Freudian theory of the memory trace:

> Suppose that there is in our soul an impressionable wax-tablet, in some more impressionable, in others less, purer in some, more impure in others, and in some harder and in some softer and in others yet a middle way . . . It is a gift, let us say, of the mother of the Muses, Mnemosyne: everything that we wish to conserve in our memories of what we have seen or heard or conceived is impressed in this wax that we present to sensations or conceptions. And of what is impressed we conserve the memory and the knowledge so long as the image (*to eidolon*) lasts. What is erased or does not succeed in impressing itself, we forget and have no knowledge of.

The story of classical psychology is, in good measure, the story of these two metaphors. We rediscover them both in Aristotle, but they are in a certain sense taken literally and inserted in an organic psychological theory in which the phantasm has a very important function, over which the exegetical effort of the Middle Ages was to toil with particular vigor. In the *De anima* (424a) the process of sensation is summed up as follows:

> We must understand as true generally of every sense that sense is that which is receptive of the form of sensible objects without the matter, just as the wax receives the impression of the signet ring without the iron or the gold . . . so in every case sense is affected by that which has colour, flavour, or sound.[4]

In the *De memoria* (450a) this impression is defined as a drawing (*zoographema*):

> The passion produced by the sensation in the soul and in the part of the body that has the sensation is something like a drawing . . . In fact the movement that is produced makes a sort of impression of the thing perceived, as do those who make a seal with a ring.

Thus Aristotle explained the mechanism of vision—arguing against those who explained it as a flux that goes from the object to the eye—as a passion impressed by color on the eye, in whose aqueous element the color reflects itself as in a mirror.

The movement or the passion produced by the sensation is then transmitted to the phantasy, which can produce the phantasm even in the absence of the thing perceived (*De anima* 428a). The exact part of the soul where the phantasms are properly located is not easy to determine; Aristotle himself confessed that "it is a problem without solution" (*pollen aporian: De anima* 432b). Aristotle was, however, certainly among the first to theorize explicitly the autonomous activity of this part of the soul: "that through which is produced in us the phantasm"

(428a). After affirming that it is diverse from sensation (because the phantasms are also produced in the absence of sensations, for example, when our eyes are closed) and that it is not possible to identify it with operations that are always true, like science and intellection (because it can also be false), Aristotle concluded (429a):

> If therefore no other thing, except for the imagination, is in fact as we have said, and possesses the characteristics we have listed, it would be a movement produced by the completed sensation. And, as the sight is the sense par excellence, the imagination (*phantasia*) has also taken its name from light (*phaos*), because without light nothing is seen. And because of the fact that the phantasms persist and are similar to sensations, animals, in performing many actions, are governed by them: some because they lack intellect, like the beasts; others because their intellect is often obscured by passions, disease, or sleep, like men.

Closely linked to the phantasy is the memory, which Aristotle defined as "the possession of a phantasm as icon of what it is a phantasm of" (a definition that permits the explanation of abnormal phenomena such as déjà vu and paramnesia).[5] This nexus is so binding that there is no memory without a phantasm, even of things that are objects of intellectual knowledge.

The function of the phantasm in the cognitive process is so fundamental that it can in a certain sense be considered the necessary condition of intellection. Aristotle went so far as to say that the intellect is a kind of phantasy (*phantasia tis*) and several times repeats the principle that, in the scholastic formulation *nihil potest homo intelligere sine phantasmata* (man can understand nothing without phantasms), will dominate the medieval theory of knowledge.[6]

But the function of the phantasm is not yet exhausted. It also has an essential role in the dream, which Aristotle defined precisely as *phantasm tis,* a kind of phantasm that appears in sleep. In fact, according to Aristotle, the movements produced by sensation remain in the organs of sense not only during waking hours, but also during sleep, just as a projectile continues to move after leaving the instrument imparting its motion (*De insomnis* 459a). The divination in dreams so dear to antiquity can be explained by the phantasms in dreams that induce us to perform, when awake, the actions we are unwittingly accustomed to associate with those phantasms, or else by means of the greater receptivity of the phantasy, during sleep or ecstasy, to external movements and emanations (*De divinatione per somnium* 463-464a).

We must here point out another aspect of the Aristotelian theory of the phantasm: its function in language. In the *De anima* (420b), Aristotle affirmed, in regard to phonation, that not all sounds emitted by an animal are words, only those accompanied by a phantasm (*meta phantasias tinos*)—because words are sounds that signify. The semantic character of language is thus indissolubly associated to the presence of a phantasm. We will see later the importance this association would acquire in medieval thought.

In the thought of Aristotle, the centrality of the phantasm in the psychic constellation is such that it may be summarized graphically in the following scheme:

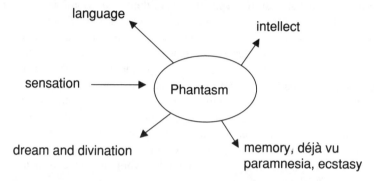

We moderns, perhaps because of our habit of stressing the rational and abstract aspect of the cognitive processes, have long ceased to be amazed by the mysterious power of the internal imagination, of this restless crowd of "metics" (as Freud would call them) that animates our dreams and dominates our waking moments more than we are perhaps willing to admit. Thus is it not immediately easy for us to understand the obsessive and almost reverential attention that medieval psychology devoted to the phantasmological constellation of Aristotle. Dramatized and enriched by borrowings from Stoicism and Neoplatonism, this constellation occupied a central position in the spiritual firmament of the Middle Ages. In this exegetical process, in which the Middle Ages concealed one of its most original and creative traditions, the phantasm is polarized and becomes the site of the soul's most extreme experiences: the place where it may rise to the dazzling limit of the divine or plunge into the vertiginous abyss of evil and perdition. This explains why no epoch has been, at the same time, both so idolatrous and so "idoloclastic" as the Middle Ages, which saw in phantasms both the *alta fantasia* (lofty phantasy) that Dante enlisted for his supreme vision and the *cogitationes malae* (evil thoughts) that torment the slothful soul in patristic writing on the capital sins, both the spiritual mediator between reason and sense that raises man along the mystical Jacob's ladder of Hugh of St. Victor and the "vain imaginations" that seduce the soul into the error Saint Augustine recognized in his own truancy among the Manicheans.

In our examination of medieval phantasmology we will begin with Avicenna, not because he was the first to give a clear formulation of it, but because his meticulous classification of the "internal sense" had so profound an influence on what has been called the "spiritual revolution of the thirteenth century" that it is possible to detect its traces even as late as the period of Renaissance humanism. In Avicenna, who, like Averroës, was also—perhaps, above all—a physician (his

Canon was used as the medical text in some European universities until at least the seventeenth century),[7] the link between faculties of the soul and cerebral anatomy, for which each faculty is localized in one of the three chambers or cavities (which a medical tradition elaborated fully in Galen identified as being in the brain), appears already well established. In this connection it is useful to remember that although today we would be astonished to find strictly medical and anatomical references in a philosophical treatise, so compact was the intellectual system of the Middle Ages that works appearing to us as philosophical or religious frequently had as their object specific questions of cerebral anatomy or clinical pathology, and vice versa. In general it is simply impossible to distinguish the philosopher from the physician (as is the case with Avicenna and Averroës, but the same can be said of a good number of the authors who fill up the volumes of Migne's *Patrologia*). Such a mixture of purely medical with what we consider to be philosophical and literary topics is also found among the poets, whose works, as we will see, are often completely unintelligible without a good understanding of the anatomy of the eye, heart, and brain, of circulatory models and of medieval embryology, not only because the poets directly referred to the physiological doctrines of their day, but because this reference was often complicated by an allegorical tendency that was exercised in a privileged way on the anatomy and physiology of the human body.

Avicenna began by dividing the external sense (*vis apprehendi a foris*) from the internal (*vis apprehendi ab intus*) and then articulated the internal sense into five "virtues" or powers:

> The first of the internal apprehensive powers is the *phantasy* or common sense, which is a power placed in the first cavity of the brain that receives in itself all the forms that are impressed on the five senses and transmitted to it. After this there is the *imagination,* the force placed in the extremity of the forward cavity of the brain, which holds what the common sense receives from the senses and which remains in it even after the removal of the sensible objects . . . [here Avicenna explains that the imagination, unlike the phantasy, is not only receptive, but also active, and that retention is different from mere reception, as is seen in water, which has the faculty of receiving images but not of retaining them] . . . After this there is the power that is called *imaginative* with respect to the vital soul and *cogitative* with respect to the human soul; it is placed in the medial cavity of the brain and composes according to its will the forms that are in the imagination with other forms. Then there is the *estimative* power, placed in the summit of the medial cavity of the brain, which apprehends the insensible intentions that are found in individual sensible objects, like the power that permits the lamb to judge that the wolf should be avoided . . . There is then the *memorial* and *reminiscent* power, which is placed in the posterior cavity of the brain and which retains what the estimative power apprehends from the insensible intentions of individual objects. The relation between this and

the estimative virtue is analogous to that between the imagination and the common sense. And the relation between it and the intentions is analogous to that between the imagination and the phantasms.[8]

Avicenna presented this quintuple gradation of the internal sense as a progressive "disrobing" (*denudatio*) of the phantasm from its material accidents. With respect to the senses, which do not strip the sensible form completely (*denudatione perfecta*), the imagination does disrobe the phantasm *denudatione vera* without, however, depriving it of material accidents, because the phantasms of the imagination are "according to a certain quantity and quality and according to a certain place." They are thus, we would say, individuated images and not abstract concepts. At the vertex of the medial cavity of the brain, the estimative power proceeds further in this "disrobing" of the phantasm, from which it apprehends the insensible intentions, such as goodness or malice, suitability or incongruity. It is only when the process of the internal sense is completed that the rational soul can be informed by the completely denuded phantasm: in the act of intellection, the form is nude and "if it were not nude, nevertheless it would become so, because the contemplative virtue strips it such that no material affection remains in it."

This psychological scheme, often simplified to a tripartite one corresponding to the three chambers of the brain in the medical tradition, reappears constantly among medieval authors. In the *Philosophia mundi* (Philosophy of the universe) of William of Conches, one of the masters in the school of Chartres in the twelfth century, the psychic process is expressed in the crude "temperamental" terms of humoral medicine:

> In the head there are three cells . . . the first is hot and dry, and is called *phantastic,* that is, visual or imaginative, because it contains the capacity of seeing and imagining, and it is dry and hot just so that it can attract the forms and colors of things. The middle cell is called *logistikon,* that is, rational: therein, in fact, is the power of discernment. What the phantastic power attracts passes into this one and here the soul discerns. It is hot and damp, so that, in discerning better, it conforms itself to the properties of things. The third cell is called *memorial,* because in it is the capacity of retaining something in the memory.[9]

The course of medieval thought can be compared, and not only in this case, with those musical compositions referred to as "variations on a theme." It works, in fact, on a given theme that reproduces and transposes through small divergences that can, in some cases, succeed in transforming completely the material from which it departs. While the Avicennian scheme is thus found, with some variations, in Albertus Magnus, Thomas Aquinas, and Jean de la Rochelle, the tripartite scheme is found in works as diverse as the *Anatomia* of Richard the Englishman, the *Opus maius* of Roger Bacon, the *Documenti d'amore* (Documents of love) of Francesco of Barberino, and the *Gloss* of Dino del Garbo to Guido Cavalcanti's canzone *Donna mi prega* (A lady asks me).

It cannot therefore surprise if an analogous psychological "theme" (here too with some significant variation) appears in the work of the thinker who perhaps more than any other mediated the reading of Aristotle in the thirteenth century and in whom Dante rightly saw the commentator par excellence of the Aristotelian text: "Averroës, who made the great commentary." In his paraphrase of the *De sensu et sensibilibus* (On the sense and sensibles), Averroës gave a compendious account of the process that begins in sensation and ends in the imagination in an exemplary synthesis of medieval psychophysiology. In this account, we immediately find the answer to the question that Giacomo da Lentini formulated in his sonnet "Or come pote sí gran donna entrare":

> The opinion of those who say that the forms of sensible objects are
> impressed on the soul with a corporal impression destroys itself . . .
> also because of the fact that the largest bodies are comprehended by
> sight through the pupil, even though it is so small . . . because of this it
> is said that these senses do not comprehend the intentions of sensible
> objects unless abstracted from matter.[10]

The eye here figures as a mirror in which the phantasms are reflected, "because water dominates in this instrument, which is pure and diaphanous, such that in it are inscribed the forms of sensible objects, as in a mirror." And as a mirror needs illumination in order to reflect images, so the eye does not see if its water (that is, the humor contained in the complex articulation of "tunics" that compose it, according to medieval anatomy) is not illuminated through the air. Averroës continued:

> Let us then say that the air mediating the light first receives the form of
> things, then yields it to the external net [*rete:* web] of the eye and this
> transmits it gradually to the last net, after which it is found in the
> common sense. In the middle, the granular [*grandinoso*] net
> comprehends the forms of things: it is like a mirror whose nature is
> intermediate between that of air and that of water. Because of this it
> receives the forms from the air, since it is similar to a mirror, and
> transmits them to the water, since its nature is common to both. The
> water, which Aristotle says is found after the granular humor, is what
> Galen calls vitreous and is the extreme portion of the eye: through it,
> the common sense sees the form. As soon as the common sense receives
> the form, it transmits it to the imaginative virtue, which receives it in a
> more spiritual way; this form thus belongs to the third order. The forms
> have in fact three orders: the first is corporeal, the second is in the
> common sense and is spiritual, the third is found in the imagination and
> is more spiritual. And as it is more spiritual than in the common sense,
> the imagination has no need of the presence of the external thing to
> render it present. Conversely, in the sense the imagination does not see

that form and does not abstract its intention except after attentive and protracted intuition. The orders of this form in these powers are therefore, according to Aristotle, as if a man took a mirror that had two facets and, looking in one of them, placed the other in the direction of the water. If now someone were to look in the second facet of the mirror, that is, in the one turned toward the water, he would see that same form described by the water of the mirror. The form of he who looks is the sensible thing, the mirror is the mediating air, and the water is the eye; the second facet of the mirror is the sensitive power and the man that comprehends it is the imaginative power. If therefore he who looks were then to look in this second mirror, the form would disappear from the mirror and from the water and he who looks in the second facet of the mirror imagining the form would remain. And thus it happens to the imaginative power with the form that is in the common sense. When the sensible object disappears, its form also disappears from the common sense and the imagination remains in the act of imagining it; that is explained by the fact that the common sense sees the form through the eye, the eye through the air, and sees it in the aqueous humor that is in the eye . . .[11]

If we have lingered over this passage of Averroës, it is because the whole cognitive process is here conceived as speculation in the strict sense, a reflection of phantasms from mirror to mirror. The eyes and the sense are both mirror and water that reflect the form of the object, but phantasy is also speculation, which "imagines" the phantasms in the absence of the object. To know is to bend over a mirror where the world is reflected, to descry images reflected from sphere to sphere: the medieval man was always before a mirror, both when he looked around himself and when he surrendered himself to his own imagination. But loving is also necessarily a speculation, not so much because, as poets repeat, "gli occhi in prima generan l'amore" (the eyes first generate love), or because love, as Cavalcanti puts it in his canzone, "vien da veduta forma che s'intende" (comes from a seen form that is understood) (that is, from a form that, according to the process we have illustrated, penetrates through the external and internal senses until it becomes a phantasm or "intention" in the phantastic and memorial cells), but because medieval psychology—with an insight that yielded one of its most fertile legacies for Western culture—conceived of love as an essentially phantasmatic process, involving both imagination and memory in an assiduous, tormented circling around an image painted or reflected in the deepest self.[12] Andreas Cappellanus, whose *De amore* (On love) is considered the exemplary theorization of the new conception of love, defined it as the *immoderata cogitatio* (immoderate contemplation) of an internal phantasm and added that "ex sola cogitatione, quam concipit animus ex eo, quod vidit, passio illa procedit" (this passion derives only from the contemplation that the mind conceives from what it saw).[13] The medieval discovery, so often (and not always cogently) discussed, was of the unreality of love, of its phantasmatic character. The novelty of the medieval conception of eros consists in this discovery, which pushes to the extreme consequences that link of desire and the phantasy that antiquity had merely foreshadowed in Plato's *Philebus,* and not, certainly, in any supposed absence of erotic spirituality in the classical world.

In all of the classical world there is nothing similar to the conception of love as a phantasmatic process, even though certain "high" theorizations of love, which have at every period found their original paradigm in Plato, are not lacking. The only examples of a "phantasmatic" conception of love are found in the late Neoplatonists and in the physicians (in a verifiable way only after the eighth century), but both cases concern "low" concepts of love, understood at times as demoniac influence, at others as nothing short of mental illness. Only in medieval culture does the phantasm emerge in the foreground as origin and object of love, and the proper situation of eros is displaced from the sense of sight to the phantasy.

It should therefore cause no surprise if, for the Middle Ages, the site of love is a fountain or a mirror; or if, in the *Roman de la Rose,* the god of love dwells near a fountain that is none other than the *miroërs perilleus* of Narcissus. We are so accustomed to the interpretation of the myth given by modern psychology, which defines narcissism as the enclosure and withdrawal in the self of libido, that we fail to remember that Narcissus was, after all, not directly in love with himself, but with his own image reflected in the water, which he mistook for a real creature. Unlike our own era (and it could not be otherwise, if we consider the importance of the phantasm in medieval psychology), the Middle Ages did not identify love of self—*filautia* (self-love) is not for the medieval mentality necessarily reproachable—but rather love for an image, an *innamorarsi per ombra* (falling in love by means of shadows) as the salient feature in the unhappy affair of Narcissus.[14] This is the reason why the fable of Narcissus has had such a persistent prominence in the formation of the medieval idea of love, so much so that the *miroërs perilleus* has become one of the indispensable accessories of the amorous ritual and the image of the youth at the fountain one of the preferred topics of medieval erotic iconography. As allegories of love, both the story of Narcissus and that of Pygmalion allude in an exemplary way to the phantasmatic character of a process essentially directed to the obsessive desire for an image, according to a psychological scheme for which every genuine act of falling in love is always a "love by means of shadows" or "through a figure," every profound erotic intention always turned idolatrously to an *ymage.*[15]

From this perspective nothing prevents us from considering the scene in which the protagonist of the *Roman de la Rose* experiences the first effects of love at the fountain of Eros-Narcissus, a fairly faithful allegory of the phantasmatic psychophysiology described by Averroës in the passage we have just examined: "aqua est oculus" (the eye is water), as Averroës said, and this explains why only when "the sun, which sees all, / casts its rays in the fountain / and the light goes to the bottom / then more than a hundred colors appear / in the crystal." The double crystal that reflects now one, now the other half of the garden, never both at once, is that of the sensitive and imaginative powers. This is understood sufficiently clearly if one remembers that, as Averroës showed with the image of the two facets of the mirror that cannot be looked at simultaneously, it is possible to contemplate the phantasm in the imagination (*cogitare*) or the form of the object in the sense, but not both at the same time.[16]

The fountain of Love, which "intoxicates the living with death," and the mirror of Narcissus both allude therefore to the imagination, where the phantasm that is the real object of love resides. Narcissus, who falls in love with an image, is the exemplary paradigm of the *fin'amors* and, at the same time, with a polarity that characterizes the psychological wisdom of the Middle Ages, of the *fol amour* that shatters the phantasmatic circle in the attempt to appropriate the image as if it were a real creature (see figure 22).

Although much remains to be clarified, we can now maintain that both the appearance of the topic of the *ymage* in the love poetry and the meeting of Eros and Narcissus at the fountain of Love are sufficiently motivated. To have made Eros himself gravitate within the constellation of the phantasm, to have led him to mirror himself in the *miroërs perilleus* of the imagination, is the great innovation of late medieval psychology and perhaps the most original contribution that it brings, almost casually, to Aristotelian phantasmology.

Before leaving Averroës, we must pause to examine an aspect of his thought that has a central importance for understanding the polemics between Averroists and anti-Averroists in the philosophy of the thirteenth century, that is, the doctrine that sees in the phantasm the point of union, the "copula," between the individual and the unique possible intellect.

This is not the place to reconstruct the famous dispute over the unity or multiplicity of the possible intellect that arose from an obscure passage of Aristotle's *De anima* and profoundly divided the intellectual life of the thirteenth century. It will suffice here to recall that Averroës, acting as mouthpiece for a profound conception (foreign to us today, but certainly among the highest expressions of medieval thought) that saw the intelligence as something unique and supraindividual — within which individual persons are simply, to use Proust's beautiful image, *colocataires* (co-tenants, co-inhabitants), each one limited to furnishing its distinct point of view to the intelligence — held that the possible intellect is unique and separate: incorruptible and eternal, it is nevertheless joined (*copulatur*) to individuals, so that each of them may concretely exercise the act of intellection through the phantasms that are located in the internal sense.[17]

Only the misconception of the role of the phantasm in the Stilnovist lyric can explain how the situation of the phantasm in the thought of Averroës should not even have been taken into consideration in the studies on the Averroism of Cavalcanti.[18] Instead, it is precisely the *copulatio* (joining) of the phantasm and the possible intellect that offered Saint Thomas the principal target for his anti-Averroist polemic. He objected that if one makes of the possible intellect something unique and separate, it is then impossible to sustain that each person can concretely understand by means of the continuity of the possible intellect with the phantasms

> unless perhaps it be said that the possible intellect is in contact with phantasms as a mirror is in contact with the man whose appearance is reflected in the mirror. But such a contact clearly does not suffice for the contact of the act. For it is clear that the action of the mirror, which is to represent, cannot on this account be attributed to the man. Whence neither can the action of the possible intellect be attributed, on account of the above-mentioned joining, to this man who is Socrates, in such a way that this man would understand. . . . For it is clear that through the intelligible species something is understood, but through the intellective power he understands something; just as also through the sensible species something is sensed, but through the sensitive power he senses something. This is why a wall in which there is color whose sensible species-in-act is in sight, is seen and does not see; but an animal having the power of sight in which there is such a species, does see. Now the aforesaid union of the possible intellect with man, in whom there are phantasms whose species are in the possible intellect, is like the union of the wall in which there is color with the sight in which is the species of its color. Therefore, just as the wall does not see, but its color is seen; so it would follow that man would not understand but that his phantasms would be understood by the possible intellect. It is therefore impossible, if one follows Averroës's position, to account for the fact that this man understands.[19]

What Saint Thomas—who here made himself the spokesman of modern subjectivism—did not seem to understand was that for an Arabic author an image might just as well be the point where who sees is united to what is seen. If, for medieval optics, the mirror was the place par excellence where the eye sees itself—*oculus videt se ipsum*—and the same person is, at once, seer and thing seen,[20] then the union with one's own image in a perfectly clear mirror often symbolized, according to a mystical tradition that profoundly influenced Arabic authors but which was also thoroughly familiar to the medieval Christian tradition, the union with the suprasensible.[21] We will see further, in the next chapter, that there are good, so to speak "scientific," reasons that make the phantasm particularly suitable to this mediating function. The image reflected in the *miroërs perilleus* of the phantasy, which we have seen fulfill such an important role in the mechanism of falling in love, thus acquires an unexpected dimension. Situated at the vertex of the individual soul, at the limit between individual and universal, corporeal and incorporeal, it appears as the sole exhausted spot of ash that the combustion of the individual existence leaves on the impassable and invulnerable threshold of the Separate and Eternal.

In the phantasmatic psychology that we have attempted to reconstruct in this chapter, there is nevertheless a point that seems not to agree with the "image in the heart" of love poetry. According to the texts we have cited, the proper place of the image is not, in fact, the heart, but one of the chambers of the brain. This divergence may leave us perplexed, if one considers that the theoretical tradition so characteristic of medieval love poetry would not have easily tolerated such a conspicuous inexactitude. A more attentive reading of the texts, however, resolves the problem without any shadow of doubt. According to medieval physiology, the seat of life is in the heart, and it is from the heart that the soul animates the whole animal. The heart is also, for that very reason, the principle and origin of those powers whose action finds their instruments elsewhere, like the nutritive power, which acts in the liver, and the imaginative and memorial powers, which act in the brain. Avicenna thus explained that although the vital principle is in the heart, "it is in the brain that is perfected the temper of the spirit that carries the sensitive power in the body." The *Colliget* of Averroës fully articulates this doctrine, placing it under the authority of Aristotle:

> It should not be forgotten that, although the chambers of the brain are
> the place where the operations of these powers are performed,
> nevertheless their roots are in the heart . . . This is explained by
> considering that these powers do not act except with the internal heat,
> and the internal heat does not reach them unless it be with the measured
> heat, and since the dative and mensural power is necessarily in the
> heart, the root of these powers is therefore in the heart. In the same
> way, since the operation of the phantasy occurs through the sign of the
> sensible objects that remains in the common sense, as is explained in
> the book on the soul, where one reads also that the place and the root of
> the common sense are in the heart, it follows that the place of the
> imaginative virtue is necessarily in the heart.[22]

The poetic theory of the image in the heart is not therefore an arbitrary invention of lovers, but is founded on a solid medical tradition; it should not come as a surprise if Dante, always so attentive to the doctrinal rigor of his own poetry, should several times make reference to it.[23] The mechanism through which a "power" can have its place and root in one part of the body and yet exercise its proper functions elsewhere is not, however, immediately obvious. Both Avicenna and Averroës referred to this phenomenon, the first speaking of a "spirit" that is perfected in the brain, and the second of an "internal heat" that originates in the heart. We have also seen Averroës underline the "spiritual" nature of the imaginative phantasm. As for the poets, they spoke often of "subtle," "animal," and "noble" spirits as if of perfectly familiar realities and appear to refer on other occasions to a spirit that enters and exits through the eyes. They thus allude to a pneumatic doctrine that we have so far omitted from consideration but which we must now face if we wish to reconstitute medieval phantasmology in its entirety. Our study, far from nearing its conclusion, is still only beginning.

Notes

1. The concept of *pseudomorphosis* was formulated by Spengler to explain what he called "Magian culture": "By the term 'pseudomorphosis' I propose to designate those cases in which an older alien Culture lies so massively over the land that a young Culture, born in this land, cannot get its breath and fails not only to achieve pure and specific expression-forms, but even to develop fully its own self-consciousness. All that wells up from the depths of the young soul is cast in the old moulds" [Oswald Spengler, *The Decline of the West*, trans. Charles Atkinson (New York: Alfred Knopf, 1926), 2:189].

2. Thus the commentary of Chalcidius to the *Timaeus* transmitted to the Middle Ages numerous other aspects of the thought of Plato; for example, the demonology of the *Epinomis*, whose wide dissemination in the Middle Ages would not be otherwise explicable.

3. Lacan's assertion can be found in, among other places, "Kant avec Sade," in *Ecrits* (Paris, 1966), 773.

4. From *Aristotle in Twenty-Three Volumes*, trans. W. S. Hett, vol. 8 (Cambridge: Harvard University Press, 1975), 137.

5. According to Aristotle (*De memoria et reminiscentia*, 451a), déjà vu is produced if, when a phantasm of sensation is being considered as a reality and not as the icon of something, one suddenly turns to considering it as the icon of something else. The phenomenon of paramnesia that is immediately thereafter attributed in the text to Antipherontes of Orea and to other "ecstatics" ("the opposite also occurs, as it did to Antipherontes of Orea and other ecstatics: they spoke of phantasms as if of the real, and, at the same time, as if they were remembering. This comes about when one takes as an icon something that is not") seems to refer to an ecstatic-mnemonic technique that enacts an intentional exchange between reality and recollection.

6. "Since it seems no object can exist separated from sensible size, it is in sensible forms that the intelligibles exist . . . One who had no sensation whatsoever would neither understand nor learn anything; and when man contemplates, of necessity he contemplates at the same time some phantasm" (*De anima*, 432a).

7. It is significant that Dante (*Inferno* IV.143-144) should name Avicenna and Averroës next to Hippocrates and Galen.

8. The Avicenna that here interests us is the *Avicenna latinus*, that is, what cultured men of the thirteenth century in the West could read. The edition consulted is *Avicennae arabum medicorum principis opera ex Gerardi cremonensis versione* (The works of Avicenna, the first among Arab physicians, from the version of Gerard of Cremona), Venetiis, 1545. For the *De anima*, the text of the critical edition of van Riet (Leuven-Leiden, 1972) has also been consulted.

The identification of the imaginative faculty, distinct from the passive phantasy (which is the not-so-remote origin of Coleridge's distinction between *fancy* and *imagination*), is a constant feature of medieval psychology. It permits us to explain, among other things, certain aspects of love *sez vezer* (without seeing), like the *domna soisebunda*, the woman made of pieces "borrowed" from other women, of the troubadour Bertran de Born.

In the vocabulary of medieval psychology, "intention" is "that which the soul apprehends from a sensible object and that has not already been apprehended from the external sense" (Avicenna). It "is not part of the thing, like the form, but rather it is the form of the knowledge of the thing" (Albertus Magnus).

9. The *Philosophia mundi* was published in the *Patrologia latina* (172, 39-102) as the work of Honorius of Autun.

10. Already in the book *De oculis* (On the eye) attributed to Galen the same problem was used to

explain that vision is not an emanation from the thing to the eye: "If therefore something is directed from the thing seen to the eye . . . in what way can it enter that narrow aperture?" (Galen, *De oculis liber,* chap. 6, in *Operum Hippocratis Coi et Galeni pergameni medicorum omnium principum,* Lutetiae, 1679, vol. 10).

11. This passage is contained in Averroës's paraphrase of the Aristotelian *De sensu et sensibilibus, in Aristotelis stagiritae omnia quae extant opera cum Averrois cordubensis . . . commentariis* (Venetiis, 1552, vol. 6).

12. The association of love and vision was already in Plato's *Phaedrus* (255c-d), in which love is compared to a "disease of the eyes" (*ophthalmia*), and it had led Plotinus to hazard a curious etymology: "Eros, whose name comes from the fact that he [or it] owes his [or its] existence to vision (*orasis*)." From this point of view, the passage from the classical conception of love to the medieval can be handily characterized as the passage from a "disease of the sight" to a "disease of the imagination"; "maladie de pensée" (disease of thought) is the definition of love in the *Roman de la Rose,* v. 4348.

13. Andreas Cappellanus, *De amore,* edited by S. Battaglia (Rome, 1947), chap. 1. "For when someone," continues the cited passage, "sees someone suitable for love and formed according to his liking, immediately his heart begins to desire her. Thereafter, as many times as he thinks of her, so much the more does he burn with love, through which he comes to a fuller contemplation. Finally he begins to contemplate the woman's shapeliness and to distinguish her limbs and to imagine her gestures and to pry into the secret parts of her body . . . "

Dante, in the canzone "Amor, da che convien pur ch'io me doglia" (Love, since after all I am required to lament), describes in minute detail the phantasmatic process of this *cogitatio immoderata:* "Io non posso fuggir, ch'ella non vegna / ne l'imagine mia, / se non come il penser che la vi mena. / L'animo folle, ch'al suo mal s'ingegna, / com'ella è bella e ria / cosi dipinge, e forma la sua pena: / poi la riguarda, e quando ella è ben piena / del gran disio che de li occhi le tira, / incontro a sé s'adira, / c'ha fatto il foco ond'ella trista incende" (vv. 16-25) ["I cannot go without her following / Into my fantasy, / Together with the thought that leads her there. / The foolish soul that to its hurt doth cling, / Forgeth its misery / Painting her as she is, guilty and fair; / Then gazeth till it can no longer bear / The fond desire it draweth through the eyes, / And into fury flies / For kindling fire wherein it sadly burns"; from *Dante Alighieri: The Minor Poems of Dante,* trans. Lorna De'Lucchi (Oxford: Oxford University Press, 1926), 163].

14. See Chiaro Davanzati: "Come Narcissi in sua spera mirando / s'inamorao per ombra a la fontana . . . " (As Narcissus gazing in his mirror / fell in love through an image, at the pool), in *Poeti del duecento,* vol. 1, 425. That this interpretation of the myth of Narcissus is a medieval discovery, to be understood in close connection with the poetic theory of the phantasmatic character of the erotic process, is evident if the medieval versions are compared to Ovid's narrative (*Metamorphoses* III.345-510), which is their source. In Ovid the theme of the reflected image is of course present, but it is not at the heart of the matter; the punishment Narcissus merits because of having refused the love of Echo is without a doubt the impossible love of self, something the youth is perfectly aware of ["iste ego sum! sensi; nec me mea fallit imago, / uror amor mei, flammas moveoque feroque" (this one is I! I sensed it, nor does my image deceive me, / I burn for my own love, I cause, and endure, the flame)]. In a precisely opposite way, when Dante wished to make the reader understand how he had mistaken the souls of the blessed for reflected images ("specchiati sembianti," mirrored appearances), the comparison that came to mind was that of defining his own error as the contrary of Narcissus's: "Per ch'io dentro a l'error contrario corsi / a qual ch'accese amor tra l'omo e'l fonte" (*Paradiso* III.17-18) ["I had made the opposite mistake to that / which kindled love in one man for his pool"; *Dante Alighieri: The Divine Comedy,* vol. 3, trans. Mark Musa (Harmondsworth: Penguin, 1984), 33]. To a medieval reader, the error of Narcissus was not so much the love of self, but the mistaking of an image for a real creature.

15. "Vos amador, que amatz per figura" (You lovers, who love through an image) is in a poem of the troubadour Ozil de Cadars; see Langfors, *Le troubadour Ozil de Cadars* (Helsinki, 1913).

16. None of the explanations yet proposed for the scene of the pool in the *Roman de la Rose* is fully convincing. C. S. Lewis, *The Allegory of Love* (Oxford, 1936), can affirm "without the shadow of a doubt" that the two stones are the eyes of the lady, on the basis of a celebrated passage of Bernart de Ventadorn: "Anc non agui de mi poder / Ni no fui meus des l'or' en sai / Que. m laisset en sos ohls vezer / En un mirahl que mout mi plai. / Mirahls, pos me mirei en te / M'an mort li sospir de preon, / Qu'aissi .m perdei cum perdet se / Lo bel Narcissus en la font" (Nevermore had I power over myself, / nor was I mine own from that time / That she let me see myself in her eyes / In a mirror that pleases me much. / Mirror, since I saw myself in you / Deep sighs have killed me, / For I lost myself as he lost himself, / The fair Narcissus, in the pool"). It has not yet been noted, I think, that Bernart does not say that the eyes of his lady are the mirror, but that he looks into them *in* a mirror ("en un mirahl"): a mirror that, if our interpretation were to prove exact, could be precisely that of the phantasy. Nor is it clear why, if the two gems were the eyes of the lady, the Rose should be reflected in them, or—above all—why they should reflect by turns one half, then the other half, of the garden.

Curiously, it has been possible, against all probability, to interpret the scene at the fountain of Narcissus as an encounter with the self and its own destiny; see E. Kohler: "The gaze in the mirror is nothing other than its meeting with its own destiny . . . The two crystals are primarily the reflections of he who sees himself in them, that is to say, the eyes of Narcissus," in Louise Vinge, *The Narcissus Theme in European Literature up to the Early Nineteenth Century* (Lund: Gleerups, 1967), 85.

As we will see in the following chapter, the conception of the phantasy as a mirror is already to be found in Synesius of Cyrene, and was transmitted by him to the Christian mystics. That the mirror in the poetry of the thirteenth century refers to the imagination can be proven from several passages. For example, in Cino da Pistoia (*Rimatori del dolce stil novo*, 209): "Fa de la mente tua specchio sovente / se vuoi campar, guardando 'l dolce viso / lo qual so che v'è pinto il suo bel riso, / che fa tornar gioioso 'l cor dolente. / / Tu sentirai cosí quella gente, / allor, come non fossi mai diviso; / ma se lo imaginar serà ben fiso, / la bella donna t'apparrà presente" (Often make of your mind a mirror, / if you wish to thrive, when gazing at the sweet face / which, I know, is there depicted: her sweet laugh, / which makes joyous the sorrowing heart. / / You will feel such of the noble one / then, as if you had never been away / but if the imagination be well fixed / the beautiful lady will appear to you); in the *Acerba* of Cecco d'Ascoli (*L'acerba*, edited by Achille Crespi, Ascoli Piceno, 1927, vv. 1959-1961): "Senza vedere, l'uom può innamorare / formando specchio della nuda mente / veggendo vista sua nel 'maginare" (Without seeing, one can fall in love / making a mirror of the bare mind, / and seeing its sights in the imagination); in Amico di Dante (*Poeti del duecento*, vol. 2, 731), the phantasy is described as a mirror held up by Love: "Talor credete voi, Amore, ch'i' dorma / che cco lo core i' penso a voi e veglio / mirandomi tuttora ne lo speglio / che 'nnanzi mi tenete e ne la forma" (You think, Love, that sometimes I sleep, / when with my heart I think of you and wake, / looking at myself all the while in the mirror / you hold before me, and in the form). This identification of the act of looking in a mirror with the imagination also permits a fresh interpretation of the figure of Oiseuse, who, in the *Roman de la Rose*, leads the lover into the garden. As Fleming has rightly observed (*The "Roman de la Rose,"* 73), the lady with the mirror is certainly not a personification of the leisure necessary to courtly love; but neither is she simply, as Fleming holds, a personification of lechery. The curious contradiction that permits a lady at her mirror to symbolize, in medieval iconography, by turns both lechery and prudence has often been noted. With conspicuous incoherence, the mirror is here in one instance a real object and, in another, a symbol of spiritual contemplation. The contradiction resolves itself if the mirror is interpreted as the imagination and, keeping in mind the polarity of the medieval concept of the phantasy, in one case as *imaginatio falsa* or *bestialis*, and, in the other, as *imaginatio vera* or *rationalis* (see Richard of St. Victor, *Beniamin minor*, chap. 16, in *Patrologia latina*, 196). This explains why it is properly Oiseuse, that is, the imagination, who leads the lover into the garden.

17. See Averroës, in *Aristotelis*, 165.

18. Bruno Nardi ("The Averroism of Dante's First Friend," in *Studi danteschi*, vol. 25, 1940, 43-79), who established the Averroism of Cavalcanti on a rigorous separation of love (with its seat in

the sensitive part) and the possible intellect, was simply unaware of the fact that the possible intellect is united to the singular individual through the phantasm that is also the origin and object of the love experience. It is evident that, if one is cognizant of Averroës, the interpretation of the celebrated Cavalcantian canzone "Donna mi prega" is entirely transformed. Even the interpretation of G. Favati ("G. Cavalcanti, Dino del Garbo, and the Averroism of B. Nardi," in *Filologia romanza*, 1955), in many respects more insightful, omits this essential point. The importance of the phantasm in the Cavalcantian doctrine of love did not escape James E. Shaw (*Cavalcanti's Theory of Love*, Toronto, 1949), who was, however, ignorant of pneumatology and, therefore, of the complexity and richness of medieval phantasmology.

19. Sancti Thomae Aquinitatis, *De unitate intellectus contra Averroistas*, critical edition by L. Keeler (Rome, 1957), 42. English translation from *On the Unity of the Intellect against the Averroists*, trans. Beatrice Zedler (Milwaukee: Marquette University Press, 1968), 50.

20. See Alexander of Aphrodisias, *De sensu communi* 42.10.

21. To H. Corbin (*En Islam iranien*, vol. 3, Paris, 1972, 65-146) is owed the exemplary reconstruction of the meaning of the theme of the mirror in Iranian and Arabic erotic mysticism. The importance of Corbin's studies for the understanding of Stilnovist lyric is yet another proof of the need for the human sciences to overcome division into specialized departments. Only a "discipline of interdisciplinarity" is adequate to the interpretation of human phenomena.

Regarding the relation of this mystical tradition and medieval Christianity, see Saint Augustine, *De Trinitate* XV, xxiii (*Patrologia latina*, 42, 1901); Isaac of Stella, *Sermo xxv* in *Sex* (*Patrologia latina* 176, 91); and other examples cited in R. Javelet, *Image et ressemblance au XIIe siècle* (Strasbourg, 1967).

22. Averrois Cordubensis, *Colliget libri VII*, Venetiis, 1552, book 2, chap. 20.

23. "per man d'Amor là entro pinta sete" ("Love's hand did trace, / O lady sweet, your very self in there"), from the canzone "La dispietata mente, che pur mira" ("The pitiless mind, that yet gazes"), v. 22 (English translation by Lorna De'Lucchi, *The Minor Poems of Dante*, 51). At other times the image is in the mind, as in the canzone "E m'incresce di me si duramente" (I pity myself so intensely), v. 43.

Chapter 13
Spiritus phantasticus

At that very moment, and I speak the truth, the vital spirit, the one that dwells in the most secret chamber of the heart, began to tremble so violently that even the most minute veins of my body were strangely affected; and trembling, it spoke these words: "Here is a god stronger than I who comes to rule over me." At that point, the animal spirit, the one abiding in the high chamber to which all the senses bring their perceptions, was stricken with amazement and, speaking directly to the spirits of sight, said these words: "Now your bliss has appeared." At that point the natural spirit, the one dwelling in that part where our food is digested, began to weep, and weeping said these words: "O wretched me! for I shall be disturbed often from now on."[1]

The foundations of this celebrated passage at the beginning of the *Vita Nuova,* where Dante registers the appearance, dressed in crimson, of the "donna della sua mente" (mistress of his mind) with a triple allegory, have been sufficiently traced by scholars, who have shown how the notion of three spirits is paralleled in the medical terminology of the period.[2] But this reconstruction is, in our opinion, incomplete, not only because it does not restore the medieval physiology of spirits in all its ramifications, but above all because the pneumatic doctrine that is expressed in this passage is in no way reducible to the medical-physiological sphere alone. Indeed, interwoven in the doctrine are, rather, *all* aspects of medieval culture, from medicine to cosmology, from psychology to rhetoric and soteriology, and it is precisely under its rubric that all these succeed in harmoniously blending together in the thrust of an edifice that is perhaps the most imposing intellectual cathedral constructed by late medieval thought. The fact that this cathedral has remained until now at least partially buried means that we have surveyed the love lyric of the duecento—its most perfect result—as we might one of those mutilated statues that time has detached from Greek temples or from the tympana of Romanesque churches and which now smile at us enigmatically in museum galleries. As Hegel noted, however, the benevolent destiny offered us by these lovely fruits severed from their tree restores to us, along with them, "neither the land that has nourished them nor the elements that have formed their substance nor the climate that gave them their individuality nor the alternation of seasons that regulated the process of their becoming." And as, in the preceding chapter, we have attempted to reconstruct the broad outlines of the medieval theory of the phantasm, we will now attempt to reevoke this "land" and this "climate" in the excavation for that pneumatic doctrine in which phantasmology is dissolved without residues.

The origin of the doctrine of the pneuma (breath, wind, spirit) must be very ancient. The passage of Aristotle frequently referred to by medieval writers is *De generatione animalium*, 736b:

> In all cases the semen contains within itself that which causes it to be fertile—what is known as "hot" substance, which is not fire nor any similar substance, but the *pneuma* which is enclosed within the semen or foam-like stuff, and the natural substance which is in the pneuma; and this substance is analogous to the element which belongs to the stars.[3]

This passage appears to presuppose the existence of a fully articulated theory and contains already the two characteristic elements of the medieval pneumatology: the astral nature of the pneuma and its presence in the sperm. It is probable that Aristotle found this theory in older medical texts, from which the Stoics also plausibly drew; the references to the pneuma in the Hippocratic corpus appear to confirm this supposition.[4] The first physician whose pneumatic doctrine we can trace with any certainty is that of Diocles of Caristo, whom Jaeger situated at the beginning of the third century B.C., contemporaneously with Zeno, the founder of the Stoa.[5] The pneumatology whose outlines we will now trace here, however, is the common patrimony of all succeeding Greek medicine, from Erasistratus to Galen. Central to this theory is the idea of the pneuma, a hot breath that originates from the exhalations of the blood or, according to others, from the external air that is continuously inhaled (or from both, according to Galen). This pneuma, a single one in Diocles of Caristo, is often distinguished (for example by Erasistratus) into a vital pneuma (*zotikos*), centered in the left ventricle of the heart, and a psychic pneuma (*psychikos*), localized in the brain. From the heart, the pneuma is diffused through the body, vivifying it and making it capable of sensation, through a circulatory system specific to the pneuma that penetrates to every part of the organism. The channels of this circulation are the arteries, which do not contain blood as the veins do, but only pneuma. Arteries and veins communicate at their extremities, which explains why, when an artery is cut and the invisible pneuma escapes, it is immediately followed by blood flowing from the veins.[6] Alterations of this pneumatic circulation produce disease: if the blood is too abundant and invades the arteries, thrusting the pneuma toward the heart, the result is fever; if, on the contrary, the pneuma is pushed so that it accumulates at the extremes of the pneumatic vessels, there is swelling.

It is plausibly from this medical doctrine that the notion of pneuma was derived by the Stoic thinkers, who made it the central principle of their cosmology and their psychology. In the thought of Zeno and Chrysippus the pneuma is a corporeal principle, a subtle and luminous body (*leptoteron soma*), identical to fire, which pervades the universe and penetrates every living thing, in some places more and in some less: it is the principle of growth and sensation. This "artisanal" (*technikon*) and divine fire is also the substance of the sun and of other celestial bodies, such that it can be said that the vital principle in plants and animals has the same nature as the celestial bodies and that a single principle vivifies the universe. This breath or fire is present in each person and communicates life to him or her: the individual soul is but a fragment of this divine principle. The pneuma is not introduced into the body from outside, however, but is "connatured" to the body of each. This permits an explanation both of reproduction, which occurs through a pneumatic current that reaches as far as the testicles and is transmitted to the offspring in the sperm, and of sensible perception, which is accomplished through a pneumatic circulation that, beginning in the heart, directs itself to the pupils (*horatikon pneuma,* the "visual" spirit of medieval physiology) where it enters into contact with the portion of air situated between the visual organ and the object. This contact produces a tension in the air that is propagated following a cone whose vertex is in the eye and whose base demarcates the visual field. The center of this circulation is in the heart, seat of the "hegemonic" part of the soul, in whose subtle pneumatic matter are impressed the images of the phantasy as the marks of writing are impressed in a wax tablet. The voice, too, is a pneuma that radiates from the hegemonic part and, through the larynx, sets the tongue in motion. Thus one single pneumatic circulation animates the intelligence, the voice, the sperm, and the five senses. After death this pneuma does not cease to exist but ascends, because of its lightness, as far as the sublunar region, where it finds its proper site, and, indestructible and immobile like the stars, nourishes itself with the effluvia that rise from the earth.

In Neoplatonism the Stoic theme of the pneuma is conceived, following a suggestion in the *Timaeus* (41e), as a vehicle (*ochema*) or subtle body that accompanies the soul during the course of its soteriological romance from the stars to the earth. Thus, in Porphyry, the descent of the soul through the planetary orbits toward its terrestrial destiny appears as the acquisition of an ethereal wrapping, of a sort of subtle pneumatic body whose substance is formed from the celestial bodies and which, in the course of its astral itinerary, is progressively darkened and moistened. After the death of the body—if the soul has known to abstain from contact with matter—it reascends to the sky along with its pneumatic vehicle; if, instead, it has not succeeded in detaching itself from matter, the pneumaochema is weighed down to the point where it is held on the earth like an oyster attached by its valves, and is led to the place of punishment.[7] During earthly life, the pneuma is the instrument of the imagination and, as such, it is the subject of dreams, of astral influences, and of the divine illuminations (in divination, when according to Iamblichus, "the ethereal and luminous vehicle circumfusing the soul is illuminated by divine light" and "the divine phantasms, moved by the will of the gods, seize our imagination"; and in ecstasy, which is explained by Iamblichus as the descent of a divine pneuma into the body).[8] The notion of pneuma also occurs in Neoplatonic demonology. Porphyry, in a passage that is certainly the origin, however mediated, of Dante's conception of the aerial body of the soul in purgatory, affirmed that the aerial body of demons alters its form according to their phantasies, reflecting itself in the surrounding air as in a mirror, so that they always appear in different forms. Iamblichus frequently referred to the luminous pneuma of demons and heroes and of the archons who reveal themselves in the epopsy, the revelatory phase of the Eleusinian mysteries.

If in Neoplatonic and Stoic pneumatology pneuma and phantasy frequently appear assimilated in a singular convergence, in the *De insomniis* of Synesius they are fused without residue in the idea of a "phantastic spirit" (*phantastikon pneuma*), the subject of sensation, dreams, divination, and divine influences, in whose sign the exaltation of the phantasy as mediator between corporeal and incorporeal, rational and irrational, human and divine, is accomplished. For Synesius the phantasy is "the sense of senses" and the nearest to the knowledge of the divine, because

> the phantastic spirit is the most common sensory medium and the first body of the soul. It conceals itself in the interior and governs the living thing as from a citadel. Nature in fact has constructed around it the fabric of the head. The hearing and sight are not truly senses, but instruments of sense, ministers of the common sense and as it were gatekeepers of the living thing, who transmit to the overlord what they perceive outside . . . The phantastic spirit is, on the other hand, a sense perfect in all its parts . . . without intermediaries, it is the closest to the soul and certainly the most divine.[9]

Precisely because it is, at the same time, the most perfect sense and the first vehicle of the soul, the phantastic spirit is the "intermediary between the rational and irrational, corporeal and incorporeal, and as if the common term through which the divine communicates with what is most remote from itself." In this ever-denser web of soteriological and psychological themes, Synesius, with a felicitous image that was to exercise an enduring influence and of which it is perhaps possible to discern an echo in Dante's "little bark of genius" (*Purgatorio* I.3), compared the phantasy to a boat in which the newborn soul descends from the celestial spheres to unite itself with the corporeal world.[10] Given that this praise of the phantasm is contained in a work on dreams ("in his waking," wrote Synesius, "man is wise, but in the dream he is a god"), it is well to remember that for Synesius too the phantastic spirit is above all the subject of dreams and the organ of divination.[11] In this connection, adopting an image that would long endure, Synesius compared the phantastic spirit to a mirror (the mirror of Narcissus is, therefore, a pneumatic mirror) that receives the *idoli* (images) emanating from things and in which, if it has been suitably purified, the prophet may discern the images of future events. Moreover, according to the Neoplatonic tradition, this spirit, during terrestrial existence, may render itself subtle and become ethereal or become darkened and ponderous. In the latter case, it becomes the simulacrum (*eidolon*) in which the soul expiates its punishment.

We have lingered over this treatise of Synesius, who was a student of the Neoplatonic martyr Hypatia and who later became a convert to Christianity,[12] because in this curious little book can be found, already formulated at least in its general outlines, the complex of doctrine that, by identifying the interior image of Aristotelian phantasmology with the warm breath (the vehicle of the soul and of life) of Stoic-Neoplatonic pneumatology, would so richly nourish the science, speculation, and poetry of the intellectual renaissance from the eleventh to the thirteenth centuries. The synthesis that results is so characteristic that European culture in this period might justly be defined as a pneumophantasmology, within whose compass—which circumscribes at once a cosmology, a physiology, a psychology, and a soteriology—the breath that animates the universe, circulates in the arteries, and fertilizes the sperm is the same one that, in the brain and in the heart, receives and forms the phantasms of the things we see, imagine, dream, and love. Insofar as it is the subtle body of the soul, it is in addition the intermediary between the soul and matter, the divine and the human, and, as such, allows the explanation of all the influxes between corporeal and incorporeal, from magical fascination to astrological inclinations.

In the transmission of this complex of doctrine, medicine earned a place in the front rank. The rebirth of pneumatology in the eleventh century began with the Latin translation by Constantine the African of the *Liber regius* of 'Ali ibn 'Abbas al-Magiusi, and reached its first culmination toward the middle of the twelfth century, with the translation of the *De differentiae animae et spiritus* of the Arab physician Costa ben Luca. In this curve of time the pneumatic physiology of the physicians exercised a profound influence on all of contemporary culture. In the *De motu cordis* of the physician Alfred the Englishman, we read:

It is necessary that the body, whose material is solid and obtuse, and the soul, which is of a very subtle and incorporeal nature, should be joined by a certain medium which, participating in the nature of both, unites in a single compact so discordant a diversity. If this medium were of a wholly incorporeal nature, it would not be distinguished from the soul;

if it were wholly subordinate to the laws of matter, it would not differ from the dullness of the body. It is therefore necessary that it be neither fully sensible nor wholly incorporeal . . . This union of extremes and organ of corporeal movement is called spirit.[13]

According to some authors (including Alfred the Englishman and his source Costa ben Luca) there are two kinds of spirit, vital and animal, but the greater part of the physicians distinguished three: the *natural spirit,* which originates in the liver (''that part where our nourishment is administered,'' in Dante's words) from the exhalations of blood, which is there digested and purified and then from the liver proceeds through the veins to all the members of the body, increasing its natural vigor; the *vital spirit,* which originates in the heart and is diffused to the whole body through the arteries, animating it; and the *animal spirit,* which arises in the chambers of the brain from a purification of the vital spirit. From the left chamber of the heart the vital spirit in fact rises to the brain through the artery, passes through its three cells, and there, ''through the power of the phantasy and the memory is again purified and further digested (*digestior purgatiorque*) and becomes animal spirit.''[14] From the brain the animal spirit fills the nerves and is radiated through the whole body, producing sensation and movement. Indeed, the optic nerve branches from the phantastic cell, then bifurcates and reaches the eyes. Through the cavity of this nerve passes the animal spirit, which here becomes still more subtle[15] and, according to one theory, emerges from the eye as the visual spirit, directs itself through the air to the object (which functions as its ''supplement''), and, once informed of the object's figure and color, returns to the eye and from there to the phantastic cell. According to another theory, the visual spirit, without leaving the eye, receives the impression of the object through the air and transmits it to the phantastic spirit.[16] An analogous mechanism accounts for hearing and the other senses. In the phantastic cell, the animal spirit enacts the images of the phantasy; in the memorial cell it produces the memory; and in the logistic cell, reason.

The entire psychological process described in the previous chapter must be translated and ''spiritualized'' in the terms of this pneumatic circulation. The psychology of Avicenna, which we previously described in purely static terms, will, when restored to its essential ''spiritual'' context, sound like this:

The similitude [of the thing] is united to the part of the spirit that bears the visual spirit . . . and penetrates to the spirit that is found in the first ventricle of the brain and is impressed on this spirit that bears the power of the common sense . . . then the common sense transmits the form to that part of the spirit that is contiguous to the spirit that bears it and impresses this form and places it thus in the formal power, which is the imaginative . . . then the form that is in the imagination reaches the rear ventricle and is united with the spirit that bears the estimative virtue through the spirit that bears the imaginative power which, in humans, is called cogitative, and the form that was in the imaginative is impressed on the spirit of the estimative virtue . . . [17]

We are now also prepared to understand the theory for which the first seat of sensation and imagination is in the heart, but the powers are actualized in the brain. The visual spirit in fact has its origin in the heart, and this same spirit, refined and purified, rises to the brain and becomes animal. A single pneumatic current circulates in the organism and in that current what can only statically be considered divided is dynamically unified.

The animal spirit naturally inheres in the sperm. Radiating itself through the body it reaches the testicles, is converted into "a milky and tenacious juice, and, coitus once completed, passes to the outside"[18] where, uniting itself to the female sperm, it forms the embryo and receives influences of the stars.

The problem that the pneumatic physiology of the physicians posed for the Christian anthropology of the Middle Ages concerned the manner in which the relation of spirit and soul was to be conceived. In his *Pantechne,* Constantine the African appeared to identify the rational spirit with intellection, a function par excellence of the rational soul, and pointed in addition to the opinion of "certain philosophers who affirm that this spirit of the brain is the soul and that it is corporeal." If Costa ben Luca already stressed the difference between the mortal and corporeal spirit and the immortal and incorporeal soul, the preoccupation over reconciling the pneumatology of the physicians with Christian doctrine is plain in William of St. Thierry, who explicitly condemned the grave error of those who identify the spirit with "that eminent part of man that makes of him the image of the incorruptible God and elevates him above all the other living creatures, to wit the rational soul." With a formula that reveals in an exemplary way the metaphysical fracture of presence that characterizes Christian ontology, he wrote, "The Author of nature has shrouded the union of the soul and the body in mystery. Ineffable and incomprehensible is the meeting of these two substances."[19]

This *mysterium ineffabile* constitutes the theme of one of the most singular works of the twelfth century: the *De unione corporis et spiritus* of Hugh of St. Victor. Hugh, like William of St. Thierry, distrusted any hasty identification of corporeal and incorporeal, and thus began with the words of the Gospel of John, according to which "what is born of the flesh is flesh, and what is born of the spirit is spirit." But over the abyss that separates the two substances, Hugh placed a kind of mystical Jacob's ladder, along which the body ascends toward the spirit and the spirit descends to the body:

If there were no intermediary between the spirit and the body, neither the spirit nor the body would have been able to meet each other. Great is the distance between body and spirit: they are distant one from the other. There is, however, something through which the spirit descends, in its turn, to approach the body . . . Not all bodies are of the same quality; some are higher, some lower, some are supreme and almost transcend the corporeal nature. Similarly also among the spirits some are higher, some lower, and some very low, almost fallen below the spiritual nature, because in this way things supreme are joined to the lowest things . . . The body rises and the spirit descends . . . The body rises through the medium of the senses, the spirit descends through sensuality . . . Think of Jacob's ladder: it rested on earth and its top touched the heavens.[20]

In quest of this Jacob's ladder, and inspired by the Neoplatonic theory of the phantastic spirit as the mediator between corporeal and incorporeal, rational and irrational, Hugh proceeded to a reevaluation of the phantasy that constitutes a decisive turn in the history of medieval culture:

Among bodies the most noble and nearest to the spiritual nature is the one that possesses a continuous movement in itself and cannot ever be stayed by an outside force. This body, insofar as it causes sensation, imitates the rational life and, insofar as it is a form of the imagination, imitates the living reason. In the body there can be nothing higher and nearer to the spiritual nature than this, in which, beyond sensation and above it, the force of the imagination originates. Such a reality is so sublime that above it no other can be found if not reason. The fiery force that has received a form from the outside is called sensation; this same form transported to the inside is called the imagination. In fact, when the form of the sensible thing, gathered from the outside by means of the visual rays, comes to be led to the eyes by the work of nature and is gathered by these, there is vision. Subsequently, passing through the seven membranes of the eyes and the three humors, finally purified and led to the inside, it reaches the brain and originates the imagination. The imagination, passing from the anterior part of the head to the central part, comes into contact with the substance of the rational soul itself and stimulates the faculty of discernment, now so purified and made subtle so as to be able to join itself without mediation with the spirit itself . . . The imagination is therefore a figure of the sensation, situated in the highest part of the corporeal spirit and in the lowest part of the rational spirit . . . In irrational animals it does not transcend the phantastic cell, but in rational animals it reaches as far as the rational cell, where it comes into contact with the incorporeal substance of the soul itself . . . Now the rational substance is a corporeal light; the imagination, insofar as it is the image of a body, is a shadow. Therefore, after the imagination has risen as far as reason, like a shadow that comes to the light and superimposes itself on the light, insofar as it comes toward the light it makes itself manifest and circumscribed, insofar as it superimposes itself on the light it darkens it, enfolds it, covers it. If reason acquires imagination through contemplation alone, the imagination acts as a garment that stands outside and enfolds it, so that reason can easily dispense with it and denude itself. If, on the other hand, reason adheres to it with delight, the imagination becomes like a skin for it, so that reason cannot detach itself without pain, because it had attached itself with love . . . Rising, therefore, from the bodies at the lowest extreme up to the corporeal spirit, there is a progression through sense and imagination, which are both in the corporeal spirit. Immediately beyond the body, there is the imaginary affection in the incorporeal spirit that the soul receives through its union with the body, and above this the reason that acts on the imagination.[21]

In the Fathers most influenced by Hugh, like Isaac of Stella and Alcher of Clairvaux, this mediating function of the phantastic spirit is reiterated and specified: "The soul that is true spirit and the flesh that is true body are united easily and appropriately at their extreme point, that is, the phantastic power of the soul, which is not a body, but is similar to the body, and in the sensuality of the flesh, which is almost spirit . . ."[22]

To measure the importance of the reevaluation of the phantasy that is accomplished in these writings, it is necessary to recall that in the medieval Christian tradition the phantasy appeared in a decisively negative light. It is not inopportune to remember in this connection that the lascivious half-naked ladies, the half-human and half-feral creatures, the terrifying devils, and the whole conglomeration of monstrous and seductive images that crystallized in the iconography of the temptations of Saint Anthony represent precisely the phantasms that the Tempter excited in the phantastic spirit of the Saint. This same vertiginous experience of the soul, with the polarizing intuition that characterizes medieval thought, then became the site of the celebration of the "ineffable union" of the corporeal and incorporeal, of light and shadow. If the spiritual mediator of this union has been identified, in the wake of Neoplatonic thought, with the phantastic pneuma, this is because not even in the most exalted Romantic theorizing has the imagination been conceived in so elevated and, at the same time, concrete a fashion as in the thought of this period, which surely more than ours deserves the name of "civilization of the image." If we keep in mind the close bond that joins love and the phantasm, it is easy to understand the profound influence that this reevaluation of the phantasy would exercise on the theory of love. Furthermore, because a positive polarity of phantasy had been discovered, it was possible, in ways we shall see, to rediscover both a positive polarity and a "spirituality" in that mortal disease of the phantastic spirit that was love.

Another aspect of the Neoplatonic theory of the phantastic pneuma that was inherited by medieval culture was the idea that it was the vehicle and the subject of magical influence. The question has often been raised as to what should be understood by the notion of magical phenomena, and, although this term is habitually used with a certain casualness, it is not clear if something such as a "magical phenomenon" is definable in itself, without recourse to a play of oppositions that vary culture by culture. Nevertheless, at least as far as the Middle

Ages are concerned, we can affirm without excessive uncertainty that to speak of magic as a sphere distinct from that of pneumatology makes little sense. In a pneumatic culture, that is, in a culture founded on the notion of spirit as *quid medium* between corporeal and incorporeal, the distinction between magic and science (and that between magic and religion as well) is of no use. Only the obsolescence of pneumatology and the consequent semantic mutation that has brought the word "spirit" to identify with the vague notion now familiar to us (and which acquired such a meaning only in opposition to the term "matter") will make possible that dichotomy between corporeal and incorporeal that is the necessary condition of a distinction between science and magic. The so-called magical texts of the Middle Ages (such as the astrological and alchemical ones) deal simply with certain aspects of pneumatology (in particular, certain influences between spirit and spirit, or between spirit and body) and, in this regard, are not essentially different from texts like the poems of Cavalcanti and Dante, which we would certainly not define as "magical." Thus the Arabic treatise known in the West by the name *Picatrix,* which exercised so much influence on Renaissance Hermetism, defines the "key of wisdom" as "the perfect nature" and this in its turn as "the pneuma of the philosopher that is united with its star" (a definition that at this point should be perfectly intelligible to our readers). The *Picatrix* then classifies the various forms of magic according to whether they have as their object "spirit from spirit" (practical magic and phantasmagoria), "spirit from body" (talismanics), or "bodies from bodies" (alchemy).[23] In particular, phenomena that we consider magical par excellence, like fascination, can perfectly well be subsumed in the doctrine of pneumatic influences and were explained as such by the medieval authors. If fascination could for a long time be placed alongside love almost as its paradigmatic model, this is because both belonged to the sphere of phantastic pneuma.[24] The opinion that "through a certain art of women and through the power of the demons men can be transformed into wolves or mules" was thus explained by Alcher as an action of demons on the phantastic spirit that, "while the body of a man reposes in a place, alive but with the senses weighed down more than in sleep, he can take on the form of a certain animal and appear as such to the senses of other men"; and by Cecco d'Ascoli as a demoniac illusion of the phantasy or as the assumption of an aerial body by a demon.[25]

The extraction of a magical sphere and literature from the bosom of medieval pneumatology was the work of a period that had lost the keys to it and could not (or would not) understand either the unity of its doctrine or the precise sense of its articulations. This process began already with scholastic theology that, while accepting the medical doctrine of spirits, attempted to isolate this doctrine in the domain of corporeal physiology and to strip it of all the soteriological and cosmological implications that made of the pneuma the concrete and real mediator of the "ineffable union" between soul and body.[26] At this point a decline began that would fatally thrust pneumatology into the half-light of esoteric circles, where it would long survive as the path, rendered impracticable, that our culture might have, but did not in fact follow. In the mainstream of thought remained only the medieval doctrine of corporeal spirits, which still survived in Descartes—and which appears still, under the name of vapors, in the *Encyclopédie*—but by this time Harvey had already furnished the new model of the circulation of the blood. Before withdrawing into the shadows, however, the idea of pneuma would yet produce a late and splendid fruit as the "spirit of love," which found its highest expression in the Stilnovist lyric.

Notes

1. *Dante Alighieri: Dante's Vita Nuova,* trans. Mark Musa (Bloomington: Indiana University Press, 1973), 3-4.

2. One representative example is G. Vitale, "Ricerche intorno all'elemento filosofico nei poeti del dolce stil novo," *Giornale dantesco* 18 (1910): 168-74, which refers above all to Albertus Magnus. Vitale saw that the spirits are not simply "personifications of the powers of the soul," but he was not aware of the link between pneumatology and the theory of the phantasy, and his conclusion shows that he held that "spirits were one of many subtleties among other subtleties, an abstraction among other abstractions, an error among other errors." Only the exemplary study of Robert Klein, "Spirito peregrino," *Revue d'Etudes Italiennes* 11 (1965): 197-236 [English translation in *Form and Meaning: Essays on the Renaissance and Modern Art* (Princeton: Princeton University Press, 1979), 62-85], has established the bases for a reconstruction of medieval pneumo-phantasmology, showing the connections between the theory of the phantasy, the Neoplatonic theory of the pneuma-ochema, and the magical and soteriological theories. Nevertheless, conceiving them as distinct "levels" only casually related to one another rather than as the articulations of a single edifice, has prevented Klein from drawing all the consequences of his discoveries, above all with respect to love poetry. For the history of ancient pneumatology, see Verbeke, *L'evolution de la doctrine du pneuma du Stoicisme à St. Augustin* (Paris-Louvain, 1945).

3. From *Aristotle in Twenty-Three Volumes,* vol. 13, trans. G. L. Peck (Cambridge: Harvard University Press, 1979), 171.

4. See Hippocratis *De flatibus* 3; *De morbo sacro* 16; *Regimen* 1, 9, 10.

5. See Jaeger, *Diokles von Karystos* (Berlin, 1938).

6. According to Galen, who attacked this theory, the pneuma circulates, mixed with blood in the veins.

7. On the theory of pneuma-ochema in Neoplatonism, see Proclus, *The Elements of Theology,* edited by E. R. Dodds (Oxford, 1963), appendix 2.

8. Iamblichus, *Les mystères d'Egypte,* critical edition and trans. by E. des Places (Paris, 1966), 117.

9. *De insomniis (Patrologia graeca,* 66, 1290).

10. Ibid., 1294.

11. When Dante (*Convivio* II.8), speaking of the "divinations of our dreams," asked himself if the organ that receives these revelations be "corporeal or incorporeal" ("and I say corporeal or incorporeal because of the various opinions that I find about it"), he must have been alluding to the dispute on the corporeal or incorporeal nature of the phantastic pneuma.

12. On the figure of Synesius as mediator between Christianity and Neoplatonism, see H.-I. Marrou, "Sinesio di Cirene e il neoplatonismo alessandrino," in *Il conflitto fra paganesimo e cristianesimo nel secolo iv* (Torino, 1968).

13. *Des Alfred von Sareshel Schrift de motu cordis* (Munster, 1923), 37ff.

14. Ibid., 45.

15. "Et cum altior et subtilior sit spiritus qui ad oculos dirigitur . . . " (And as the spirit that is

directed to the eyes is higher and subtler . . .) (John of Salisbury, *De septem septenis*, in *Patrologia latina* 199, 952). This is the subtle spirit of the Stilnovists; see Guido Cavalcanti, "E quel sottile spirito che vede" (And that subtle spirit that sees), in *Rimatori del dolce stil novo*, 38; "Pegli occhi fere un spirito sottile" (Through the eyes strikes a subtle spirit), in ibid., 39.

16. The mechanism of vision and the optical problems linked to it, from illusions to refraction in mirrors, are among the most passionately discussed subjects in a "contemplative" culture like that of late antiquity and the Middle Ages. The form in which late antiquity passed the problem onto the Middle Ages is summarized in the commentary of Chalcidius to the *Timaeus* (*Timaeus Platonis sive de universitate interpretibus M.T. Cicerone et Chalcidio una cum eius docta explanatione*, Lutetia, 1563, 142ff.); in Galen (*De Hippocratis et Platonis placitis*, book 7, chaps. 4-5; also *De oculis liber;* both in *Operum*, vol. 5); and in Nemesius (*Nemesii episcopi Premnon physicon a N. Alfano archiepiscopo Salerni in latinum translatum*, recognovit C. Burckhardt, Leipzig, 1917, 75 ff.). Without a clear knowledge of these pneumatic theories it is simply impossible to read the poetry of the thirteenth century, and, in particular, the Stilnovists. For example, the ecstatic phenomenon described by Dante in *Vita Nuova* XIV (the "spirits of sight" out of their instruments) can be understood only in relation to this "spiritual" conception of vision.

17. Avicenna, *De anima* III.8.

18. *Galeno ascriptus liber de compagine membrorum*, chap. 11 (in *Operum*, 332).

19. William of St. Thierry, *De natura corporis et animae* (*Patrologia latina*, 180, 712). On this problem, see the observations of V. Liccaro in Hugh of St. Victor, *I tre giorni dell'invisibil luce. L'unione del corpo e dello spirito* (Florence, 1974), 195-96.

20. *De unione corporis et spiritus* (*Patrologia latina*, 177, 285).

21. Ibid., 287-88.

22. Alcher of Clairvaux, *Liber de spiritu et anima* (*Patrologia latina*, 40, 789).

23. *Picatrix: Das Ziel des Weisens, von Pseudo-Magriti* (London, 1962), 7 and 205.

24. The relation of love, which is born from the gaze, to fascination through the eyes is already in Plutarch, *Symposiaka problemata*, book 5, p. 7: *de iis qui fascinare dicuntar* (of those who are said to fascinate): "The sight, which is marvelously mobile and wandering, thanks to the spirit that rays a fiery dart from the eyes, spreads a certain marvelous force, through the effect of which mortals achieve and suffer many things . . . Those who touch or listen are not wounded as are those who gaze or are gazed at fixedly . . . The sight of beautiful things, notwithstanding it should strike the eyes from a distance, kindles an inner fire in the spirits of lovers."

25. Alcher of Clairvaux, *Liber de spiritu et anima*, 798; Cecco d'Ascoli, in the Commentary to the *Sphere of Sacrobosco*, in *L'acerba*.

26. Thus Saint Thomas (*De spiritualibus creaturis*, article 7) answered negatively to the question "Utrum substantia spiritualis corpori aereo uniatur" (whether the spiritual substance is joined to an aerial body), and Albertus Magnus (*De spiritu et respiratione* I.i.8) denied that the spirit is the *medium* of the union of soul and body.

Chapter 14
Spirits of Love

This ample and lively scene should serve as the backdrop for our study of the pneumatology of Dante and the Stilnovists. The "three spirits" of the beginning of the *Vita Nuova* do not play an isolated or a purely ornamental allegorical role, but, like the statement of a theme at the beginning of a sonata, they are woven into a context where all the registers of the pneumatic doctrine can be expected to play, from physiology to cosmology, from psychology to soteriology. And, as Klein well discerned, the sonnet "Oltre la spera che più larga gira" (Beyond the sphere which makes the widest round), which concludes the *Vita Nuova,* gathers these motifs together in a synthesis that, in many respects, compendiously anticipates the ecstatic voyage of the *Commedia*. The "pilgrim spirit" that, emerging from the heart (the seat, as we know, of the vital spirit), accomplishes its celestial voyage ("beyond the sphere which makes the widest round") and, as Dante informs us, a "thought," that is, an imagination, or rather, as we can now define it with more precision, a phantastic spirit, can detach itself from the body and receive the form of its vision in such a way ("in such a quality") that "my intellect cannot understand it." (We know from Avicenna that the intellect cannot receive the phantasm unless the phantasm is abstracted from the sensible qualities; but precisely this limitation here establishes the visionary capacity of the phantastic spirit and its superiority, almost, over the intellect.) This concept of the phantastic spirit as the seat and vehicle of the celestial influences, which we have already come across in Synesius, was explicitly affirmed by Dante in the seventeenth canto of the *Purgatorio* in the celebrated invocation of the "imaginative" power, where he asks himself what moves the phantasy when, caught up in its vision, it cannot be moved by the sense:

O imaginativa che ne rube
talvolta sí di fuor, ch'om non s'accorge
perché dintorno suonin mille tube,
   chi move te, se 'l senso non ti porge?
Moveti lume che nel ciel s'informa
per sé o per voler che giú lo scorge. (*Purgatorio* XVII.13-18)

[O imagination, that do sometimes so
snatch us from outward things that we give no heed,
though a thousand trumpets sound around us,
who moves you if the sense affords you naught? A light
moves you which takes form in heaven, of itself, or by a will
that downward guides it.][1]

The solidarity of the astral theme of the Neoplatonic pneuma-ochema with the psychological theme of the phantastic spirit was still alive in Dante when he wrote, in the *Convivio* (II 6.9), that "this spirit comes by the rays of the star."

In canto XXV of the *Purgatorio* Dante expressed, through the mouth of Statius, the pneumatic theory of the embryo, which we have already encountered in the medical tradition, and that of the aerial body of the soul beyond the grave, which is familiar to us from Porphyry and Synesius. The "perfect blood, which is never drunk / by the thirsty veins" (vv. 37-38) is not simply the blood, as is often repeated, but the spirit that, as we know, is formed from the purest and most digested part of the blood, and, having descended to the testicles and changed into semen, forms the embryo, joining itself "in natural vessel" with "[the] other's blood" (v. 45). The doctrine of the "shade" of the souls in purgatory is but a singular transcription of the Neoplatonic idea of the pneuma as a simulacrum in which the soul expiates its punishment (that Origen, Avicenna, and later Ficino would develop in the direction of the purely phantastic reality of infernal torments), and the "figuring itself" of the shade "according to how desires and other affections afflict us" is but an echo of the Porphyrian theory of the "aerial body" of the demons, so malleable that it changes form according to their phantasies.

The entirety of Stilnovist lyric should be placed under the standard of this pneumatic constellation and only within its orbit does that lyric become fully intelligible. When Cavalcanti speaks of "subtle spirits," of "little spirits," and of "spirits of love" we should not forget what distant but coherent harmonics we are meant to hear resonating in these words. The poet was not referring, as some have thought, to a medical doctrine, more or less seriously and not without eccentricity; but rather to a unitary system of thought in whose orbit, as we will see, poetry itself, insofar as it is dictated by inspiring love, finds its proper place and its most pregnant meanings. Thus, for example, a sonnet like "Pegli occhi fere un spirito sottile" (Subtle the spirit striking through the eyes), so obsessively dominated by the word "spirit," has frequently been considered too obscure and extravagant not to contain a parodic (indeed, self-parodic) intention. Yet, restored to the pneumatological context that we have attempted to reconstruct, not only does the poem appear comprehensible, but it presents itself as a rigorous description of the pneumatic mechanism of Eros and a true and proper translation into pneumatic terms of the phantasmatic psychology of love:

> Pegli occhi fere un spirito sottile,
> che fa 'n la mente spirito destare,
> dal qual si move spirito d'amare,
> ch'ogn'altro spiritel[lo] fa gentile.

> Sentir non pò di lu' spirito vile,
> di cotanta vertú spirito appare:
> quest'è lo spiritel che fa tremare,
> lo spiritel che fa la donna umíle.

> E poi da questo spirito si move
> un altro dolce spirito soave,
> che sieg[u]e un spiritello di mercede:

> lo quale spiritel spiriti piove,
> ché di ciascuno spirit'ha la chiave,
> per forza d'uno spirito che 'l vede.

> [Subtle the spirit striking through the eyes
> Which rouseth up a spirit in the mind
> Whence moves a spirit into love inclined
> which breeds in other spirits nobilities
> No turbid spirit hath the sense which sees
> How greatly empowered a spirit he appeareth;
> He is the little breath which that breath feareth,
> Which breedeth virginal humilities.
> Yet from this spirit doth another move
> Wherein such tempered sweetness rightly dwells
> That Mercy's spirit followeth his ways,
> And Mercy's spirit as it moves above
> Rains down those spirits that ope all things else,
> Perforce of One who seeth all of these.][2]

The subtle spirit that penetrates through the eye is the visual spirit that, as we know, is *altior et subtilius* (higher and subtler); "striking" through the eye, it arouses the spirit found in the cells of the brain and informs it with the image of the lady. From this spirit, love is born (the "spirit of loving"), which refines and makes tremble every other spirit (that is, the vital and natural ones). Guido was so obsessed with pneumatics that he continually translated the psychological process into his "spiritual" terms: the arrows of love, which Alexander of

Aphrodisias had already identified with the glances of lovers,[3] became, in the Stilnovists, an influence from pneuma to pneuma,[4] and the internal image, the phantasm, was always conceived as a phantastic pneuma, included in a circulation that is both exasperated and fulfilled in the amorous motion of the spirits. Therefore the phantasm, the object of love, was for Cavalcanti literally "formed of desire" ("forming of desire a new person"; "made playfully in figures of love").[5] Indeed, the experience of the pneumatic cycle that goes from the eyes to the phantasy, from the phantasy to the memory, and from the memory to the whole body, seems to be Cavalcanti's fundamental experience, such that the perfect symmetry of spirit and phantasm, which had been condensed in the Neoplatonic formula of the phantastic pneuma, is always discernible in detail. We can easily recognize in the ballad "Veggio negli occhi de la donna mia" (Light do I see within my lady's eyes) an almost point-by-point comparison to the pneumatic mechanism of the preceding sonnet, except that in the ballad the genesis of love is described in phantasmatic terms. In the sonnet the subtle spirit strikes through the eyes and arouses the spirit in the mind, but in the ballad the image that seems to detach itself from the lady's visage impresses its figure in the phantasy. In the sonnet, the procession of the spirits one from the other is matched by the successive germination of the images of "new beauty" in the ballad:

Veggio negli occhi de la donna mia
un lume pien di spiriti d'amore,
che porta uno piacer novo nel core,
sí che vi desta d'allegrezza vita.

Cosa m'aven, quand'i' le son presente,
ch'i' no la posso a lo 'ntelletto dire:
veder mi par de la sua labbia uscire
una sí bella donna, che la mente
    comprender no la può, che 'mmantenente
ne nasce un'altra di bellezza nova,
da la qual par ch'una stella si mova
e dica: «La salute tua è apparita.»

Là dove questa bella donna appare
s'ode una voce che le vèn davanti
e par che d'umiltà il su' nome canti
sí dolcemente, che, s'i' 'l vo' contare,
    sento che 'l su' valor mi fa tremare;
e movonsi nell'anima sospiri
che dicon: «Guarda; se tu coste' miri,
vedra' la sua vertú nel ciel salita.»

[Light do I see within my lady's eyes
And loving spirits in its plenisphere
Which bear in strange delight on my heart's core
Till Joy's awakened from that sepulchre.
That which befalls me in my lady's presence
Bars explanations intellectual,
I seem to see a lady wonderful
Forth issue from her lips, one whom no sense
Can fully tell the mind of and one whence
Another fair, swift born, moves marvelous
From whom a star goes forth and speaketh thus:
"Lo, thy salvation is gone forth from thee."
There where this lady's loveliness appeareth,
There's heard a voice which goes before her ways
And seems to sing her name with such sweet praise
That my mouth fears to speak what name she beareth,
And my heart trembles for the grace she weareth,
While far in my soul's deep the sighs astir
Speak thus: "Look well! For if thou look on her,
Thus shall thou see her virtue risen in heaven."][6]

Never, perhaps, does the medieval supremacy of the imaginary and its "optic" interpenetration with the real find such an animated and at the same time meticulous expression as here: the appearance of the phantasm in the phantasy is hardly fixed in the memory when suddenly, as in a game of mirrors, an image of "bellezza nova" (new beauty) is formed in the intellect (new, because it has been denuded, as we know, from material modifications), and is the bearer of salvation because in that image the possible intellect—separate and unique, according to Avicenna—is united to the individual.

The famous canzone "Donna me prega," the axis of Cavalcanti's *trobar clus* ("closed," obscure style of making poetry), is nevertheless clearly illuminated if we restore it to the complex of doctrine that we have attempted to resuscitate. The double aspect—phantasmatic and pneumatic—of eros is evoked in the double genesis of love suggested by verses 16-18 and 21-23: to the pneumatic-astral aspect correspond the verses " . . . so formed—like / a diaphane by light—of a darkness / which from Mars—comes, and stays," and to the phantasmatic-psychological corresponds the verse "It comes from a seen form that is intended." [Here "is intended" does not of course mean "comes to be understood," but corresponds perfectly, *a parte obiecti* (with respect to the object), to the phrase "tragge intenzione" (draws forth the intention) from the eighteenth canto of Dante's *Purgatorio*.] The rigorously phantasmatic character of the amorous experience is reiterated in the canzone in terms so extreme that even the sense of sight, since it is only an incidental cause of falling in love, is now excluded as inessential (cf. v. 65: "and, [I say to] who hears well, the form is not seen") in the proud awareness of the self-sufficiency of the imagination: "Out of color, divided from essence / fixed—in a dark medium, it [love] abrades light." Only the knowledge of the pneumo-phantastic in all of its articulations permits the resolution of the long-standing debate between the supporters of a Platonic-contemplative interpretation of the Cavalcantian theory of love and the supporters of an opposing view. There are not "two loves" (love-as-contemplation and concupiscent love), but a "single amorous experience" that is, at the same time, contemplation [in that it is the obsessive *cogitatio* (meditation) of the internal phantasm] and concupiscence (in that the desire has as its origin and immediate object the phantasm: "that is the phantasy that gives rise to the whole desire," in the words of Jean Gerson). The so-called Averroism of Cavalcanti does not consist, as has been affirmed, in a limitation of the erotic experience to the sensitive soul, which would entail as a consequence a pessimistic conception of eros and a rigorous separation from the possible intellect. On the contrary, it consists, as we have seen, in the fact that the phantasm (the phantastic pneuma), origin and subject of love, is precisely that in which, as in a mirror, the union (*copulatio*) of the individual with the unique and separate intellect is accomplished.[7]

But Dante too conceived of love in this way when he linked together its genesis and nature in the four exemplary tercets he put in the mouth of Virgil:

> Vostra apprensiva da essere verace
> tragge intenzione, e dentro a voi la spiega,
> sí che l'animo ad essa volger face;
>   e se, rivolto, inver' di lei si piega,
> quel piegare è amor, quell' è natura
> che per piacer di novo in voi si lega.
>   Poi, come 'l foco movesi in altura
> per la sua forma ch'è nata a salire
> là dove piú in sua matera dura,
>   cosí l'animo preso entra in disire,
> ch'è moto spiritale, e mai non posa
> fin che la cosa amata il fa gioire. (*Purgatorio* XVIII.22-33)

[Your faculty of apprehension draws an image
from a real existence and displays it within you,
so that it makes the mind turn to it;
and if, thus turned, the mind inclines toward it,
that inclination is love, that inclination is nature
which is bound in you anew by pleasure.
Then, even as fire moves upwards
by reason of its form, being born to ascend thither
where it lasts longest in its matter,

so the captive mind enters into desire,
which is a spiritual movement, and never rests
until the thing loved makes it rejoice.][8]

If the genetic process of love is here described in the phantasmatic terms of the
psychology that is by now familiar to us, as the soul's inclination and turning,
almost as if in a mirror, around the phantasm "intended" in the mind, love itself
is defined as a "spiritual movement" and inserted in the movement of pneumatic
circulation.

The sociological hypothesis that sees courtly love as primarily a social phenomenon has so insistently dominated research on the origins of love poetry that
very rarely has an analysis of its structural elements as they appear in the texts
themselves been undertaken. Just as the rigorously phantasmatic character of amorous experience, notwithstanding its explicit and unequivocal affirmation by the
poets, has almost always eluded coherent research (because of the misunderstood
supposition that a phantastic experience was necessarily irrelevant for the understanding of a "social phenomenon"), so too the pneumatic nature of love, even
when it has been understood, has been reduced to the limits of an entirely sec-
ondary medical theory, thanks to the projection of the dualistic soul/body scheme
on a conception whose intention was precisely to mediate and overcome this opposition. We can now affirm without hesitation that the Stilnovist theory of love
is, in the sense we have demonstrated, a *pneumo-phantasmology,* in which the
theory of the phantasm, of Aristotelian origin, is fused with Stoic-medical-
Neoplatonic pneumatology in an experience that is, jointly and in equal measure,
a "spiritual movement" and a phantasmatic process. Only this complex cultural
inheritance can explain the characteristic dimension, both real and unreal, physiological and soteriological, objective and subjective, that erotic experience retains in the Stilnovist experience. The object of love is in fact a phantasm, but this
phantasm is a "spirit," inserted, as such, in a pneumatic circle in which the limits separating internal and external, corporeal and incorporeal, desire and its
object, are abolished.

The union of phantasmology and pneumatology has already been accomplished, as we have seen, in the medical tradition and in the Neoplatonic doctrine
of the "phantastic spirit" and had led to that reevaluation of the phantasy as the
mediator between body and soul and as the seat of magical and divine influences,
which finds its exemplary model in the work of Hugh of St. Victor. But in what
way did the "phantastic spirit" become a "spirit of love"? If the meeting between Eros and the phantasm took place near the *miroërs perilleus* of Narcissus,
in what circumstances did the winged god, armed with arrows, make his entrance
into the severe pneumatic doctrine? And in what measure is this convergence between love and pneuma an original discovery of the poets of love?

The pneumo-phantastic character of Eros had been recognized by a medical
tradition in which the passions of the mind were firmly inscribed in the circula-

tion of the spirits. "For sexual excitement is due to breath (pneuma); the penis proves this, as it quickly increases from small to large because of the breath in it," we read in a passage of Aristotle's *Problems* concerning the calamitous erotic inclination of melancholics. In Galen the erotic pneumatology maintains all of its physiological crudity and the "spiritual movement" of love is of a piece with the erection of the member and the formation of the sperm:

> When someone is through one of the five senses stimulated to love, the heart is strongly shaken and from this shaking two spirits are born, hot and dry. One of these, the more subtle, reaches the brain; the other, which is more dense, diffused through the nerves immediately reaches the member and, insinuating itself between the nerves and the membranes that form it and coil around it, makes it erect . . . the first spirit, which we said was found in the brain, receiving from this [brain] a certain humidity, reaches the spinal marrow through the kidneys . . . and passing through two channels pours itself into the testicles . . . [9]

In the field of the theory of fascination, love, as we have seen, had been considered for some time as a pneumatic penetration through the glance, which "kindles an internal fire in the mind of the lover."

Only with the Stilnovists, however, was the theory of the pneuma fused with the theory of love. They had the intuition of a polarity—the same that would later lead the humanists to reevaluate melancholy positively—in which the obsessive emphasis of a pathological experience well known to medical diagnostics goes hand in hand with its soteriological ennoblement; thus mortal disease and salvation, obscuration and illumination, privation and fulfillment, appear problematically and inextricably joined. The proof of this polarity is contained in a chapter of the history of medicine in which love assumes the dark saturnine mask of a malady "similar to melancholy" that desiccates the face and eyes of lovers and plunges them into madness and death. This malady appears, in medieval medical treatises, under the name of *amor hereos* (heroic love).

Notes

1. English translation from *Dante Alighieri: The Divine Comedy: Purgatorio,* trans. Charles S. Singleton (Princeton: Princeton University Press, 1973), 179.

2. English translation from *The Sonnets and Ballads of Guido Cavalcanti,* trans. Ezra Pound (Westport, Conn.: Hyperion Press, 1983), 27.

3. "leva pharetra sagittis referta pluribus, quoniam principio amor per radium oritur unum oculorum; statim quippe ut quis aspexit, amavit; post frequentes ad rem amatam radios mittit, quasi tela jactat . . . " The passage is in book 1 of the *Problems* of Alexander of Aphrodisias, in response to the question: "Cur amantium extremae partes modo frigidae sunt, modo calidae?" (Why are the extremities of lovers sometimes hot and sometimes cold?) Latin translation by Angelo Poliziano in Angeli Politiani, *Opera,* Lugduni, 1537, vol. 2, 263-64a.

4. The pneumatic mechanism of falling in love, constantly mentioned in Cavalcanti (in *Rimatori del dolce stil novo,* XI, vv. 9-11; XII, vv. 9-12; XXVIII, vv. 4-7), recurs in Dante and the Stilnovists.

5. Ibid., XXIX, v. 17; XXXI, v. 22.

6. *The Sonnets and Ballads of Guido Cavalcanti,* 83.

7. This situation of the phantasm also permits the understanding of the nexus between the theory of love and the Averroist assertion—now well documented for Cavalcanti's milieu as well; see P. O. Kristeller, "A Philosophical Treatise from Bologna Dedicated to G. Cavalcanti," in *Studi in onore di B. Nardi,* vol. 1 (Florence, 1955), 425-63—that ultimate happiness can be attained in this life and consists in the contemplation of the separate substances. The nexus is provided by the fact that, through the contemplation of the phantasm that is the object of love, the actual contemplation of the separated substances becomes possible. See Saint Thomas, *Summa contra gentiles,* book 3, chap. 43, citing the opinion of Averroës: "Oportet igitur quod, quum intellecta speculativa sint nobis copulata per phantasmata, quae sunt quasi quoddam subjectum eorum, etiam intellectus agens continuetur nobiscum, in quantum est forma intellectorum speculativorum . . . Unde cum ad intellectum agentem pertineat intelligere substantias separatas, intelligemus tunc substantias separatas, sicut nunc intelligimus intellecta speculativa; et hoc erit ultima hominis felicitas, in qua homo erit sicut quidam deus" ["Consequently, since these same principles (speculative principles) are joined to us by phantasms, which are a kind of subject thereof, it follows that the active intellect also is joined to us, being the form of those principles . . . Consequently, since it belongs to the active intellect to understand separate substances, . . . just as now we understand speculative knowledge. This will be man's ultimate happiness, wherein man will be a god as it were"; *Saint Thomas Aquinas: The Summa Contra Gentiles,* trans. English Dominican Fathers, vol. 3 (London: Burns, Oates and Washbourne, 1928), 97].

8. *Dante Alighieri: The Divine Comedy: Purgatorio,* trans. Charles S. Singleton, 191.

9. *Galeno ascriptus liber de compagine membrorum,* chap. 11.

Chapter 15
Between Narcissus and Pygmalion

His love is here indeed heroic and divine; and so I wish to take it, although because of it he call himself subject to so many torments; because every lover, who is disjoined or separated from the beloved (to whom, as he is joined in his affections, he wishes he might be joined in effect), suffers heartache and pain, tortures and torments himself: not because he loves, considering that he feels his love to be nobly and worthily employed, but because he is deprived of that fruition, which he would obtain if he were to reach that goal to which he inclines. He does not sorrow because of desire, which animates him, but because of the difficulty of his zeal, which puts him on the rack. Let others then judge him unhappy in his place because of this appearance of ill fate, as if it had condemned him to such pains; because he will not for that fail to recognize the debt that he has to love, and thank it for having presented to the eyes of his mind an intelligible species, in which, while in this earthly life, enclosed in this prison of flesh, girded by these tendons and nerves, and steadied by these bones, it is allowed to him to contemplate more highly the divinity than if any other species and similitude of it were offered.[1]

The origin and meaning of the expression "heroic love" in Bruno's text, and in particular in this passage of the *Furori,* has not to my knowledge been studied. The vague semantic connotation of the adjective "heroic" in modern use has evidently been accepted as more than sufficient for the understanding of the text. What has not been realized is that, by so doing, we lose precisely the significance that the choice of expression must have had for Bruno—who had by no means invented it, but had received it or, better, diverted it from an ancient and still living tradition.

In fact the expression "heroic love" has a long history that does not refer us, as we might expect, to the bright and luminous world of the heroes, but to the dark and sinister realm of medical pathology and Neoplatonic demonology.[2] The reconstruction of this history constitutes a confirmation of what Aby Warburg had already demonstrated for the history of images, that is, that Western culture develops and transforms itself through a process of "polarization" of the received cultural tradition.[3] This does not mean that there are not creative and revolutionary moments of that history (the history of the expression "heroic love" illustrates just such a moment), but simply that—because every culture is essentially a process of transmission and of *Nachleben* (afterlife)—creation and revolution work in general by "polarizing" what is given by tradition, until arriving, in certain cases, at the complete semantic inversion of these givens. European culture is, despite everything, conservative, and it is conservative precisely to the extent that it is progressive and revolutionary.

If we open a treatise of medieval medicine to the section devoted to cerebral pathology, after the chapters given over to mania and melancholy, we almost inevitably happen upon the *rubric de amore qui hereos dicitur* (or *de amore heroico*). The *Lilium medicale* of Bernard Gordonio, professor at Montpellier about 1285, describes the disease in these terms:

> The disease called *hereos* is a melancholy suffering caused by love for a woman.
>
> *Cause*. The cause of this affliction is a corruption of the estimative faculty (of discernment) by means of a form and a figure that remains strongly impressed in it. When someone is seized by love for a woman, he strongly conceives of her form, her figure, and manner, because he thinks and believes that she is the most beautiful, the most venerable, the most extraordinary, and most endowed in body and soul; and because he ardently desires her, without measure or hesitation, thinking that if he could satisfy his desire, he would reach his blessedness and his happiness. And so altered is the judgment of his reason, that it continually imagines the form of the lady and abandons all of its activities, such that, if someone speaks to him, he scarcely manages to understand. And as he is in incessant meditation, his condition comes to be defined as a melancholy affliction. And it is called *hereos* because lords and nobles, because of the abundance of their delights, habitually fell prey to this malady, and as happiness is the perfection of love, so *hereos* is the perfection of love.
>
> The power of discernment, which is the highest of the sensitive powers, commands the imaginative and the concupiscible; the concupiscible in turn the irascible, and the irascible that power that moves the muscles. Because of this the whole body then [when afflicted

with *hereos*] moves without any rational order and runs night and day
from street to street without heeding heat and cold and all dangers . . .

Signs. The symptoms [of this disease] are the omission of all sleep,
food, and drink; and the whole body weakens, except for the eyes. The
sufferers have profound and hidden imaginings with sorrowful sighs;
and if they hear songs about separations caused by love, immediately
they begin to weep and become saddened; if on the other hand they hear
of loves reestablished, they immediately laugh and sing. Their pulse is
variable and disordered; but it becomes rapid, frequent, and strong if the
lady they love is named or if she passes in front of them . . .

Prognosis. The prognosis is that if they are not cured they fall into
mania or die.

Cure. The sufferer either obeys reason or does not. In the first case
he should be removed from that false imagination at the hands of a
man whom he fears and he should be made ashamed by words and
admonitions showing him the dangers of the world, of judgment day,
and the joys of paradise. In case he should not obey reason, if he is a
young man on whom the whip may still be used, he should be
frequently and strongly flogged until he is all beaten and bruised; then
he should be told something very sad, so that the greater sorrow will
obscure the lesser. Or he should be told something very pleasing, for
example that he has been made seneschal or bailiff or that he has been
assigned a large benefice . . . Then he should be kept busy with some
necessary activity . . . and he should be taken to distant places so that
he should see various and diverse things . . . Then he should be
encouraged to love many women, such that by love for one he will be
distracted from his love for the other, as Ovid says: I urge you to have
two lovers, or even more if possible. It is also helpful to change habits
and to meet with friends, to go to places where there are flowering
meadows, hills, woods, scents, and beautiful things to see, birdsong and
instrumental music . . . finally, if there is no other remedy, we request
the help and advice of old women, so that she [the beloved] should be
defamed and dishonored . . . Find therefore a hideous old woman with
big teeth and a beard, with an ugly and vile dress and who carries under
her lap a cloth soiled with menses; in the presence of the lady, let the
old woman begin to mar the lady's blouse saying that she is scabby and
a drunkard, that she wets her bed, that she is epileptic and shameless,
that in her body there are enormous growths full of stench and other
disgusting things about which old women are well informed. If he is not
persuaded by this, then the old woman should suddenly bring forth the
soiled cloth in front of his face, crying out: thus is your ladyfriend,
thus. And if by this he is not persuaded to abandon her, then he is not a
man, but an incarnate devil.[4]

The attentive reader will have immediately noticed that Gordonio's description contains nearly all the elements of the erotic theory that we have attempted

to reconstruct in the preceding pages. Above all the phantasmatic aspect of the amorous experience, which was one of the most tenacious acquisitions of the love-psychology of the poets, is here explicitly reconfirmed. The disease of *hereos* is in fact located by Gordonio in the imagination, or rather, more precisely, in the *estimativa*,[5] which, in the psychology of Avicenna, is the faculty situated at the summit of the middle cavity of the brain that apprehends the insensible intentions in sensible objects and judges their goodness or evil, suitability or unsuitability. This topological specification is not without import, because it is precisely this estimative or evaluative faculty [defined as "la virtù che consiglia / e de l'assenso de' tener la soglia" (the power that advises / and guards the threshold of consent)] that Dante evoked to establish the liberty and responsibility of the love experience in the passage of the *Purgatorio* (XVIII.35-36) where, in the mouth of Virgil, Dante patently repudiates "la gente che'avvera / ciascun amor in sé laudabil cosa" (the people who confirm / every love as praiseworthy in itself). In Dante's sonnet "Per quella via che la bellezza corre" (Along that way which beauty runs) the tower that opens when the soul consents and that is instead closed before the joyful phantasm of Lisetta, alludes to this faculty, whose seat is in that same part "dove amore alberga" (where love resides).

According to the physicians, the eclipse of this faculty sets in motion the pathology of *amor hereos*. The error of the estimative faculty (commanding the imagination, which is, in its turn, placed above the other powers) releases desire,[6] and desire drives imagination and memory to turn obsessively around the phantasm that impresses itself ever more strongly, in a vicious circle in whose orbit Eros comes to assume the dark saturnine mask of the melancholic pathology. The exalted overestimation of the object of love, which is among the most characteristic intuitions of the love poets, finds thus its prosaic explanation precisely in the defect of the estimative power ("he thinks and believes that she is the most beautiful, the most venerable, the most extraordinary, and most endowed in body and soul"). But even more surprising is finding *locus amoenus,* which is perhaps the most persistent and exemplary *topos* of Provençal lyric, among the remedies the physicians most insistently recommended for curing *amor hereos*. "It is beneficial," wrote the physician Valesco of Taranta, "to walk through meadows, orchards, and woods with friends and companions, in flowering gardens where birds sing and nightingales are heard . . . " The conjunction of the *locus amoenus* with the supreme exaltation of amorous *joi* (joy, pleasure) so characteristic of the poetry of the troubadours, appears in this light as a kind of self-conscious reversal of, and defiant challenge to, the remedies of love recommended by the physicians. Perhaps by way of an analogous denial of the therapeutic pretenses of the physicians ("he should be told something very pleasing, for example that he has been made seneschal or bailiff or that he has been assigned a large benefice"), the poets did not tire of repeating that no circumstances, not even those of the emperor, compare with the joy of love.

Even the extravagant cure recommended by Gordonio, that of the ugly crone who, through the grotesque contrast of her person, dims and extinguishes the effects of the overestimation of the love object, is not without its counterpart in the love poetry. Specifically, it permits us to read in a new way Cavalcanti's sonnet "Guarda, Manetto, quella scrignutuzza" (Come, Manetto, look upon this scarecrow), whose playful intent is clarified precisely in reference to an absolutely serious medical therapy. The radical treatment Guido suggests to Manetto is in fact precisely that proposed by the doctor of Montpellier: the repugnant sight of the "little scarecrow" next to the "lovely noble lady" will have the inevitable effect of curing with a guffaw any love malady or melancholic disease whatsoever ("you wouldn't be in such a fierce rage / or be so anguished because of love / or so wrapped up in melancholy"). "And if by this he is not persuaded to abandon her," the voice of Gordonio's clinical experience disconsolately concludes, "then he is not a man, but an incarnate devil."

In the pathology of *amor hereos* we also find the second essential element of the theory of love, that is, its pneumatic character. Arnaldo of Villanova, in the *De amore qui heroycus nominatur* (Of the love called heroic), which is perhaps the fullest treatment of the subject, traced the cause of the error of the estimative power to a defect not of the faculty itself, but to its instrument, that is, to the spirits that flow "copious and almost boiling" in the central cavity of the brain, which does not succeed in cooling them, "such that they confuse the judgment and, as it were inebriating them, deceive men and lead them astray."[7] Precisely because of this excess of heat and dryness, the forward cell of the brain, in which the imagination resides, dries out and retains more strongly the phantasm that torments the erotic passion. The whole complex mechanism of sighs, so ceremoniously presented in the experience of the poets, finds its detailed pneumatic explanation in the works of the physicians.[8]

If what we have said is true, we can affirm that something similar to the love experience as the poets would come to understand and describe it made its appearance in Western culture, in a pathological form, as early as the ninth century in the sections on cerebral diseases found in medical treatises. We find almost all the elements that characterize the noble love of the poets in the gloomy syndrome "similar to melancholy" that the physicians outlined under the rubric of *amor hereos,* but with a negative connotation. This means that the reevaluation of love effected by the poets beginning in the twelfth century did not arise from a rediscovery of the "high" conception of Eros that the *Phaedrus* and the *Symposium* had bequeathed to the Western philosophical tradition, but from a polarization of the mortal "heroic" disease of the medical tradition that, in the encounter with what Warburg would have called the "selective will" of the period, underwent a radical semantic reversal. Just as, two centuries later, the humanists, following a tradition whose emblem has forever fixed itself on the winged genius of Dürer's *Melencolia,* modeled the physiognomy of their loftiest human ideal, the contemplative man, on the grim saturnine features of what an ancient medical tradition considered the most wretched of temperaments, so too the poets fashioned what would become the noblest spiritual experience of modern European man in the mold of a mortal illness of the imagination. Indeed, given the substantial affinity between melancholy and *amor hereos,* we can say that only because the poets, beginning in the twelfth century, enacted an audacious and radical reversal of the medical theory of heroic love was it possible for the humanists, two centuries later, to proceed with their own reassessment of the saturnine temperament.

Thus what had been, in Plato, a clear opposition between two "Loves" (which had a distinct genealogy going back to two Venuses, the celestial and the vulgar, or *pandemia*) became in the Western tradition a single Eros strongly polarized in the lacerating tendencies between two oppositely valued extremes. The Freudian idea of the libido, with its essentially unitary connotation but which may orient itself in opposing directions, appears in this perspective as a late but legitimate descendant of the medieval idea of love. And it is to the fact that the highest moral ideal is indivisible from a "low" and phantasmatic experience, that we likely owe the ambiguous character of every modern Western conception of happiness, in contrast to the Greek contemplative ideal of *theoria* as *teleia eudaimonia* (perfect happiness), still alive in the medieval concept of the separated intellect. That, at least from the twelfth century onward, the idea of happiness should appear intertwined with the notion of the restoration of the "sweet play" of Edenic innocence—that happiness should be, in other words, inseparable from the project of a redemption and a fulfillment of the corporeal Eros—is the specific trait (even if rarely perceived as such) of the modern Western conception of happiness. This is in accordance with a code that, formulated already in Dante's figure of Matelda, reappears in the Renaissance topic of the ecstatic dancing "nymph" and has its final symbolic offshoots in the *Fêtes galantes* of Watteau and the bathers of Cézanne. Although remote from its originary impulse, the lucid poetic project of love as fulfillment and restoration of Edenic innocence still survives unconsciously in the contemporary aspiration to a liberation of sexuality as the condition of happiness.

If it is true that, in the history of culture, the great innovations are frequently effected departing from elements received from tradition, it is equally true that the "polarizations" through which a period affirms its own novelty with respect to the past are, in general, rendered possible by the preexistence, in the bosom of the inheritance transmitted by tradition, as a potential tension, which comes to be reactualized and polarized in its encounter with the new epoch. (Aby Warburg used to speak, in this connection, of cultural symbols as "dynamograms" or electric condensers that transmit an electric charge in all its tension, but without characterizing it semantically as positive or negative.) Thus the reassessment of melancholy was certainly one of the means through which humanism affirmed its own new attitude toward the world. That reassessment, however, was indubitably made possible by the existence, in the classical concept of the black bile, of an ambiguity that was already present in Aristotle (whose *Problems* states that those who have the most genius belong to this most wretched of temperaments). The continuity of this ambiguity is attested by, among other things, the double polarity of *tristitia-acedia* in the patristic tradition. The pathological figure of *amor hereos* also contains in itself such a potential tension. In this case, however, the tension reflects an origin extraneous to the medical orbit in the strict sense that, through the demonological classification of cosmic theurgy, reconnects itself with Neoplatonic thought. Thus, despite everything, the dark figure of love as a disease (and, through it, the poetic theory of love) reattaches itself, albeit by oblique and mediated ways, to the inheritance of the philosopher who had made of love the highest initiatory experience of the soul. Curiously, this connection concerns not celestial love, but its homonym on the other side, that "love of the diseased part" of which the physician Eurixymachus spoke in the *Symposium*.[9]

The proof of this origin is furnished by the very name of *amor hereos*. Lowes claims that the name *hereos* derives from a mistaken Latin transcription of the Greek *eros*, of which he thinks he discerns traces in a Latin manuscript of the sixth century containing a highly inaccurate transcription of the *Synopsis* by the Greek physician Oribasius. Lowes's hypothesis, beyond its failure to explain the singularly bilingual term *amor hereos*, also disregards the explicit affirmations of the medical sources that invariably understand the term *hereos* through its association with *herus* (*erus*) or *heros*. The adjective *heroycus* found, among other places, in Arnaldo of Villanova, can only derive from this term. The semantic convergence of love and the hero, already found in an imaginary etymology from Plato's *Cratylus*, where Socrates playfully derives the word hero (*hērōs*) from love (*erōs*) "because the heroes are generated by Eros,"[10] has been plausibly fulfilled in the context of a Neoplatonic rebirth of the popular cult of heroes and of theurgic demonology. The "spirits of the deceased" linked to ancient local cults,[11] and which the Hippocratic treatise on the sacred malady already listed among the causes of mental sickness, are here inserted in the hierarchy of the superhuman creatures that proceed from the One and that reveal themselves in theurgic practices. The *De mysteriis* of Iamblichus minutely describes what distinguishes the epiphany and influence of heroes with respect to demons and to archons, and Proclus, speaking of the demonic hierarchies ecstatically extended toward the divine, said that "the army of the heroes moves drunken, together with the angels and demons, around beauty."[12] In his commentary on the *Carme aureo* (Golden poem or song) of Pythagoras, Hierocles defined the heroes as "an intermediate race of rational natures who occupy the place after the immortal gods, precede human nature, and conjoin the latter with the former." In the wake of the fantastic etymology of the *Cratylus* (but with a semantic intensification that bears witness to the new role that the heroes played in the Neoplatonic revival), he explained the phrase "illustrious heroes" (*agathoi heroes*) of the Pythagorean poem in the following manner: "For good reason they are called *illustrious heroes*, in that they are good (*agathoi*) and luminous (*photeinoi*) and never touched by vice or forgetfulness; heroes (*heroes*) in that they are loves (*eroes*) and lovers (*erotes*), as it were the dialectical beloved ones and lovers of god, who take us from this earthly sojourn and elevate us to the divine city."[13] From this point of view, the heroes were identified by Hierocles with the angels of Hebrew and Christian theology: "Sometimes they are also called angels, in that they manifest and announce to us the rules of the blessed life." This passage shows that the juxtaposition of the hero and love was originally made in a positive constellation of ideas, and that only through a lengthy historical process, which includes the encounter with theurgic magic and the conflict with Christianity, does "hero-eros" acquire the negative valuation that survives as sole component in the medical doctrine of *amor hereos*.

The passage of the *Epinomis* where Plato, in classifying five species of living things and the elements corresponding to them (fire, ether, air, water, earth), named an intermediate species between the ethereal demons and the earthly creatures probably influenced the construction of the Neoplatonic hierarchy of demons. The passage is as follows:

> After them and below them, come in order the daemons and the creatures of the air (*aerion genos*), who hold the third and midmost rank, doing the office of interpreters, and should be peculiarly honored in our prayers that they may transmit comfortable messages. Both sorts of creature, those of aether and those of air, who hold the rank next to them, we shall say, are wholly transparent; however close they are to us, they go undiscerned. Being, however, of a kind that is quick to learn and of retentive memory, they read all our thoughts and regard the good and noble with signal favor, but the very evil with deep aversion. For *they* are not exempt from feeling pain, whereas a god who enjoys the fullness of deity is clearly above both pain and pleasure, though possessed of all-embracing wisdom and knowledge. The universe being thus full throughout of living creatures, they all, so we shall say, act as interpreters, and interpreters of all things, to one another and to the highest gods, seeing that the middle ranks of creatures can flit so lightly over the earth and the whole universe. [*Epinomis,* 984e-985b, in *The Collected Dialogues of Plato,* ed. E. Hamilton and H. Cairns (Princeton: Princeton University Press, 1961), 1526-27]

The mediating function that the *Epinomis* assigns to the aerial demons corresponds perfectly to what in the *Symposium* (202e) is attributed, using almost the same words, to love ("Possessing what power?" . . . "Interpreting and transporting human things to the gods . . . ").[14] It is presumably this correspondence that has facilitated the movement toward a progressive identification of love and the aerial demon. A passage of Chalcidius (who transmitted to the Middle Ages the demonology of the *Epinomis*) says of the aerial demon: "In that it is closer to the earth, it is the most suitable to the passions of the affections."[15] In Apuleius (who, because of the polemic with Augustine, was quite familiar to Christian thinkers), although on the one hand the mediating function of the demons and their identification with the aerial element are precisely reaffirmed, on the other hand Love is explicitly classified among the aerial demons and in fact occupies an eminent position among them: "There is . . . a higher and more august kind of demons, who, freed from the corporeal chains and bonds, are charged with a determinate power: among these are Sleep and Love . . . "[16]

In Psellus, a father of the church and late Neoplatonic philosopher, the negative polarity of demonology, already present with an impressive wealth of detail in Porphyry's *De abstinentia* (where, among other things, the elaboration of love potions is put under the influence of malefic powers), appears already fused with the doctrine of the phantastic spirit as the vehicle of fascination and falling in love. At the same time there is an accentuation of the obscure and sinister character of the aerial demon, who now becomes the specific agent of the erotic pathology, of its phantasms and ravings. According to this theory, the aerial demon (known simply as "aerial") acts on the human phantastic spirit and

> as air in the presence of light, assuming form and color, transmits these to those bodies that are by nature disposed to receive them (as in the case of mirrors), so too the bodies of the demons, taking from the interior phantastic essence the shapes, colors, and the forms they wish, transmit them to our spirit, suggesting to us actions and thoughts and exciting in us forms and memories. They thus evoke images of pleasures and of passions in both the sleeping and the waking and frequently arouse our loins and inspire us to unhealthy and evil loves.

The identification of the aerial demon and Eros is so complete that Psellus explicitly affirmed that the aerial demons shoot "fiery arrows" that are highly reminiscent of the fiery spiritual darts of the god of love.[17]

It is not easy to specify at what moment the "aerial demon" of the *Epinomis,* of Chalcidius, and of Psellus became identified with the "hero" resuscitated by the ancient popular cults. Certainly the heroes, according to a tradition that for Diogenes Laertius goes back as far as Pythagoras, already offer all the characteristics of aerial demonicity: they dwell in the air and influence men by inspiring them with signs indicating disease and health.[18] The identification with the aerial demon is attested by an etymology whose origin is probably Stoic and which is frequently found in the fathers of the church from Augustine on. In book 10, chapter 21 of the *De civitate Dei* (The city of God), which contains a passionate refutation of Neoplatonic theurgy, Augustine defined the Christian martyrs as "nostros heroas" (our heroes):

> "Hero" is said to be derived from the name of Juno. The Greek name of Juno is Hera, and that is why one or another of her sons was called Heros, according to Greek legend. This myth evidently signifies, though in cryptic fashion, that Juno is assigned the power over the air . . . Our martyrs, in contrast, would be called "heroes" if (as I said) the usage of the Church allowed it, not because of any association with the

demons in the air, but as the conquerors of those demons, that is, of the "powers of the air." [19]

This triple semantic patrimony Eros-hero-aerial demon, blending itself with an ancient medical theory (of which there are already traces in Plutarch and Apuleius)[20] that conceived of love as a disease, emerges in the sinister and "demoniac" image of an Eros that Plutarch, outside of any Christian influence, already described as a small monster equipped with fangs and claws.[21] Thus in the context of Neoplatonic tradition a "low" figure of Eros-hero-aerial demon had already taken shape, which undermined men by inspiring in them insane passions. This figure, joined with the ancient Hippocratic belief that saw in the heroes a cause of mental illness, is probably the source, if not the very formulation *amor hereos* of the medical tradition, then at least of its interpretation as *amor heroycus,* heroic love.[22] Heroic love is not initially the noblest and loftiest love, but the low and dark passion inspired by the hero-aerial demon. Just as the humoral theory of melancholy was linked to the sinister influence of the noonday demon (the reincarnation of Empusa, a figure belonging to the spectral retinue of Hecate, who was also a cause, according to Hippocrates, of nightmares and mental disease), so the medical doctrine of *amor hereos* expressed the pathological and negative polarity of the influences of Eros-hero-aerial demon. This heroic-demoniac figure of Eros, with fangs and claws, must have furnished the iconographic model for that "lowly and mythographic" Cupid that Panofsky thought to be at the origin of the representation of Love with claws in place of feet in the Giottesque allegory of chastity and in the fresco in the castle of Sabbioneta. He attempted to reconstitute its prototype through the illustration of the *Documenti d'amore* of Francesco of Barberino, which shows Love, with claws and with a bow, standing on a galloping horse. Panofsky did not succeed in identifying the model of this curious iconographic type, but he held that it "must have been imagined well before Barberino wrote his treatise, though certainly not before the thirteenth century."[23] In reality, as we have seen, a "demonic" image of Eros had already been fashioned—at least in the literary sources—in late antiquity, within the orbit of Neoplatonic theurgy. This image led Plutarch to attribute fangs and claws to Eros; it also, at a certain point, had been included in the medical theory of *amor hereos*. The origin of the unusual motif of Eros standing on a horse should likely be sought in the context of idolopoietic theurgy, in a passage of Proclus.[24] We must learn to see these obscure and demonic traits behind the noble appearance of the god of love of the poets. Only if it is understood that the theory of love is a bold polarization of "heroic-demonic" love and of love as a disease will it be possible to measure the revolutionary and novel character of a conception of love that despite changes during the passing of seven centuries, is still, with all of its ambiguities and contradictions, substantially ours. Only this proximity to a morbid and demonic experience of the imagination can at least partially explain the medieval discovery of the phantasmatic character of the process of love, which had remained so peculiarly obscured in the classical tradition. If, instead, a "high" model (for example, Platonizing Christian mysticism, and beyond that, the Platonic theory of celestial love) is posited as an origin, then we cannot understand what is unique and specific in the discovery of the poets. It should not be forgotten, of course, that a positive polarity was potentially implicit, as we have seen, in the same cultural tradition in which the "lowly" image of Eros had been forming, from Neoplatonic theurgy to pneumo-phantasmology. Just as Neoplatonic phantasmatic theurgy had certainly contributed to the formation of erotic soteriology, so too the reevaluation of the "phantastic spirit," achieved in the alchemical crucible in which Neoplatonism joined itself in fertile union to Christian thought, has undoubtedly influenced the poetic reevaluation of love. In fact the positive polarization of Eros coincides in the poets with the decline of its phantasmatic character. If the physicians suggested coitus as the principal cure for *amor hereos* and recommended whatever might withdraw the patient from his or her "false imagination," the love of the poets was instead rigorously and obsessively maintained within the phantasmatic circle. Thus the "mortal malady" of the imagination must be traversed completely, without avoiding or skipping, because, along with lethal danger, it also contains the ultimate possibility of salvation. From this point of view, Narcissus and Pygmalion appear as the two extreme emblems between which is situated a spiritual experience whose crucial problem can be formulated in the following questions: How can one recover from *amor hereos* without transgressing beyond the phantasmatic circle? How can one appropriate the unappropriable object of love (that is, of the phantasm) without ending up like Narcissus (who succumbs to his own love for an *ymage*) or like Pygmalion (who loved a lifeless image)? How, that is, can Eros find its own place between Narcissus and Pygmalion?

Notes

1. G. Bruno, *De gli eroici furori*, part I, dialogue 3, in G. Bruno, *Opere italiane*, vol. 2 (Bari, 1925), 339.

2. J. L. Lowes, "The 'Loveres Maladye of Hereos,' " in *Modern Philology* 11 (April 1914); 491-591, deserves credit for having reconstructed the semantic history of the expression *amor hereos*, with respect to its occurrence in Chaucer's "Knight's Tale." Unfortunately Lowes's study has remained unknown to Romance philologists and Italianists. Nardi, who cites the *De amore heroyco* of Arnaldo of Villanova in his study on "L'amore e i medici medioevali," in *Saggi e note di critica dantesca* (Milano-Napoli, 1964), 238-67, does not question the origin of the expression and betrays his ignorance of Lowes's study.

3. The rediscovery of Goethe's notion of polarity, directed toward a global comprehension of our culture, is among the most fertile legacies that A. Warburg has left to the science of culture. On the concept of polarity in Warburg's work see the passages cited in Ernst H. Gombrich, *A. Warburg: An Intellectual Biography* (London, 1970), 241 and 248. On the thought of Warburg see G. Agamben, "A. Warburg e la scienza senza nome," in *Prospettive settanta* (July-September 1975).

4. The description quoted from Gordonio generally agrees with that of Arnaldo of Villanova (Arnaldi Villanovani, *Praxis medicinalis*, Lugduni, 1586). The most ancient descriptions are perhaps those in the *Pantechne* and the *Viaticum* of Constantine the African (c. 1020-87): the first is a trans-

lation of the *Liber regius* of the Persian physician 'Ali ibn 'Abbas al-Magiusi (known to the Latins as Haly Abbas), and the second is from an Arabic treatise composed in the second half of the tenth century.

5. Arnaldo locates the same source; more generically, other physicians speak of a *corruptio virtutis imaginativae* (corruption of the imaginative power).

6. With profound intuition, medieval psychophysiology made the desire (*vis appetitiva,* appetitive power) depend on the imagination. See Jean de la Rochelle, *Tractatus de divisione multiplici potentiarum animae,* edited by P. Michaud (Paris, 1964): "vis appetitiva et desiderativa, que, cum ymaginatur forma que appetitur aut respuitur, imperat alii virtuti moventi ut moveat . . . " (the appetitive and desiring power, which, when it imagines a form that it desires or rejects, commands the other movable powers that it move). Thus also Arnaldo of Villanova in his *De coitu*: "Tria autem sunt in coitu: appetitus ex cogitatione phantastica ortus, spiritus et humor" (There are three things in coitus: appetite born from phantastic contemplation, spirit, and humor).

7. Arnaldo of Villanova, *De amore qui heroycus nominatur,* chap. 2, in Arnaldi Villanovani, *Praxis medicinalis.*

8. Arnaldo continued, in the same chapter: "Similiter, et in absentia rei desideratae tristatur et cum ad comprehensum, diu cordis recreatione copiosus aer attractus, forti spiritu cum vaporibus diu praefocatis interius expellatur, oritur in eisdem alta suspiriorum emissio" (Similarly, in the absence of the thing desired one is saddened; and as, for the sake of the embrace, copious air is attracted for the refreshment of the heart, that by means of the strong spirit with long heated vapors it should be more deeply expelled, a deep emission of sighs is also born from them).

9. *Symposium,* 186b.

10. *Cratylus,* 398c-e.

11. On the cult of the heroes, the information provided by E. Rohde is still useful; see *Psyche* [Freiburg im Breisgau, 1890-94; English translation, *Psyche: The Cult of Souls and the Belief in Immortality among the Greeks* (New York: Harcourt, Brace, 1925)]. On the heroes as causing mental diseases, see Hippocratis, *De morbo sacro,* book 1, chap. 6, 360, and the observations of E. R. Dodds, *The Greeks and the Irrational* (Berkeley/Los Angeles, 1951), 72.

12. Iamblichus, *Les mystères,* II.6 and passim; Proclus, *In Platonicum Alcibiadem de anima atque daemone,* in aedibus Aldi, Venetiis, 1516 (Latin translation by Marsilio Ficino).

13. Hieroclis *Commentarium in Aureum carmen* III 2.

14. English translation from *Symposium* in *Plato in Twelve Volumes,* vol. 3 (Cambridge: Harvard University Press, 1979), 179.

15. *Timaeus Platonis sive de universitate,* 97.

16. Apulei Madaurensis platonici, *Liber de deo Socratis* (Amsterdam, 1662), 336.

17. Psellus, *De daemonibus,* Latin translation by Marsilio Ficino, in aedibus Aldi, (Venetiis, 1516), 51.

18. Diogenes Laertius, VIII 32.

19. English translation by H. Bettenson (Penguin, 1972), 401.

20. In a fragment of the lost treatise *On Love* (Stobaeus, IV 20.67), Plutarch wrote: "According to some love is a disease, according to others a desire, friendship, madness . . . " Apuleius, in the *De philosophia morali,* spoke of an "Amor teterrimus" (most loathsome love) as an "aegritudo corporalis" (bodily sickness).

21. Plutarch (in Stobaeus, IV 20.68): "Which are the teeth and the talons of love? Suspicion, jealousy . . . "

22. It is worth noting, among the possible explanations of the term *hereos,* that in the *Chaldean Oracles* the aerial demon appears with the spelling *eerios.* See *Oracles chaldaiques,* critical text and translation by E. Des Places (Paris, 1971), fragments 91 and 216, and Ruth Majercik, *Julianne, the Theurgist: The Chaldean Oracles—Text, Translation, and Commentary* (London/New York: Brill, 1989).

23. E. Panofsky, *Studies in Iconology: Humanistic Themes in the Art of the Renaissance* (New

York: Harper and Row, 1972), 119.

24. *In Platonis rem publicam*, I, p. 111, Kroll; *Oracles chaldaiques,* fragment 146: "The invocation said, you will see a fire similar to a boy who rushes by and leaps on the waves of the air; or verily a fire without form from which a voice breaks; or an abundant light that will wind itself shrieking on the ground; or a horse more resplendent than the light; or again *a burning boy who rides on the swift back of a horse, covered in gold or else naked, or with a bow in his hand and his feet on the horse's back."* If this hypothesis were valid, it would suggest a possible connection between the theory of love and the idolopoietic Neoplatonic theurgy and would place in a new light the "idolatric" character that love, insofar as it is a phantasmatic process, possesses in medieval culture. That love was brought into proximity with idolatry is testified, in addition to the frequent references of the poets to Narcissus and Pygmalion that we have seen, by the representations of lovers as idolaters (see, for example, in figure 23 the birth salver attributed to the Master of St. Martin in the Louvre, which shows some celebrated lovers in the act of adoring a winged and naked female figure, at whose sides stand two lovers with talons). It is worth pointing out that idolatry (or better, idololatry) did not in the late Middle Ages properly designate the adoration of material images, but rather that of mental images. See Peter Lombard, *In epistolam I ad Corinthios,* in *Patrologia latina,* 191, 1602: "Idolum enim hic appellat speciem quam non vidit oculus, sed animum sibi fingit" (here he calls an idol an image not seen by the eye, but fashioned for itself by the mind); also *Commentarius in Psalmum LXXIX,* in ibid., 191, 772: "Quod enim quisque cupit et veneratur, hoc illi deus est . . . Illi autem cogitant recentem deum, et alia huiusmodi fingunt in corde; et ita ipsi sunt templa simulacrorum . . ." (What each desires and venerates, this is a god to him . . . They, however, conceive of a recently [made] god, and differently from the former manner they fashion [it] in the heart; and so they themselves are the temples of idols). As to the Neoplatonic theurgy (which the cited passage from Proclus refers to), this was precisely a mystical practice founded on the hallucinatory evocation of phantasms or mental images. The numerous references in Gnostic texts to the "image" and to the union with the "image" in the "nuptial chamber" presumably allude to a mystical-phantasmatic practice of analogous type. The poetic theory of love, situated on such a basis, would reveal all of its soteriological implications. On the persistence of such "idolatric" practices in the circle of Marsilio Ficino, see D. P. Walker, *Spiritual and Demonic Magic from Ficino to Campanella* (London: Warburg Institute, 1958).

Chapter 16
The "Joy That Never Ends"

> E io a lui: «I' mi son un che, quando
> Amor mi spira, noto, e a quel modo
> ch'e' ditta dentro vo significando».

> [And I to him: "I am one who, when
> Love inspires me, takes note, and in the manner
> that he dictates within I go signifying."]

This tercet of the *Purgatorio* (XXIV.52-54) has been so often cited and commented on that any attempt to make it speak in a new way may rightly appear foolhardy. Yet if it is placed against the background of what we have attempted to bring to light in the preceding chapters, the verses shed their metaphoric character and no longer appear merely as a scarcely credible anticipation of the Romantic theory of immediate expression or of the modern poetics of the objectification of feelings, but rather as a rigorous development of the pneumatological doctrine in a concept of the poetic sign that is in fact the keystone of the entire pneumophantastic edifice.

The exegesis of this passage has generally been dominated by the semantic suggestion implicit in the interpretation of the expression *"Amor mi spira"* according to the vague metaphorical meaning of the verb *ispirare* (to inspire) in modern usage as "to infuse or instill." This expression should instead be restored to the context of a pneumatological culture in which the metaphorical sense was not yet divided from the proper one. In the context of pneumatic psychophysiology, it would be sufficiently clear from the preceding chapters that we can understand Dante's use of the Italian verb *spirare* here by its more common

124

meaning, "to breathe." Love "breathes" (*spira*) because it is essentially and properly a "spiritual motion" (to use Dante's own expression), just as the word "spirit" (*spirito*), in Dante's Stilnovist vocabulary, should always be understood in reference to a culture that immediately perceived in the term the entire gamut of pneumatic (or rather, pneumo-phantasmatic) resonances.

Nevertheless, in the passage at hand, Dante undoubtedly links the (in)spiration of love to a theory of the linguistic sign: indeed he defines his own making of poetry as the notation and signification of the dictation of inspiring love. How can the (in)spiration of love, that is, the pneumo-phantasmatic character of the process of love, be the foundation of a theory of poetic language? The answer to this question presupposes the reconstruction of a chapter of medieval semiology that is an integral part of the theory of the "phantastic spirit" and that constitutes perhaps the most original contribution brought by the poets of the *stil nuovo* to that theory.

The definition of language as a sign is not, as is well known, a discovery of modern semiology. Before its formulation by the thinkers of the Stoa, it was already implicit in the Aristotelian definition of the human voice as *semantikos psophos*, "significant sound." We read in the *De anima:* "Not every sound produced by the animal is voice (a sound can be produced with the tongue, or even coughing), but it is necessary that whoever makes the air vibrate should be animate and have phantasms; the voice is in fact a significant sound and not only air that is breathed . . . " (4206). The "semantic" character of human language is thus explained by Aristotle in terms of the psychological theory that we know, with the presence of a mental image or phantasm, so that, if we wish to transcribe into Aristotelian terms the algorithm now usually used to represent the notion of sign (S/s, where s is the signifier and S the signified), it would be configured as follows: P/s, where s is sound and P the phantasm.

The Aristotelian definition of language is reiterated in a passage of the *De interpretatione* that has exercised so decisive an influence on medieval thought that it may be said that all of medieval semiology developed as a commentary upon it. In Boethius's Latin translation the passage reads as follows: "sunt ea, quae sunt in voce, earum quae sunt in anima passionum, notae" (those things that are in the voice are the signs of the passions in the soul). The expression "passions in the soul" would seem to refer, according to the definition of the *De anima,* to the images of the phantasy, but if we keep in mind the ambiguous status of the phantasy in Aristotle's thought, suspended in the no-man's-land between sensation and intellection, it will not surprise us that disputes regarding the precise meaning of the words "passions in the soul" were quick to flare up. In his commentary on the *De interpretatione* Boethius discussed these disputes, writing that "some hold that the words signify the sensations, others, the phantasms." Following an intellectualistic tradition that would later characterize the scholastic theory of language, he polemicized at length with the defenders of this interpretation, attempting to demonstrate that by "passions in the soul" Aristotle intended neither the sensations nor the phantasms, but the intellections: "Nouns and verbs do not signify something imperfect, but perfect: therefore Aristotle rightly affirms that everything concerning nouns and verbs is not the sign of sensations or imaginations, but only the qualities of the intelligibles."[1]

This interpretation of the Aristotelian theory of language in scholastic semiology is perfectly exemplified in the *De interpretatione* of Albertus Magnus. Here the theory of the sign is articulated according to the gradations of the psychological process by now familiar to us:

> The external object impresses itself and acts in some way on the soul
> and inflicts on it a passion, since the soul is passive and receptive with
> respect to the mind and the intellect. And, since the intellect undergoes
> and receives from the external thing in such a way, the forms and the
> intentions produced in the soul from things are called passions. And since
> articulated words cannot be formed if not by that which understands and
> conceives the external object and receives the passion according to the
> form of the thing known, the words are brought into being by the
> intellect: the intellect does not constitute the articulated word except to
> signify the species of the thing and the passion that it conceives within
> itself from the thing . . . Thus what is in the word, constituted by the
> intellect to signify, is a notation of the passions received in the soul
> from things; the thing in fact generates its species in the soul, and the
> intellect, informed of this species, institutes the word. Because of this
> the passion of the soul is a species of the thing; and the signifying word
> instituted by the intellect, when thus informed, expresses the notation of
> the passion which is in the soul. So the same word becomes the sign
> and the similitude of the thing in he who hears it. Therefore that which
> is the notation of the passion on the lips of the speaker, is the sign and
> the similitude of the things in the ears of the listener. In this way words
> are the notations of the passions that are in the soul.[2]

The intellectualistic stamp that had led Boethius to exclude the phantasm from the sphere of the signified, is emphasized by Albert to the point of denying the relevance, for a theory of the linguistic sign, of the "passions of the mind" in the sense that we give this expression today. Albert in fact distinguished two senses of the term "passion":

> In one sense we call passion the form that the object impresses on the
> passive power, whether it be sensible or intelligible, as the visible object
> inflicts a passion on the sense and the intelligible object on the possible
> intellect. In another sense we call passion a motion of the soul by which
> it is moved through the body and manifests its motion with the
> movements of the spirit and the blood, as one says the passion of wrath,
> the passion of concupiscence, the passions of joy, sadness, mercy, fear,
> and other things of the kind; in that sense in which we say, in other
> words, to suffer what is moved according to the diastole and systole of

the heart: but it is not in this sense that we are here speaking of passion.[3]

Against the background of this theory of the linguistic sign we should situate what Dante says in the tercet of the *Purgatorio* that we are examining. From this point of view, his words do not appear to contain at first glance any new elements: "I take note" and "I go signifying" in fact correspond precisely to the scholastic definition of language as notation and sign of a passion of the soul. But a more attentive examination reveals a radical divergence from the scholastic definition. The scholastic interpretation, as we have seen, identified the *passio animae* (passion of the soul) with the *species intelligibilis* (intelligible species) and affirmed the intellectual origin of linguistic signs, explicitly excluding the *motus spirituum* (movements of the spirit)—wrath, desire, joy, and so on—from the orbit of the theory of language. Dante instead characterized poetic expression precisely as the dictation of an inspiring love. In doing so, however, he did not express an individual intuition or an art of poetry, but, by situating himself outside of scholastic semiology, reinserted the theory of language into that pneumophantastic doctrine that we have seen play such an essential part in the love lyric.

In the context of this theory, the voice appeared from the outset as a pneumatic current originating in the heart, which, passing through the larynx, excited the motion of the tongue. In his *De Hippocritis et Platonis placitis,* Galen dwelled at length on the physiology of the human voice, and informs us in minute detail of the dispute dividing those who argued that the vocal pneuma originated in the heart from those who placed its origin instead in the brain.[4] If we keep in mind the pneumatic nature of the phantasm (the "phantastic spirit") that is, at once, the origin and the object of the erotic desire, defined, in its turn, as a "spiritual motion," the connection of language with the (in)spiration of love will once again appear a coherent and complex doctrine, one that is at the same time a physiology, a doctrine of the "beatitude of love" and a theory of the poetic sign. This explains why the link of the (in)spiration of love with poetic language is affirmed not only in Dante, but should be a commonplace among the love poets, for whom the voice, moreover, is explicitly said to proceed from the heart.[5] We can thus easily understand why, in the works of Cavalcanti, it is the "spirits" who speak, and why Cino, in a sonnet that seems to take up and refine Dante's program, could say of love that "dal suo spirito procede / che parla in me, ciò ch'io dico rimando" (from its spirit proceeds / that speaks in me, what I say in rhyme).[6]

The pneumatic doctrine that posited the spirit as *quid medium* between soul and body and thus attempted to fill in the metaphysical fracture between visible and invisible, corporeal and incorporeal, appearance and essence, and to make speakable and understandable "the union of these two substances" that, in the words of William of St. Thierry, "God has surrounded with mystery," was redirected by the love poets. They situated poetic language, insofar as its production is a pneumatic activity, in the mediating position that had belonged to "spirit." By conceiving of poetry as the dictation of inspiring love, they thus came to confer on it the highest status that could be attributed to it, situating the space of the poem, in the imaginary Jacob's ladder of Hugh of St. Victor, at the extreme limit of the corporeal and incorporeal, sensible signifier and rational signification, where, just as the phantasy does for Hugh, poetry "informs the corporeal spirit and comes into contact with the rational spirit."[7]

Eros and poetry, desire and poetic sign are thus linked and involved through their common participation in a pneumatic circle within which the poetic sign, as it arises from the spirit of the heart, can immediately adhere both to the dictation of that "spiritual motion" that is love, and to its object, the phantasm impressed in the phantastic spirits. In this way, the poets freed themselves from the "primordial positing of the signified and the signifier as two orders distinguished and separated by a barrier resisting signification," which, in its fidelity to the original metaphysical positing of the word as "signifying sound," governs every Western conception of the sign.[8] The pneumatic link, uniting phantasm, word, and desire, opens a space in which the poetic sign appears as the sole enclosure offered to the fulfillment of love and erotic desire in their roles as the foundations and meaning of poetry, in a circulation whose utopian topology can be imperfectly exemplified in the following diagram:

This can also be displayed as a Borromean knot where desire and word are pulled together by the phantasm:

The inclusion of the phantasm and desire in language is the essential condition in order that poetry can be conceived as *joi d'amor* (joy of love, love's joy). Poetry is then properly *joi d'amor* because it is the *stantia* (chamber) in which the beatitude of love is celebrated.[9] Dante expressed this singular mutual implication of Eros and poetic language with his usual clarity when he affirmed, in a fundamental passage of the *Vita Nuova,* that the goal and the beatitude of his love are to be found in "those words that praise my lady" (XVIII 6). If Dante could say that the fulfillment of love lies in the poetic word and, at the same time, conceive of poetry as love's (in)spiring dictation, it is because this hermeneutic circle contains the most essential truth of the *dolce stil nuova*—which, in distinguishing itself from scholastic semiology, appears as the supreme achievement of pneumo-phantasmology.

In this way the poetic word was presented as the site where the fracture between desire and its unattainable object (which medieval psychology, with its profound intuition, had expressed through its identification of Eros with the youth "who so much loved his shadow, that he died") is healed, and the mortal "heroic" disease, through which love assumes the saturnine mask of melancholic delirium, celebrates its rescue and ennoblement. That *versuum recitatio* (recitation of verses) and *cantus seu instrumentorum suavitas* (sweetness of song or instruments) that the physicians advised as remedies for *amor hereos* thus became the instruments of a superior spiritual "healing." In poetic practice, understood as the signification of the (in)spiration of love, Narcissus in fact succeeds in obtaining his own image and in satisfying his *fol amour* in a circle where the phantasm generates desire, desire is translated into words, and the word defines a space wherein the appropriation of what could otherwise not be appropriated or enjoyed is possible. This is the circle where phantasm, desire, and word weave themselves together "as tongues enlace in the kiss,"[10] of a love that "sua semper sine fine cognoscit augmenta" (always knows its increase without end)[11] and that constitutes the greatest possible approximation in this life to the "sweet play" of innocent love in Eden.

The legacy that the love lyric of the Duecento has imparted to European culture is not, however, so much a certain conception of love as the nexus of Eros and poetic language, the *entrebescamen* of desire, phantasm, and poetry in the *topos outopos* of the poem. If one wished to seek, in the exemplary wake of Leo Spitzer, a *trait éternel* (eternal signature) of Romance poetry, this nexus could certainly furnish the paradigm capable of explaining not only the *trobar clus* as a "specifically Romance tendency toward precious form,"[12] but also the analogous tension in Romance poetry in the direction of the self-sufficiency and absoluteness of the poetic text. The *trobar* is *clus* because the endless union of desire and its object is celebrated in its closed pneumatic circle; the typically medieval conception of the phantasmatic character of love finds its resolution and fulfillment in poetic practice. Over the course of a poetic process whose emblematic temporal extremes are Petrarch and Mallarmé, this essential textual tension of Romance poetry will displace its center from desire to mourning: Eros will yield to Thanatos its impossible love object so as to recover it, through a subtle and funereal strategy, as lost object, and the poem will become the site of an absence yet nonetheless draws from this absence its specific authority. The "rose" whose quest governs the poem of Jean de Meung thus becomes *l'absente de tout bouquet* (the absent from any and all bouquets) that exalts in the text its *disparition vibratoire* (vibratory disappearance) so as to mourn a desire imprisoned like a "swan" in the "ice" of its own dispossession.

But in the poetry of (in)spiring love—whose situation on the highest finial of the pneumo-phantasmological edifice has been the goal of our research—desire, supported by a conception that constitutes the sole coherent attempt in Western thought to overcome the metaphysical fracture of presence, celebrates, for perhaps the last time in the history of Western poetry, its joyful and inexhaustible "spiritual union" with its own object of love, with that "joy that never ends." This remains the always vital and luminous project against which our poetic culture will have to measure itself, if and when it succeeds in stepping backward and beyond itself toward its own origin.

Notes

1. *In librum Aristotelis De interpretatione libri sex* (*Patrologia latina*, 46, 406).
2. *De interpretatione*, treatise 2, chap. 1, in Beati Alberti Magni, *Opera omnia*, Lugduni, 1651.
3. Ibid., chap. 2.
4. *De Hippocratis et Platonis placitis*, book 2, 98ff. (in *Operum*). See also Chalcidius: "Vocem quoque dicunt e penetrali pectoris, idest corde, mitti, gremio cordis nitente spiritu . . . " (They also say the voice is emitted from the depths of the breast, that is, the heart, [from] the spirit impelling in the bosom of the heart) (*Timaeus Platonis*, 135).
5. See, for example, Guido Cavalcanti (*Rimatori del dolce stil novo*, XXXVI): "Tu, voce sbigottita e deboletta, / ch'esci piangendo de lo cor dolente" (You, weak and dejected voice, who emerge weeping from the sorrowing heart).
6. Guido Cavalcanti, XXI and XXV (*Rimatori*. pp. 39, 41), and Cino da Pistoia, CLX (*Rimatori*, p. 212).
7. The definition of love that Dante gives in the *Convivio* (III 2.3) as "unimento spirituale de l'anima e de la cosa amata" (spiritual joining of the soul and the thing loved) is, once again, to be taken literally; the adjective "spiritual" alludes here to the pneumo-phantasmatic link that mediates the amorous union.
8. J. Lacan, "L'instance de la lettre dans l'inconscient," in *Ecrits* (Paris, 1966), 497. On the metaphysics of the sign in Western thought, see chap. 17 in part 4 of this volume.
9. The Provençal word *joi*, which summarizes in itself the fullness of the erotic-poetic experience of the troubadours, is also etymologically linked to a linguistic practice in that it presumably derives from *Jocus*, and so opposed, in its meaning of "word-play" to *Ludus*, "bodily play." See Camproux, "La joie civilisatrice des troubadours," in *La table ronde*, n. 97, January 1956; and Guittone d'Arezzo, in *Poeti del dolce stil novo*, 244: "gioiosa gioi'," "gioia in cui viso e gioi' tant'amorosa," "gioi' di dire."

In the expression *joi d'amor* the genitive is to be taken also in the subjective sense: poetry is "love's joy" as the Greek statues were *agalma tou theou*, image and joy of the god (*agalma* derives from *agallomai*, "I rejoice, exult"). The love poetry of the thirteenth century, with the preeminence it accords to the image of the heart, appears from this point of view as a *Nachleben* (afterlife) of Greek statuary, in the sense in which Clement of Alexandria (*Protrepticus*, chap. 4) could say that the god of the Christians is an *agalma noeton*, a mental image. On the concept of *agalma*, see the reflections of Kerényi in *Agalma, eikon, eidolon*.

The usage of the word "stanza" to indicate a part of the canzone or poem derives from the Arabic term *bayt*, which means "dwelling place," "tent," and at the same time "verse." According to Arab authors, *bayt* also refers to the principal verse of a poem composed in praise of a person to whom one wishes to express desire, and in particular the verse in which the object of desire is expressed. (See the entry for *bayt* in E. W. Lane, *Arab-English Dictionary.*)

10. Consider the beautiful image of Bernart Marti (ed. Hoepffner, Paris, 1929, 11): "C'ausi vauc entrebescant / los motz e l so afinant: / lengu'entrebescada / es en la baizada" (Thus I go interweaving / words and finishing the sound: / the tongue is woven / in the kiss). The topological weave of this *entrebescamen* of love is expressed in exemplary fashion in the hieroglyphic of Horapallo that signifies "Love." See Ori Apollinis Niliaci, *De sacris Aegyptiorum notis,* Parisiis, 1574, 55r and the figure opposite the frontispiece; see also figures 24 and 25.

11. "Amor enim iste sua semper sine fine cognoscit augmenta, et ejus exercuisse actus neminem poenituisse cognovimus" (This love always knows its increase without end, and we never heard that anyone regretted having performed its act), from Andreas Cappellanus, *De amore,* II, 6. This is the "gioi che mai non fina" (joy that never ends) of Guido delle Colonne (*Poeti del duecento,* 99).

12. Leo Spitzer, *L'interpretazione linguistica delle opere letterarie,* in *Critica stilistica e semantica storica* (Bari, 1965), 66.

Part IV
The Perverse Image:
Semiology from the Point of View of the Sphinx

The perverse image seemed both and neither . . .
Dante, *Inferno* XXV.77-78

Chapter 17
Oedipus and the Sphinx

I.1. The essence of the emblematic tradition is so extraneous to the ideology prevalent today that, despite the exemplary defense of Benjamin,[1] its rigorous exposition is again necessary. The studies that, following the fruitful path of Aby Warburg, have on more than one occasion focused on the emblematic project, have not only failed to make it more familiar, but, if possible, have made it more foreign to us.[2] In this case, what was hiding in the detail was not, in fact, the "good God" but the vertiginous space of that which, before the veil was removed that distorted its contours, necessarily appeared as a Satanic fall of intelligence and as a demonic distortion of the nexus that unites every creature to its own form, every signifier to its own signified. In his *Aesthetics,* Hegel interpreted the "uneasiness"[3] our culture experiences with regard to symbols: "in themselves alone these productions say nothing to us; they do not please us or satisfy us by their immediate appearance, but by themselves they encourage us to advance beyond them to their meaning which is something wider and deeper than they are" [G. W. F. Hegel, *Aesthetics,* trans. T. M. Knox (Oxford: Oxford University Press, 1975), 1:308]. After defining the symbol as a sign, that is, as the unity of a signified and its expression, Hegel then identified its specific character in the persistence of a "partial discord" and a "struggle" within the sign between form and signification.[4]

The same "uneasiness" that the symbolic form brings scandalously to light has accompanied Western reflection on signification since the beginning, and its metaphysical residue has been absorbed, without benefit of inventory, by modern semiology. Insofar as the duality of thing manifesting and thing manifested is implicit in the sign, it remains something double and fragmented, but insofar as this duality is manifested in the one sign, it is rather something rejoined and united. The *sym*bolic, the act of recognition that reunites what is divided, is also the *dia*bolic that continually transgresses and exposes the truth of this knowledge.

The foundation of this ambiguity of signifying resides in that original fracture of presence that is inseparable from the Western experience of being. Because of that fracture, all that comes to presence comes there as to the place of a deferral and an exclusion, in the sense that its manifestation is simultaneously a concealment, and its being present, a lack. This originary co-belonging (*coappartenenza*) of presence and absence, of appearance and concealment was expressed by the Greeks in their intuition of truth as *'alétheia* (revelation), and on the experience of this fracture the discourse that we still call with the Greek name "love of wisdom" is founded. Only because presence is divided and unglued is something like "signifying" possible; and only because there is at the origin not plenitude but deferral [whether this is taken to mean the opposition of being and appearance, the harmony of opposites, or the ontological difference between being (*Sein*) and an entity (*Seiende*) is there the need to philosophize.

Early on, however, this fracture was dismissed and eclipsed through its metaphysical interpretation as the relation of truer being to less true, of paradigm to copy, of latent to sensible manifestation. In the reflection on language, which has always been par excellence the plane on which the experience of the original fracture is projected, this interpretation is crystallized in the notion of the sign as the expressive unity of the signifier and the signified. In this way the fracture of presence takes on the aspect of a process of "signification," and signification is interpreted on the basis of the unity of the signifying form and the signified content joined one to the other in a relation of "manifestation" (or eclipse). This interpretation, whose possibility is only implicit in the Aristotelian definition of language as *semantikos psophos* (signifying sound), acquires normative value in the course of the nineteenth century in the constitution of a dogma that today still prevents access to an authentic understanding of signification. According to this conception, which has found in aesthetics its exemplary crystallization, the highest relation between form and the signified, and that to which every signification generally tends, is that in which the sensible appearance is wholly identified with the signified and the signified is wholly absorbed in its manifestation. To this perfect unity, in which the signified is still in part hidden, the symbolic is opposed as something imperfect that must be superseded. Hegel, in his *Aesthetics,* identified the work of art as the model for such a superseding of the symbol:

> The symbolic, that is to say, in our meaning of the word, at once stops
> short of the point where, instead of indefinite, general, abstract ideas, it
> is free individuality which constitutes the content and form of the
> representation. . . . Meaning and sensuous representation, inner and
> outer, matter and form, are in that event no longer distinct from one

another; they do not announce themselves, as they do in the strictly symbolic sphere, as merely related but as *one* whole in which the appearance has no other essence, the essence no other appearance, outside or alongside itself. (*Aesthetics* 1:313)

The original deferral of presence, which is properly what deserved to be questioned, is thus dismissed and confined in the apparent evidence of the expressive convergence between form and content, exterior and interior, manifestation and latency, although nothing in principle requires the consideration of "signifying" as an "expression" or an "eclipse." In modern semiology, the forgetting of the original fracture of presence is manifested precisely in what ought to betray it, that is, in the bar (/) of the graphic S/s. That the meaning of this bar or barrier is constantly left in shadow, thus hiding the abyss opened between signifier and signified, constitutes the foundation of that "primordial positing of the signified and the signifier as two orders distinguished and separated by a barrier resisting signification," a position that has governed Western reflection on the sign from the outset, like a hidden overlord. From the point of view of signification, metaphysics is nothing but the forgetting of the originary difference between signifier and signified. Every semiology that fails to ask why the barrier that establishes the possibility of signifying should itself be resistant to signification, falsifies, with that omission, its own most authentic intention. In Saussure's formula, "linguistic unity is double," the accent has been placed now on the pole of the signifier, now on that of the signified, without ever putting into question the paradox, insuperable for Saussure, that had testified on behalf of his own formulation. Whether the relation indicated by the barrier is in fact conceived as a conventional substitution or as the amorous aesthetic embrace of form and signified, in either case what remains obscured is precisely the abyss of the original division of presence over which signification installs itself. The question that remains unasked is the only one that deserved to be formulated: why is presence deferred and fragmented such that something like "signification" even becomes possible?

I.2. The origin of this dissimulation—effected by the expressive unity of signifier and signified—of the fracture of presence was prefigured by the Greeks in a mythologeme that has always held a particular fascination for our culture. In the psychoanalytical interpretation of the myth of Oedipus, the episode of the Sphinx, although necessarily of essential importance for the Greeks, remains obstinately in the shadows; but it is precisely this aspect of the life of the hero that must here be put in the foreground. The son of Laius resolves in the simplest way "the enigma proposed by the ferocious jaws of the virgin," showing the hidden meaning behind the enigmatic signifier, and, with this act alone, plunges the half-human, half-feral monster into the abyss. The liberating teaching of Oedipus is that what is uncanny and frightening in the enigma disappears as soon as its utterance is reduced to the transparency of the relation between the signified and its form, which the signified only apparently succeeds in escaping.

Nevertheless, what we can discern in the archaic enigmas shows not only that the signified must not have preexisted its formulation (as Hegel believed), but that the knowledge of that formulation was in fact unessential. The supposition of a solution "hidden" in the enigma belongs to a subsequent age that no longer understood what the enigma brought to language, that no longer had any knowledge of enigmas except in the degraded forms of the riddle and the guessing game. Not only was the enigma thought to be much more than mere amusement, but experience of it always meant the risk of death.[5]

What the Sphinx proposed was not simply something whose signified is hidden and veiled under an "enigmatic" signifier, but a mode of speech in which the original fracture of presence was alluded to in the paradox of a word that approaches its object while keeping it indefinitely at a distance. The *ainos* (story, fable) of the *ainigma* is not only obscurity, but a more original mode of speaking. Like the labyrinth, like the Gorgon, and like the Sphinx that utters it, the enigma belongs to the sphere of the apotropaic, that is, to a protective power that repels the uncanny by attracting it and assuming it within itself. The dancing path of the labyrinth, which leads into the heart of that which is held at a distance, is the model of this relation with the uncanny that is expressed in the enigma.[6]

If the above is true, the sin of Oedipus is not so much incest as it is hubris toward the power of the symbolic in general (the Sphinx is thus truly, according to Hegel's suggestion, "the symbol of the symbolic"), which he has misperceived by interpreting its apotropaic intention as the relation of an oblique signifier and a hidden signified. Oedipus's gesture inaugurates a breach in language whose metaphysical legacy is extensive: on the one hand, the symbolic discourse of the Sphinx, whose essence is coding and concealment, and which employs "improper" terms; on the other hand, the transparent discourse of Oedipus, employing proper terms, which is expression or decoding. Oedipus thus appears in our culture as "civilizing hero" who, with his answer, provides the enduring model for the interpretation of the symbolic. (This model is related to the "signifying" of alphabetic writing, whose invention the Greek tradition attributed to the ancestor of Oedipus, Cadmus, whose descendants maintained a relation with writing and signification that has not yet been studied. The son of Cadmus, Polydorus, is also called Pinacos, "the man of the written tablets," and Labdacus, father of Laius, derives his name from the letter lambda. All of this testifies to the importance of this aspect of the mythologeme, which Freudian interpretation has left in the dark.) Every interpretation of signifying as the relation of manifestation or expression (or, inversely, of coding and eclipse) between a signifier and a signified (and both the psychoanalytic theory of the symbol and the semiotic theory of language belong to this type) places itself necessarily under the sign of Oedipus; under the sign of the Sphinx must be placed every theory of the symbol that, refusing the model of Oedipus, focuses its attention above all on the barrier between signifier and signified that constitutes the original problem of signification.

Next to this Oedipal dismissal of the original fracture of presence, another interpretation does in fact remain in reserve, so to speak, in the tradition of Western thought. This alternative appears at an early date in the light of the Heraclitean project of an utterance that neither "hides" nor "reveals" but rather "signifies" the unsignifiable conjunction (*synapsis*) between presence and absence, between the signifier and the signified. Heraclitus frequently—and the practice earned him his reputation for obscurity—referred to such utterance by establishing proximities between contraries and by creating oxymorons in which opposites do not exclude each other, but point toward their invisible contact points.[7]

From this point of view it is significant that Aristotle, in order to characterize the enigma, employed an expression that undoubtedly retraces what Heraclitus said about putting together opposites. In the *Poetics* (58a), Aristotle defined the enigma as a *ta adynata synapsai,* "a putting together of impossible things." For Heraclitus, every signifying is, in that sense, a *ta adynata synapsai,* and every authentic signifying is always "enigmatic." The divine *semainein,* to which fragment 93 alludes, cannot in fact be interpreted in the sense that metaphysics has rendered familiar, as a relation of manifestation (or eclipse) between signifier and signified, exterior and interior, but, on the contrary, its intention is characterized precisely in opposition to the *legein* (saying) and to the *kryptein* (hiding), as a glimpse into the abyss opened between signifier and signified, all the way to the "god" that appears between them.[8]

This glimpse is what a semiology freed from the mark of Oedipus and faithful to the Saussurian paradox would finally bring to the "barrier resistant to signification." This barrier, without itself ever coming into language, dominates Western reflection on the sign, and its dismissal is the foundation for the primordial position of the signifier and the signified that belongs in an essential way to metaphysics. By permitting itself to be captured in the labyrinth, drawn in by the *ainos* of the emblematic form, this chapter has attempted to point toward the originary apotropaic stage of language in the heart of the fracture of presence, in which a culture that had paid its debt to the Sphinx could find a new model of signification.

Notes

1. The defense alluded to here is that contained in the *Ursprüng des deutschen Trauerspiel* (1928) (Frankfurt am Main: Surkamp, 1963). This is surely the least popular of Benjamin's works, but it is perhaps the only one in which he fulfilled his most profound intentions. In its structure, this work reproduces the laceration of the emblem to such an extent that one can say of emblem what Benjamin himself said of allegory: "Allegory opens into nothingness. Evil *tout court*, which allegory oversees as a permanent profundity, exists only within allegory, is only and exclusively allegory—it signifies something different from what it is. In other words, it signifies precisely the nonbeing of what it represents . . . Knowledge about evil has no object . . . It is gossip in the profound sense that Kierkegaard intended this word."

2. Warburg's interest in symbols naturally led him to become interested in impresas, emblems or devices accompanied by mottoes. His peculiar approach to images can indeed be characterized by saying that he looked at every image as if it were an impresa that transmitted to the collective memory an engram charged with vital tension.

On emblems, in addition to the study of Mario Praz, *Studies in Seventeenth Century Imagery, Studies of the Warburg Institute,* vol. 3 (London, 1939), see, among others, E. H. Gombrich, "Icones Symbolicae, The Visual Image in Neoplatonic Thought," *Journal of the Warburg and Courtauld Institute* 11 (1948), and R. Klein, "La théorie de l'expression figurée dans les traités italiens sur les imprese," *Bibliothèque d'Humanisme et Renaissance,* vol. 19 (1957).

3. "Thus when we first enter the world of [symbolism], our footing is not really secure; we feel that we are wandering amongst *problems*" (*Aesthetics* 1:308).

4. "If we ask, within these boundaries which have been indicated, for a narrower principle of division for symbolic art, then, in so far as symbolic art just struggles towards true meanings and their corresponding mode of configuration, it is in general a battle between the content which still resists true art and the form which is not homogeneous with the content either. . . . In this respect the whole of symbolic art may be understood as a continuing struggle for compatibility of meaning and shape, and the different levels of this struggle are not so much different kinds of symbolic art as stages and modes of one and the same contradiction [of incompatibility between meaning and shape]" (*Aesthetics* 1:317-18).

5. The inability to resolve the enigma had as its consequence death by despair. According to Greek tradition, Homer and Calchas died this way.

6. On the closeness of the dance and the labyrinth, see Kerényi, *Labyrinth-Studien* (Zurich, 1950), 77: "All research on the labyrinth ought properly to begin with the dance."

7. Heraclitus (fragment 10): "Things put together (*synapseis*): whole-not whole, concordant-discordant, consonant-dissonant; from all things the one and from the one all things."

8. "The Lord, whose oracle is at Delphi, neither says (*legei*) nor conceals (*kryptei*), but signifies (*semainei*)."

Chapter 18
The Proper and the Improper

II.1. The originary doubleness of the metaphysical conception of signifying manifests itself in European culture as the opposition of the proper and the improper. "Duplex est modus loquendi," one reads in the *De veritate* of Saint Thomas Aquinas, "unus secundum propriam locutionem; alius modus est secundum figurativam, sive tropicam, sive symbolicam locutionem" ["In matters dealing with God there are two different ways of speaking: (1) In proper language . . . and (2) In figurative, transferred, or symbolic language"].[1] The impossibility, for our culture, of mastering this antinomy is witnessed by the constant alternation of epochs of the improper, in which the symbolic-emblematic occupies the central place in culture, and epochs of the proper, in which the improper is pushed to the margins, without either of the two discourses succeeding in entirely reducing its own double.

The foundations of a theory of the improper, which furnished the theological justification for the Renaissance and baroque obsession with emblems no less than for the exalted allegoresis of medieval mysticism, are found sketched in the apocryphal corpus that goes under the name of Dionysus the Areopagite. This justification is formulated as a kind of "principle of incongruence," according to which—since in reference to the divine, negations are truer and more congruous than affirmations—a representation that proceeds by discrepancies and shifts would be more adequate to its object than a representation that proceeds by analogies and resemblances. In other words, precisely its inadequacy with respect to its mystical object confers on the incongruous symbol what might paradoxically be defined as a "congruence by discrepancy" that permits the mind to raise itself, in an anagogical leap of love, from the shadowy corporeal world to the contemplation of the intelligible.[2] Ten centuries later, Hugh of St. Victor defined the mystic power of the incongruous with almost the same words used by the Areopagite:

> Dissimilar figures distract our mind from material and corporeal things more than do similar ones, and do not allow it to rest in itself. The reason for this is that all created things, though perfect, are separated from God by an infinite gap . . . so that the knowledge of God—which, denying in this manner all His perfections, transmits what He is not—is more perfect than that which, affirming what He is not, by means of such small perfections attempts to explain what thing God might be.

Between the first half of the sixteenth and the second half of the seventeenth centuries, that is, in the period in which the modern scientific image of the world was being formed, European culture was dominated to such an extent by the topic of the incongruous that this period could be defined, in the words of Herder, as "the epoch of the emblem." The emblem is in fact the central figure to which this period entrusted its most profound cognitive project and, also, its most intimate malaise. The studies of Giehlow have shown the decisive influence exercised over the formation of sixteenth-century emblematics by a pseudoepigraphical corpus, the *Hyeroglyphica* of Horapollo, which was composed at the end of the second or perhaps even during the fourth century A.D. and contained what claimed to be an interpretation of the Egyptian hieroglyphs. On the fecund misunderstanding of an explanation of the "sacred signs" of the Egyptian priests, the humanists founded the project of a model of signification in which not the convergence and unity of appearance and essence, but their incongruence and displacement, became the vehicle of a superior knowledge: one in which the metaphysical difference between corporeal and incorporeal, matter and form, signifier and signified, both tended toward the maximum divergence and, at the same time, came together. It does not appear fortuitous, from this point of view, that the emblematists referred constantly to the emblem as a compound of soul (the motto) and body (the image)[3] and to their union as "mystical mixture" and "ideal man." Metaphor, as the paradigm of signifying by improper terms (and according to baroque theorists, both the emblem and the impresa fall under this framework), becomes thus the principle of a universal dissociation of each thing from its own form, of every signifier from its own signified. In emblems, in the "amorous and heroic" *imprese,* in the blazons (heraldic arms) that now mask with their *picta poesis* (painted poetry) all the aspects of profane life, as in the *acutezza* (sharp wit, ingenuity) that is employed to the end of all signification, the link that joins each object to its own appearance, each creature to its own body, each word to its own signified is radically called into question. Each thing is true only to the extent to which it signifies another, and each thing is itself only if it stands for another. For the allegorical project of the baroque, this mortification of the proper form is a token of redemption that will be rescued on the Last

Day, but whose cipher is already implicit in the act of creation. God appears thus as the first and supreme emblematist, an "arguto favellatore" (subtle, witty fabulist) as we read in the *Cannocchiale aristotelico* (Aristotelian telescope) of Tesauro, "wittily expressing to men and angels his lofty concepts with various heroic emblems and symbolic figurations." The sky "is a vast sky-blue shield, where ingenious nature traces out what she meditates, forming heroic emblems and subtle, mysterious symbols of her secrets."[4]

Caricature, which was born precisely in this era, is the moment when emblematic displacement reaches the human figure. This renders plausible the hypothesis, still not confronted by scholars, that the origin of the "figura caricata" (charged, caricatured figure) is to be linked to the prohibition—an integral part of the emblematic code—against describing the human body except partially: "corpus humanum," we read in the rules of Petrus Abbas, "integrum pictura esse non potest, pars corporis, oculus, cor, manus tolerari potest" (the whole human body must not be in a picture; a part of the body—eye, heart, hand—can be tolerated). The root of the prohibition that prevented the displacement of the human figure from its proper signification (except by recourse to a fetishistic device widely used by the emblematists) was the biblical "in his image and likeness," which, directly linking the human form to its divine creator, irrevocably guaranteed its identity. The displacement of the human figure from this theological "signified" must therefore have appeared as the demoniac act par excellence, which explains the monstrous and caricatural aspect with which the devil is outfitted in Christian iconography. The inexplicable delay attending the appearance of caricature in European culture is not to be sought, as Gombrich and Kris have suggested, in a supposed belief in the magical efficacy of the image,[5] but in the fact that, outside of the emblematic cosmos, the displacement of the human figure necessarily implied a blasphemous project. Only in an epoch like that of the emblems, intimately accustomed to discern in incongruence the model of truth, could a caricature appear more similar to the person than the person itself. Caricature is, in the human sphere, what the emblem is in the sphere of objects. As the emblem had called into question the nexus of things with their proper forms, so, with apparent frivolity, caricature separated the human figure from its signified; but, since this figure already bore inscribed its allegorical cipher, only by twisting and altering its proper lineaments could it acquire a new emblematic status. Man, created in the image and likeness of God, "per malitiam diaboli depravatus venit in longuinquam regionem dissimilitudinis" (depraved by the malice of the devil came into a distant region of unlikeness). This "region of unlikeness" is the *regnum peccati* (kingdom of sin) "in which the memory is scattered, the intellect is blinded, the will is troubled."[6] And nevertheless, according to the implicit wisdom of the emblematic project, this displacement is also a token of redemption, this unlikeness a superior likeness.

It is therefore not surprising that, with the disappearance of baroque allegoresis, the emblematic form, which estranges each signifier from its own signified, begins to be disturbing. Creuzer's *Simbolica* and the *Fisiognomica* of Lavater are the last imposing attempts to grasp a superior knowledge in emblematic displacement: both end in parody and uncomprehension. The unease that Hegel avowed with respect to the symbolic and his diffidence toward the allegorism of the Romantic avant-garde are symptoms of the new attitude that was manifested through firm mastery of the proper form. It is significant that, after describing the Sphinx as the figure in which "the symbolic as such . . . becomes a riddle," Hegel opposes it with Oedipus, the champion of Enlightenment, whose response brings "the light of consciousness . . . the clarity which makes its concrete content shine clearly through the shape belonging and appropriate to itself, and in its [objective] existence reveals itself alone" (*Aesthetics* 1:361).

With this development, however, the world of emblematic figurations, in which an entire era had seen the most "acute" expression of human spirituality, is not simply abolished. The world now becomes the warehouse of jetsam where the uncanny fishes for its scarecrows. The fantastic creatures of Hoffmann and Poe, the animated objects and caricatures of Grandville and Tenniel, and Odradek's bobbin in Kafka's tale are, from this point of view, a *Nachleben* of the emblematic form, neither more nor less than certain Christian demons represent a "posthumous life" of the pagan divinities. In the form of the uncanny, which invades daily life with increasing force, the symbol presents itself as the new Sphinx threatening the citadel of reason. Freud is the Oedipus who proposes the key intended to dissolve the enigma and free reason from its monsters. The conclusions of his studies on the uncanny are therefore particularly interesting to us. Freud saw in the uncanny (*Unheimliche*) the estranged familiar (*Heimliche*):

> For this uncanny is in reality nothing new or alien, but something which is familiar and old-established in the mind and which has become alienated from it only through the process of repression. This reference to the factor of repression enables us, furthermore, to understand Schelling's definition of the uncanny as something which ought to have remained hidden but has come to light.[7]

This formula, which also sums up Freud's attitude toward symbols, which he constantly linked to the mechanism of repression, allows us to ask why modern culture should have so obstinately identified the symbolic with the uncanny. Perhaps the reason for this "uneasiness" with respect to the symbolic resides in the fact that the apparent simplicity of the scheme with which our culture interprets signification conceals the repression of a more familiar and original kind of signifying, one that does not tamely allow itself to be reduced to our cultural scheme. We should learn to see something intimately human behind the feral traits of the monster in which "the human spirit tries to push itself forward, without coming to a perfect portrayal of its own freedom and animated shape, because it must still remain confused and associated with what is other than itself" (*Aesthetics* 1:361).

II.2. The Oedipal interpretation of the speech of the Sphinx as a "coded speech" secretly governs the Freudian conception of the symbol. Psychoanalysis in fact presupposes the splitting of discourse into an obscure speech by means of improper terms, based on repression (which is that of the unconscious), and into a clear speech of proper terms (which is that of consciousness). The passage ("the translation") from one discourse to the other properly constitutes analysis. This necessarily presupposes a process of "desymbolization" and of progressive reduction of the symbolic: the "drying of the Zuider Zee," which according to Freud substantiates the psychoanalytic process, is, once concluded, the equivalent of a complete translation of unconscious symbolic language into conscious sign. The myth of Oedipus therefore dominates the horizon of analysis in a manner much more profound than its critics heretofore thought. Not only does it furnish the content of interpretation, it guides and structures the fundamental attitude of analytic discourse itself in its self-positioning before the Sphinx of the unconscious and its symbols. As Oedipus discovers the hidden meaning of the enigma of the Sphinx, and, in so doing, frees the city from the monster, so analysis rediscovers the latent thought behind the manifest symbolic cipher and "heals" the neurosis.

It is therefore not simply a coincidence if the essential processes of symbolism brought to light by Freud correspond point by point, as has been observed, to the catalogue of tropes of the old rhetoric.[8] The territory of the unconscious, in its mechanisms as in its structures, wholly coincides with that of the symbolic and the improper. The emblematic project, which dissociates every form from its signified, now becomes the hidden writing of the unconscious, while the emblem books exit the libraries of educated persons and enter the unconscious, where repression incessantly traces its blazons and *imprese*.

The orthodox psychoanalytical theory of symbolism[9] that is expressed in Jones's apodictic affirmation—"only what is repressed comes to be symbolized"— and that sees in every symbol the return of the repressed in an improper signifier, does not exhaust the Freudian theory of the symbol. In fact, on several occasions Freud described symbolic processes that do not allow themselves to be reduced to Jones's formula. One of these is the *Verleugnung* of the fetishist.

According to Freud, the perversion of the fetishist arises from the refusal of the boy to become cognizant of the woman's (the mother's) lack of a penis. Faced with the perception of this absence, the boy refuses to admit its reality, because to do so would be to admit a threat of the castration of his own penis. From this point of view the fetish is nothing but "the substitute for the woman's (the mother's) penis that the little boy once believed in and—for reasons familiar to us— does not want to give up."[10] Nevertheless the meaning of the child's refusal is not as simple as it might seem and rather implies an essential ambiguity. In the conflict between perception of reality that moves him to renounce his phantasm, and his counterdesire that moves him to renounce his perception, the boy in fact does neither one nor the other, or, rather, he does both at once, arriving at a unique compromise. On the one hand, with the help of a particular mechanism, he repudiates the evidence of his senses; on the other, he recognizes and assumes the reality of that evidence by means of a perverse symptom. The space of the fetish is precisely this contradiction; the fetish is simultaneously the presence of that nothingness that is the maternal penis and the sign of its absence. As both a symbol of something and its negation, the fetish can maintain itself only with the provision of an essential laceration, in which the two contrary reactions constitute the nucleus of a true and proper splitting of the ego (*Ichspaltung*).

It is clear that the mechanism of *Verleugnung* will not yield to interpretation according to the scheme of a return of the repressed in the guise of an improper signifier. Indeed, it is plausibly because of Freud's awareness that repression (*Verdrangung*) is inadequate to account for the phenomenon that he has recourse to the term *Verleugnung*. Not only is there no substitution of one signifier for another in the *Verleugnung* of the fetishist—indeed the signifiers maintain themselves through a reciprocal negation—but neither can one properly speak of repression, because the psychic content is not simply pushed back into the unconscious, but is, in some way, affirmed to the same extent that it is denied (which does not mean, however, that it is conscious). The dynamic mechanism of this process could be represented in the following way:[11]

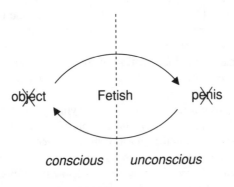

Here we find something analogous to what occurs in the *Verneinung,* that is, in those negation-admissions with which the patient confesses to the analyst what he or she is apparently denying. Freud defined this process as "lifting of the repression, though not, of course, an acceptance of what is repressed," and Hippolyte spoke of "a utilization of the unconscious, maintaining, however, repression."[12] The *Verleugnung* presents us with a process in which, by means of a symbol, man succeeds in appropriating an unconscious content without bringing it to consciousness. Just as the *imprese* display in the blazon the most intimate personal intentions without translating them in the proper terms of the discourse of reason, so too the fetishist emblematizes his most secret fears and desires in a symbolic blazon that allows him to come into contact with them without their entering his consciousness. In this gesture of the fetishist, who succeeds in appropriating his own hidden treasure without unearthing it, the ancient apotropaic wisdom of the Sphinx, which repels by receiving and receives by repelling, once again comes to life. And just as the analyst can perhaps learn something from the pervert as far as pleasure is concerned, so too perhaps Oedipus can learn something from the Sphinx about symbols.

II.3. Insofar as the "difference" between the signifier and the signified reaches its maximum in the emblematic form, this form constitutes the domain par excellence where a science of signs that had truly become aware of the Saussurian paradox of "double unity" might have exercised itself. Yet, even after the studies of baroque theorists, of the mythologues, and of the Romantic critics, a merely sufficient semiological analysis precisely of the emblematic form is still lacking. Weighing on the numerous recent attempts to interpret metaphor is the initial metaphysical positioning of the problem as the relation of the proper and the improper, which was already implicit in the Aristotelian definition of metaphor as the "transport" of an "extraneous" noun.[13] In the course of Western reflection on the sign, this position translates into the prejudice that there are two terms in a metaphor, one proper and the other improper, and that the movement or substitution of one for the other constitutes the metaphorical "transport." This formulation works to the detriment both of Jakobson's definition of metaphor as the "attribution of a signifier to a signified associated by resemblance to the primary signified" and of the definition of metaphor as the semic intersection (based on a metonymy) of two terms, according to the following scheme:[14]

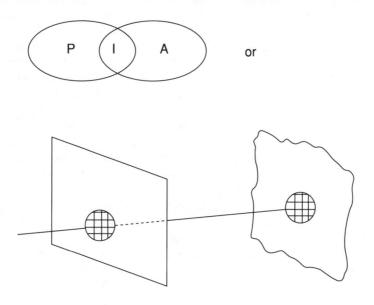

What remains obscured in both cases is that the "resemblance" and the semic intersection do not preexist the metaphor, but are rendered possible by it and assumed subsequently as its explanation, just as Oedipus's answer does not preexist the enigma, but, having been created by it, pretends, with a singular begging of the question, to offer its solution.

What the scheme proper/improper prevents us from seeing is that in metaphor nothing is really substituted for anything else, because there is no proper term that the metaphorical one is called upon to replace. Only our ancient Oedipal prejudice—that is, an a posteriori interpretive scheme—makes us discern a substitution where there is nothing but a displacement and a difference within a single signifying act. Only in a metaphor already crystallized by usage (which is therefore no longer a metaphor at all) is it possible to distinguish a proper and an improper signified: in an originary metaphor it would be useless to look for something like a proper term.

The inadequacy of the Oedipal scheme of the proper and the improper to grasp the essence of metaphor is particularly evident in the emblem: the "painted" or "enacted" metaphor. It would seem to be possible to recognize a proper and improper term, exemplified in the "soul" and the "body" of the emblem, but, after the briefest look—which the emblematic tradition invites—into the labyrinth, it is apparent that the emblem provides for no positive substitution of one term for the other. Rather, the space of the emblem is the purely negative and insubstantial space of a process of difference and reciprocal negation-affirmation. Thus the "body" and the "soul" are in a relation to one another that is, simultaneously, one of explanation and of eclipse (a "shadowing over by explaining" and an "explaining by shadowing over," in the words of a seventeenth-century treatise), without either of the two projects prevailing completely over the other (which would signify, in fact, the death of the emblem). The theoreticians of the impresa insistently repeat that the emblematic "marvel" (*meraviglia*) "is not born from the obscurity of words, or from the recondite nature of things, but from the coupling and mixture of both one and the other. Because of this a third is constituted, of diverse nature from them, producing that marvel."[15] Nevertheless one would search in vain in this "third" for something positive, for it is but the difference and the reciprocal negation-affirmation of the other two. The same can be said for that emblazoning of the human figure that is, as we have seen, the caricature. The exemplary success of Philipon's celebrated "pear," which represents King Louis Philippe as a pear (or vice versa), consists precisely in the fact that we find ourselves confronted neither with a pear nor with Louis Philippe, but with the emblematic tension that arises from their confusion-difference.

If this is true, the operation of the emblematic form appears to be surprisingly similar to that of the fetishist *Verleugnung* as described by Freud. Moreover, *Verleugnung* offers a model for the interpretation of metaphor that escapes the traditional reduction of the problem and in the light of which *the metaphor becomes in the realm of language what the fetish is in the realm of things*. As in

Verleugnung there is not simply a ''transport'' from a proper to an improper signified, but rather a process of never-substantializable negation between an absence and a presence (because the fetish is both that nullity that is the maternal penis and the sign of its absence). Therefore, in the emblematic form, there is neither substitution nor transport, but only a game of negation and difference, irreducible to the exchange of proper and improper. And since the fetish, because of its essential contribution, cannot maintain itself except on condition of a laceration, in which the two contrary reactions constitute the nucleus of what Freud called ''the splitting of the ego'' (*Ichspaltung*), therefore the emblematic form is erected over a true and proper fracture of the semiotic *synolon* (union of matter and form).

The displacement of metaphor is not, in fact, between the proper and the improper, but within the metaphysical structuring of signification itself. Its space is determined by a reciprocal exclusion of the signifier and the signified, and in this space emerges the original difference on which every signification is founded. Nietzsche, in his projected *Philosophenbuch,* rightly saw in metaphor the originary phenomenon of language and in the ''rigid columbarium'' of proper terms nothing else than the residue of a metaphor.[16] In contrast to the Sphinx and its metaphorical discourse, Oedipus appears like Nietzsche's deaf man, who, before the figure of Chladni produced on the sand by sound waves, pretends to know what it is that is called sound. The Aristotelian definition of the enigma as a *synapsai ta adynata,* ''a putting together of impossible things,'' well grasps the central paradox of signification that metaphor unmasks: the *semainein* is always originally a *synapsis* of *adynata,* a connection of impossibles—not a relation of manifestations, in itself nonproblematic, between signifier and signified, but a pure barrier. The ''sharp wit'' (*acutezza*) of the ''divine fabulist'' who, according to Tesauro, ''wittily expresses to men and angels his lofty concepts,'' buries its point (*acutezza,* according to the profound intuition of a seventeenth-century dictionary, to be understood etymologically as the act of piercing and opening) precisely in this juxtaposition of signifier and signified. Metaphor, caricature, emblem, and fetish point toward that ''barrier resistant to signification'' in which is guarded the original enigma of every signifying act. It is this barrier that we must now investigate.

Notes

1. Sancti Thomae, *De veritate,* q. 23, a. 3. The English translation is from Saint Thomas Aquinas, *Truth,* vol. 3, trans. Robert W. Schmidt (Chicago: Henry Regnery Co., 1954), 104.

2. ''Since then the negations of the divine are true and the affirmations incongruous, manifestation through dissimilar figures is more appropriate for the unspeakable things that are hidden . . . The anagogical wisdom of the holy theologians rightly employs differences, not permitting that which is material in us to adhere to those undecorous images, but exciting and stimulating the superior part of the soul with the very deformity of the figures, such that it will seem neither licit nor plausible, not even to those who are tied to matter, that such absurd forms should be akin to the truth of divine contemplations'' (Psuedo-Dionysus the Areopagite, *De coelesti hierarchia,* chap. 2, 3).

3. "The symbol consists of pictures and words, or, as the vulgar might say, body and soul" (Petrus Abbas, in *C.F. Menestrerii Philosophia imaginum,* Amsterdam, 1695); "giusta proportione di anima e di corpo" (The just proportion of soul and body) (Paolo Giovio, *Dialogo del'imprese militari et amorose,* Venezia, 1557).

4. Emmanuele Tesauro, *Cannocchiale aristotelico, o sia idea delle argutezze heroiche vulgarmente chiamate imprese e di tutta l'arte simbolica et lapidaria contenente ogni genere di figure e inscrittioni espressive di arguti e ingegnosi concetti esaminate in fronte co' rettorici precetti del divino Aristotele* (Aristotelian telescope, or idea of the heroic conceptions commonly called emblems and of all the symbolic and lapidary art containing every kind of figure and inscription expressive of clever and ingenious concepts examined in the light of the rhetorical precepts of the divine Aristotle), Torino, 1652.

5. E. H. Gombrich and E. Kris, "The Principles of Caricature," in Ernst Kris, *Psychoanalytic Explorations in Art* (New York, 1952).

6. Peter Lombard, cited in R. Javelet, *Image et ressemblance au XII siècle. Du saint Anselme à Alain de Lille* (Strasbourg, 1967), 240ff.

7. "Das unheimliche," originally published in *Imago* 5 (1919). The English translation is from "The Uncanny," in *The Standard Edition of the Complete Psychological Works of Sigmund Freud,* trans. and edited by James Strachey (London: Hogarth Press, 1955), 241.

8. From E. Benveniste, in "Remarques sur la fonction du langage dans la decouverte freudienne" (*La psychanalyse* 1, 1956); reprinted in E. Benveniste, *Problèmes de linguistique générale* (Paris, 1966). The importance of this essay can be judged from the fact that it anticipates by a year the essay of Lacan in which his ideas on the "signifier" are fully developed ("L'instance de la lettre dans l'inconscient," in *La psychanalyse,* 1957). Since then, the notion of a "rhetoric of the unconscious" has become common among psychoanalysts and linguists, although without anyone having made the decisive step showing that the unconscious does not *have* a rhetoric, but *is* a rhetoric.

9. It is worth specifying that our criticism is directed at this orthodox conception of symbolism, and not at the Lacanian interpretation of Freud.

10. From *The Standard Edition of the Complete Psychological Works of Sigmund Freud,* vol. 21, 152-153.

11. It follows from the diagram that the fetish is not identified with the object, but is situated, in a sense, in the interval opened by the reciprocal negation (indicated by the sign X) of the object and the maternal penis.

12. The quotation from Freud is from "Negation," *The Standard Edition of the Complete Psychological Works of Sigmund Freud,* vol. 19, 236. Jean Hippolyte, "Commentaire parlé sur la Verneinung de Freud," in Lacan, *Ecrits,* 887.

13. *Poetics,* 1557b.

14. Roman Jakobson's definition is in "A la recherche de l'essence du langage," *Diogène* 51 (1965). For the second definition, see A. Henry, *Métonimie et métaphore* (Paris, 1971). The tenacity of the dogma of substitution is such that traces can be discerned of it even in Lacan, who wrote that the metaphor "arises from two signifiers of which one is substituted for the other, taking its place in the signifying chain" (*Ecrits,* 507). He adds, however, that "the hidden signified remains present thanks to its (metonymic) connection with the rest of the chain." It is in the paradox of a substitution in which the substituted remains present that the secret of metaphor is to be sought.

15. Scipione Ammirato, *Il rota ovvero delle Imprese* (Florence, 1598).

16. "What then is truth? A multitude of metaphors in motion, of metonymies, of anthropomorphisms, in short: a sum of human relations that have been poetically elevated, transposed, adorned, and that, after long use, seem firm, canonical, and binding to a given people . . . While every metaphor of the intuition is individual and without equal and, because of this, can escape every determination, the great edifice of concepts displays the rigid regularity of a Roman columbarium and breathes forth in its logic the severity and frigidity that are proper to mathematics. Whoever is impregnated with this frigidity will hardly believe that the concept, bony and octagonal like a die, and,

like the die, immovable, is rather nothing more than *the residue of a metaphor* . . . Only through the forgetfulness of this primitive world of metaphors, only through the invincible belief that *this* sun, *this* window, *this* table is a truth in itself, in short only because man forgets himself as a subject and, in particular, as a subject of artistic creation, can he live in a world of repose and security'' [the fragments of the *Philosophenbuch* are in vol. 10 of the Kröner edition of the works of Nietzsche: A. Kröner, *Werke* (Leipzig, 1903-26)].

Chapter 19
The Barrier and the Fold

III.1. The notion of the sign on which modern semiology is based is founded on a metaphysical reduction of signification that remains as yet unknown to "the science that studies the life of signs in the domain of social life."[1] This reduction, whose roots are sunk deep in the history of Western philosophy, was made possible by the special circumstances of the first appearance of the text around which the modern semiological project has been formed. It is well known and unnecessary to emphasize here that the courses presented by Ferdinand de Saussure in Geneva from 1907 to 1911 were not intended for publication and that he had in fact explicitly ruled out the possibility of publishing them.[2] What needs emphasis is that these courses represented the culminating moment of an intellectual crisis, an impasse, the experience that constitutes perhaps the most essential aspect of Saussure's thought. The publication of the *Cours,* in the circumstances of 1915, reveals precisely this experience of a radical aporia, presenting as a series of positive results what was in reality the final reef against which Saussure had shipwrecked at the conclusion of a voyage begun almost fifteen years before, during the period of his studies on Baltic intonation. Saussure represents in fact the precious instance of a philologist who, caught in the net of language, felt, as Nietzsche did, the insufficiency of philology, and who had to become a philosopher or succumb. Saussure did not abandon linguistic study as Nietzsche had done, but, closing himself for thirty years in a silence that appeared inexplicable to many, interrupted only by the publication of mélanges of brief technical notes, the *enfant prodige* who had renewed the study of Indo-European linguistics with the brilliant *Mémorie sur le système primitif des voyelles* (Report on the primitive vowel-system) pursued to the limit an exemplary instance of the impossibility of a science of language within the Western metaphysical tradition.[3]

The documents of this crisis were long ago published by Benveniste and then reiterated in a memorable article by him without, however, his having fully appreciated their consequences.[4] The critical edition of the *Cours* edited by Rudolf Engler was published in 1967 in the only appropriate way, that is, as a synopsis of all the sources from which the 1915 text was derived, and lends urgency to the reassessment of the place of the *Cours* in the history of modern linguistics.[5] To the extent that it reflects the authentic thought of Saussure, the *Cours* cannot be considered during the subsequent years as the foundation of semiology; if anything, the *Cours* puts semiology radically into question. It does not contain the origins of semiology, but, in a certain sense, its closure.

The first document in what has been defined as "the drama of Saussure"[6] is found in a letter to Meillet written in 1894, when Saussure was working on his study of intonation and accent in Lithuanian, a study that would never be published. With uncharacteristic bitterness, Saussure confessed his discouragement before the "ineptie absolue" (absolute ineptitude) and contradictions of linguistic terminology:

> I am extremely disgusted with all of that and with the difficulty found
> in general in writing ten lines on the subject of linguistic facts that
> might have a common sense. Preoccupied for a long time above all
> with the logical classification of these facts . . . I increasingly see the
> immensity of the work that would be necessary to show to the linguist
> what he is doing . . . and, at the same time, the vanity of all that, in
> the final analysis, can be done in linguistics . . . This will end despite
> myself in a book in which, without enthusiasm or passion, I will
> explain why there is not a single term used in linguistics to which I
> would assign any meaning whatsoever. And only after having done this,
> I confess, will I be able to resume my work at the point where I have
> left off.[7]

This book was never written, but the notes and sketches that remained from it and that later were conflated in the course on general linguistics show Saussure's lucid awareness of an impasse not merely in his work, but in the science of language in general:

> Behold our profession of faith in linguistic matters: in other fields,
> one can speak of things "according to this or that point of view," being
> certain of finding a secure ground in the object itself. In linguistics, we
> deny on principle that objects are given, that there are things that
> continue to exist when one passes from one order of ideas to the next,
> and that one may consequently be permitted to consider "things" in
> diverse orders, as if they were given in themselves . . .
>   The truly ultimate law of language, at least so far as we dare to
> speak of it, is that there is never anything that can reside in a *single*

term, and this because of the fact that linguistic symbols have no relation to what they ought to designate, thus that *a* is incapable of designating something without the help of *b,* and likewise *b* without the help of *a,* or in fact that both of them are without value except through their reciprocal difference, or that neither of the two has value, whether it be through any part of itself (for example, "the root," etc.), except by means of this same plexus of eternally negative differences.

It is astonishing. But where in truth would the possibility of the contrary lie? Where would be for a single instant the point of positive irradiation in all of language, once granted that there is no vocal image that responds more than any other to what it must say?[8]

In his lectures, Saussure was certainly influenced by the didactic need to veil his doubt regarding the possibility of finding a positive term in language. Nevertheless, the critical edition of the *Cours* shows that the paragraph in which the sign is presented as something positive does not exactly reflect the notes of the students. Where the text of the *Cours* says "as soon as the sign is considered in its totality, we are in the presence of something positive in its order," the notes say more cautiously:

Thanks to the fact that these differences condition one another, we would have something that can resemble positive terms by placing in juxtaposition a certain difference of the idea with a certain difference of the sign.[9]

And further on:

But the signifier and the signified contract a bond by virtue of determinate values born from the combination of a quantity of acoustic signs with a quantity of excerpts that can be made from the mass. What would be necessary for this relation of signifier and signified to be intrinsically given? Above all it would require that the idea be determined in advance, and it is not . . . It would require above all that the signified were something to be determined in advance, and it is not. Therefore this relation is but another expression of the values taken in their opposition.[10]

If language is the absolutely insubstantial space of these "eternally negative differences," the sign is certainly the last element that could offer that "point of positive irradiation" within language on which a linguistic science finally liberated from the "ineptitude of current terminology" might be constructed. Insofar as it determines the double status of the linguistic unit, however, the sign is rather the site of absolute difference, where the metaphysical fracture of presence comes to light in the most blinding way. A decisive passage in the notes testifies that its very nature as a sign language is, for Saussure, something beyond grasp:

Language is nothing but a particular case of the theory of signs. But precisely because of this fact alone, language finds itself in the absolutely impossible situation of being something simple (or directly graspable in its mode of being by our understanding), while at the same time, in the general theory of signs, the particular case of the vocal signs is the most complex of all the known particular cases, like writing, cipher, and so on.[11]

Far from simplifying the linguistic act, the inclusion of language in the semiological perspective makes it something impossible. The science of the sign will only be able to attain its critical phase through the awareness of this impossibility (whose origin, as the history of the notion of the sign demonstrates, from the Stoa to medieval logic, has its basis in the essential solidarity of every interpretation of signifying with the metaphysical interpretation of presence). Saussure, who had reached the point of no return in his knowledge of language, where one is "abandoned by all the analogies of heaven and earth,"[12] spoke—with apparently paradoxical expressions that recall the Aristotelian definition of the enigma as the "putting together of impossible things"—of a "plexus of eternally negative differences," of a "stable bond between things that preexist the things themselves," of a double unity "that has an obverse and reverse." What weighed upon him most was the avoidance of substantializing the terms of that scission that had revealed itself to him as coessential to language. He was gesturing toward that difference and that "connection of impossibles" that has been covered and repressed in modern semiology with the "barrier resisting signification." In the semiotic algorithm, the barrier that separates the signifier and the signified is there to show the impossibility for the sign to produce itself in the fullness of presence. To isolate the notion of sign, understood as a positive unity of *signans* and *signatum,* from the original and problematic Saussurian position on the linguistic fact as a "plexus of eternally negative differences" is to push the science of signs back into metaphysics.[13]

III.2. The claim that there is a close relationship between the history of Western metaphysics and the interpretation of signification as the unity of a signifier and a signified is explicitly affirmed by a critical tradition whose project is formulated as the substitution of a science of writing (grammatology) for the science of signs (semiology). According to this project, metaphysics is founded on the privileged status of the signified, understood as the fullness of presence, with respect to the signifier, which is an external trace. This privilege is the same one that establishes the superiority of the *phoné* over the *gramma,* of the spoken word over the written, in the tradition of Western metaphysics. The specific character of the grammatological project is expressed, however, in the affirmation according to which the originary experience is always already trace and writing, the signified always already in the position of signifier. The illusion of a full and originary presence is the illusion of metaphysics, which is embodied in the double structure of the sign. The closure of metaphysics, and of the semiotics in solidarity with it, implies the awareness that there is no possible origin beyond the signifier and the trace: the origin is an *architrace,* which in the absence of an origin establishes the very possibility of appearance and signification.[14]

By restoring the originary character of the signifier, the grammatological project effects a salutary critique of the metaphysical inheritance that has crystallized in the notion of sign, but this does not mean that it has really succeeded in accomplishing that "step-backward-beyond" metaphysics—with greater prudence, the philosopher on whose thought that critique is based hesitated to declare that step complete or even merely possible.[15] Metaphysics is not, in fact, simply the interpretation of the fracture of presence as a duality of appearance and essence, of signifier and signified, of sensible and intelligible; rather, that the original experience be always already caught in a fold, be already simple in the etymological sense (*sim-plex,* "once pleated"), that presence be always already caught in a signification: this is precisely the origin of Western metaphysics. Placing writing and the trace in an initial position means putting the emphasis on this original experience, but not transcending it. Both *gramma* and *phoné* in fact belong to the Greek metaphysical project, which, defining "grammar" as the reflection on language and conceiving of the *phoné* as *semantiké* (that is, as the sign of a "writing in the soul"),[16] thought of language from the outset from the point of view of the "letter." The metaphysics of writing and of the signifier is but the reverse face of the metaphysics of the signified and the voice, and not, surely, its transcendence. Even if it were possible to reveal the metaphysical inheritance of modern semiology, it would still be impossible for us to conceive of a presence that, finally freed from difference, was only a pure and undivided station in the open. What we can do is recognize the originary situation of language, this "plexus of eternally negative differences" in the barrier resistant to signification (that Oedipal repression has made inaccessible). The originary nucleus of signification is neither in the signifier nor in the signified, neither in writing nor in the voice, but in the fold of the presence on which they are established: the *logos,* which characterizes the human as *zoon logon echon* (living thing using language), is this fold that gathers and divides all things in the "putting together" of presence. And the human is precisely this fracture of presence, which opens a world and over which language holds itself. The algorithm S/s must therefore reduce itself to simply the barrier (/) but in this barrier we should not see merely the trace of a difference, but the topological game of putting things together and articulating (*synapseis*), whose model we have attempted to delineate in the apotropaic *ainos* of the Sphinx, in the melancholic profundity of the emblem, in the *Verleugnung* of the fetishist.

In the dawning language of Greek thought, this "articulation" of presence took the name of *harmonia.* Around the Indo-European roots of this word we find a constellation of terms that points toward a cardinal notion of the universe of the

Indo-European peoples: that of the just order that governs the rhythm of the universe, from the movements of the stars to the succession of seasons and the relations among humans and gods.[17] What interests us here, however, is less the centrality of this concept than that the idea of the "just order" should present itself from the beginning of Greek speculation as an articulation, an agreement, a juxtaposition (*harmodzo* and *ararisco* originally meant "join" or "connect" in the carpenter's sense),[18] that the perfect "jewel" of the cosmos implied therefore for the Greeks the idea of a laceration that is also a suture, the idea of a tension that is both the articulation of a difference and unitary. Heraclitus alluded to this "most beautiful" and "invisible" articulation in the fragments (8, 51, 54) where *harmonia* is not simply harmony in the sense familiar to us, but the name of the principle itself of the "just" station or situation in presence. That this articulation, which, for Heraclitus, still belongs to the tactile-visible sphere, should then be transferred to the numerical-acoustic sphere, testifies to a decisive turn in Western thought, where it is still possible to discern the solidarity between signification and metaphysical articulation, in the passage from the visible to the acoustic aspect of language.

Only when we have arrived in the proximity of this "invisible articulation" will be be able to say we have entered into an area from which the step-backward-beyond of metaphysics, which governs the interpretation of the sign in Western thought, becomes really possible. We can for the moment perhaps only have an intuition of what might be a presence restored to the simplicity of this "invisible harmony": the last Western philosopher recognized a hint of this harmony in a painting by Cézanne in the possible rediscovered community of thought and poetry.[19] Faithful in this to the apotropaic project, whose signification had appeared to the dawning age of Greek thought as a mode of speaking that was neither a gathering nor a concealment, we cannot but approach that which must, for the moment, remain at a distance.

Notes

1. F. de Saussure, *Cours de linguistique générale*, critical edition by R. Engler (Wiesbaden, 1967), chap. 3, 3.

2. "As for a book on this subject," he had declared to his friends and pupils, "one cannot dream of it: it must give the definitive thought of its author" (R. Engler, Preface to the *Cours*, ix). Sechehaye and Bally, the curators of the edition of 1915, expressed their surprise in their preface when, in searching for Saussure's notes for the *Cours*, they found nothing that corresponded to the notes of his students: "F. de Saussure destroyed completely his hasty scribblings where he traced out day by day the sketch of his exposition." It is probable that this destruction was not merely casual.

3. See the impressions of Meillet, perhaps the greatest of his students: "He [F. de Saussure] had produced the best book on comparative grammar ever written, had sown ideas and set down solid theories, had made his mark on numerous pupils, and nevertheless he had not completely fulfilled his destiny," from A. Meillet, "Ferdinand de Saussure," in *Linguistique historique et linguistique générale*, vol. 2 (Paris, 1952), 183. The "myth" of Saussure, already present in this article (Meillet speaks of Saussure's "blue eye full of mystery") is still active in the form of the "three portraits" in an article by Benveniste from 1964: "First the brilliant beginner, 'beautiful as a young god,' who

makes a stunning entrance into the discipline; then, according to a portrait painted by his brother during the Paris years, the meditative and secretive young man, already tense with his internal necessity; and at last the final image of the aging gentleman, of dignified manner, a little weary, bearing in his dreaming, anxious look the question on which his life would thenceforth fix itself" ("F. de Saussure à l'Ecole des Hautes Etudes," in *Annuaire de l'Ecole pratique des Hautes Etudes, 1964-65*).

4. First, "Notes inédites de F. de Saussure," *Cahiers F. de Saussure* 12 (1954), followed by "Saussure après un demi-siècle," *Cahiers F. de Saussure* 20 (1963; republished in Benveniste, *Problèmes de linguistique générale*, vol. 1, 32-45).

5. This critical edition of Engler is the only one that can be defined as critical in the rigorous sense.

6. "This silence hid a drama which must have been painful; it was aggravated with the years and never had an outcome" [Benveniste, *Problèmes de linguistique générale*, 37; English translation from *Problems in General Linguistics*, trans. Mary Elizabeth Meek (Coral Gables, Fla.: University of Miami Press, 1971), 33].

7. "Lettres de F. de Saussure à M. Meillet," *Cahiers F. de Saussure* 21 (1964).

8. "Notes inédites de F. de Saussure," 63.

9. Saussure, *Cours*, 272.

10. Ibid.

11. "Notes inédites de F. de Saussure," 64-65.

12. "We are on the contrary profoundly convinced that whoever treads on the territory of language, may be said to be abandoned by all the analogies of heaven and earth" ("Notes inédites de F. de Saussure," 64).

13. To E. Benveniste (that is, to a linguist who has brought about, in our view, a new "situation" of the science of language) we owe the most lucid perception of the inadequacy of the semiotic perspective in the narrow sense for giving an account of the linguistic phenomenon in its wholeness. Benveniste's distinction of a double *signifiance* of language (that he defined as *semiotic mode* and *semantic mode*, the first of which must be "recognized" and the second "understood," and between which there is no transition) and his search for an "other aspect" to the problem of meaning, for which the semiotic notion of the sign (as positive unity of signifier and signified) is no longer valid, point toward the same area that we have here attempted to configure by opposing the Oedipal notion of signifying to that of the Sphinx.

14. See Jacques Derrida, *De la grammatologie* (Paris, 1967); English trans., *Of Grammatology*, trans. Gayatri C. Spivak (Baltimore: Johns Hopkins, 1977).

15. Like much of contemporary French philosophy, the thought of Derrida too has its basis, more or less openly declared, in that of Heidegger.

16. Already Aristotle referred the semantic character of human language to the phantasy, whose images, according to a metaphor found in Plato, are conceived as "a writing in the soul."

17. This constellation of terms, which derives from the root *ar-*, includes, among others, Vedic *rta*, Iranic *arta*, Latin *ars, ritus, artus*, Greek *ararisko*; see E. Benveniste, *Le vocabulaire des institutions indo-européenes*, vol. 2 (Paris, 1969), 101.

18. Leo Spitzer, *Classical and Christian Ideas of World Harmony* (Baltimore, 1963).

19. "In the late work of the painter is the fold / of that which comes to presence and of presence itself / become simple, 'realized,' healed, / transfigured in an identity full of mystery. / Does a path open up here, that leads to the co- / belonging of poetry and thought?" from M. Heidegger, "Cézanne," in *Gedachtes*, in Ren Char, *L'Herne* (Paris, 1971).

Index

Compiled by Hassan Melehy

159

Theory and History of Literature

Giorgio Agamben teaches philosophy at the Collège International de Philosophie in Paris and at the University of Macerata in Italy. He has written numerous books. Also published in translation by the University of Minnesota Press are *Language and Death: The Place of Negativity* (1991) and *The Coming Community* (1993).

Ronald L. Martinez is associate professor of Italian at the University of Minnesota.